Managing Projects with
Microsoft® Project 98

For Windows™

Gwen Lowery
Rob Ferrara

 VAN NOSTRAND REINHOLD

I⊤P® A Division of International Thomson Publishing Inc.

New York • Albany • Bonn • Boston • Detroit • London • Madrid • Melbourne
Mexico City • Paris • San Francisco • Singapore • Tokyo • Toronto

Microsoft, Microsoft Access, Microsoft Excel, and Microsoft Word are registered trademarks and Windows, Microsoft Outlook, and Microsoft SQL Server are trademarks of Microsoft Corporation.

Copyright © 1998 by Gwen Lowery

I(T)P®   International Thomson Publishing Company.
         The ITP logo is a registered trademark used herin under license.

All rights reserved. No part of this work covered by the copyright hereon may be reproduced or used in any form or by any means—graphic, electronic, or mechanical, including photocopying, recording, taping, or information storage and retrieval systems—without the written permission of the publisher.

The ideas presented in this book are generic and strategic. Their specific application to a particular company must be the responsiblity of the management of that company, based on management's understanding of their company's procedures, culture, resources, and competitive situation.

Printed in the United States of America.

Visit our Web site at www.vnr.com.

For more information contact:

Van Nostrand Reinhold
115 Fifth Avenue
New York, NY 10003

Chapman & Hall GmbH
Pappalallee 3
69469 Weinham
Germany

Chapman & Hall
2-6 Bounday Row
London SEI 8HN
United Kingdom

International Thomson Publishing Asia
60 Albert Street #15-01
Albert Complex
Singapore 189969

Thomas Nelson Australia
102 Dodds Street
South Melbourne 3205
Victoria, Australia

International Thomson Publishing Japan
Hirakawa-cho Kyowa Building, 3F
2-2-1 Hirakawa-cho, Chiyoda-ku
Tokyo 102 Japan

Nelson Canada
1120 Birchmount Road
Scarborough, Ontario
M1K 5G4, Canada

International Thomson Editores
Seneca, 53
Colonia Polanco
11560 Mexico D.F. Mexico

1 2 3 4 5 6 7 8 9 10 IPC 01 00 99 98 97

Library of Congress Cataloging-in-Publication Data available

ISBN 0-442-02552-1

Contents

Introducing Microsoft Project 98

A friend of mine, I'll call him Joe, was the lead engineer in a highly creative team of computer-chip designers. Joe reveled in the give-and-take of team brainstorming sessions and immersed himself in the design and development of each chip his team developed. But despite loving his job, he'd often grumble, "I wish someone else could handle the management part and free me to do the engineering part only."

One day Joe got his wish—or very nearly. He stopped by my office to pick me up for lunch and saw some curious-looking tables, charts, and graphs radiating from a program on my computer screen. "What's that?" he asked. I gave him a brief demonstration.

I showed Joe how to use the program to easily create a project schedule, assign people to tasks, track progress, communicate important information among team members, and even how to access useful documents on the World Wide Web. When the demonstration ended, Joe exclaimed, "That's it! I've found someone to manage my projects for me. Why didn't you tell me before? And you call yourself a friend?"

The "someone" that Joe found to manage his projects is Microsoft Project 98.

Using Microsoft Project is like having your own project management assistant. It helps you create project plans of any size, track progress, solve problems before they wreck the deadline or the budget, and communicate project information quickly and easily. If you've never used Microsoft Project but are familiar with other Microsoft programs, such as Microsoft Excel and Microsoft Word, you'll have a head start getting up and running with Microsoft Project.

WHAT'S NEW IN MICROSOFT PROJECT 98

Microsoft Project 98 includes a number of new features and enhancements that enable you to manage projects more easily and effectively than ever. This section covers the new features in Microsoft Project 98, which are grouped into the following categories:

- Creating project plans and tracking progress.
- Managing resources and costs.
- Working with the Internet.
- Sharing project information.
- Using new and enhanced Microsoft Project tools.

Create Project Plans and Track Progress with Ease

Microsoft Project has been redesigned to calculate task durations and schedules with the results you expect. Plus, it provides a number of new ways to schedule, link, and track tasks.

- **Effort-Driven Scheduling** This scheduling method, on by default, enables you to increase or decrease the duration of a task by adding or removing resources. The amount of work calculated for the task remains fixed.

- **Task Types** Microsoft Project uses the formula *duration = work/resource units* to schedule tasks. By default, units are fixed, so Microsoft Project calculates duration. But you can choose which part of the equation Microsoft Project calculates for a task by choosing its task type: fixed duration, fixed units, or fixed work.

- **Cross-Project Task Dependencies** Show dependencies between projects and between the tasks in different projects by linking tasks between projects.

- **Multiple Critical Paths** If your project plan includes several phases or projects that occur at the same time, you can create a separate sequence of tasks for each phase or project and display the critical path of each task sequence on the Gantt Chart view.

- **Links Can Take Precedence over Fixed-Date Constraints** A fixed-date constraint forces Microsoft Project to schedule a task on or near a date you specify, no matter how the schedule changes. But now you can choose to have schedule changes override constraint dates, enabling Microsoft Project to automatically recalculate a constrained task's start and finish dates.

- **Multiple Baselines** See how your project plan has evolved over time by saving up to 10 interim plans and comparing them with your original baseline plan.

- **Progress Lines** See whether all tasks in a project are ahead or behind schedule as of a specified date by displaying progress lines. Displayed on the Gantt Chart view, a progress line is a vertical, zig-zagging line that represents the degree to which tasks are ahead or behind schedule.

- **Increased Consolidation Limits** Insert up to 1,000 projects into a consolidated project file. The exact number of projects you can include in a consolidated project depends on the available memory in your computer.

Manage Resources and Costs Efficiently

For many managers, effective resource and cost management are essential for successful project management. Microsoft Project provides a number of new ways to help you manage resources and costs.

- **Task Splitting** Show discontinuous work on a task by splitting it. A split task appears as a split Gantt bar on the Gantt Chart view. A gap between two parts of the bar represent time when work isn't being done on the task.

- **Resource Contouring** If a resource follows a certain hourly pattern over the life of a task, you can match the resource's assigned hours on a task to the actual hours spent on the task each day by applying a *resource contour*. Microsoft Project provides you with several predefined resource contours to choose from.

- **Resource Start and Finish Dates** To make sure that you assign a resource to a task only when the resource is available, you can specify the date a resource starts working on the task and the date the resources stops working on the task.

- **Improved Resource Leveling** Level resources your way. Look for overallocations on a minute-by-minute to month-by-month basis, level all or part of your project, create splits in remaining work, and level resources from your project's finish date rather than its start date.

- **Multiple Resource Rates** Specify a different pay rate for each kind of job performed by the same resource, and then let Microsoft Project apply the correct rate to each task the resource works on.

- **Variable Resource Rates** Specify pay rate increases or decreases and the dates they go into effect. When a new pay rate goes into effect, Microsoft Project uses the new pay rate to calculate resource costs.

- **A Resource Usage View with Task Details** See a list of resources showing assigned tasks grouped under each resource, a table of resource information, and a set of details about resources and their assigned tasks. The improved Resource Usage view shows the total number of hours worked by each resource in a given time period, and breaks down those hours by task.

- **A Task Usage View with Resource Details** See a list of tasks showing assigned resources grouped under each task, a table of task information, and a set of details about tasks and their assigned resources. Use the new Task Usage view to enter and edit task and resource information together, see how many hours each resource is scheduled to work on particular tasks, and set work contours.

- **Improved Resource Pooling** View and edit resource information from all the projects that share a resource pool without opening all of the sharing project files.

- **User–Entered Actual Costs** Enter actual costs manually, rather than having Microsoft Project calculate them automatically.

Enrich Project Plans with Internet Information

To manage projects more effectively, you can tap into the tremendous resources that are available on the Internet. If your computer's connected to the Internet, you can use Microsoft Project to visit and establish links to web sites on the World Wide Web.

- **Publish Projects on the Web** Save your projects in HTML (Web) format and your Gantt Chart views in GIF format and publish project information on the World Wide Web.

- **Link Web Documents to Your Project Plan** Insert a link to a web document in your project plan. With a click of the link, you're at the document's web site. Link web documents that are of interest to you, clients, and team members.

- **Use the New Web Toolbar** Include information from the web and other projects by embedding *hyperlinks* into your project plan. You can find web and hyperlinking tools on the Web toolbar.

Share Project Information with Improved Importing and Exporting, Workgroup, and Intranet Support

Sharing project information effectively is the key to project success. Microsoft Project provides you with several new and improved ways to share project information with people, projects, and other programs.

- **Import and Export as Easily as You Open and Save** When you import data, you use the Open command. When you export data, you use the Save As command. Microsoft Project makes importing and exporting nearly as easy as opening and saving a project file.

- **Use Import/Export Maps for Exchanging Selected Data** When you're importing or exporting only part of the information that's in a project plan, you match a field in Microsoft Project to its counterpart field in another program by using an *import/export map*. The data is inserted into the correct field, even if the fields have different names.

- **New Database Format** Use the new Microsoft Project Database (MPD) file format for exporting project files to databases.

- **Set up a Workgroup on the System of Your Choice** Set up a workgroup that uses a MAPI-compliant e-mail system, an intranet, the World Wide Web, or all three. A workgroup is a group of project participants—you and your team members—that's connected to the same communications system. Using Microsoft Project's workgroup features, you can send and receive assignment information in special workgroup messages.

- **Out-of-the-Box Web Solution** If you decide to set up a workgroup based on an intranet system but there's no intranet system at your organization, you can set up an intranet site for communicating and tracking project status by installing the Microsoft Personal Web Server that comes with Microsoft Project.

Use Features That Help You Work Faster and Smarter

Microsoft Project provides you with a number of features that enable you to work fast and smart.

- **Spend Less Time Typing** Enter data quickly by using new features that make it unnecessary to type. For example, to enter a date in a date field, you can pick the date from a miniature calendar. And in many numerical fields, you can enter a number by using a spin control: a pair of up and down arrows that you can click to increase or decrease the value in the field.

- **Filter Quickly with AutoFilters** Choose as your criterion any value that appears in a column in a sheet view, and filter for that value instantly.

- **Display Commonly Used Views Fast** Click the view you want on the View Bar, located on the left side of the screen.

- **Include Pictures in Headers, Footers, Legends, and Notes** Insert graphics files or paste pictures into headers, footers, legends, and notes.

- **Keep Tabs on Tasks, Resources, and Assignments** Check the icons in the new Indicators field to see if there's something you need to know about a task, resource, or assignment. These icons are called *indicators*. By positioning the pointer over an indicator, important information about the task, resource, or assignment appears.

- **Printing Improvements** Change the size of views and reports on both postscript *and* non-postscript printers.

WHAT'S COVERED IN THIS BOOK

Managing Projects with Microsoft Project provides concise and in-depth coverage of the topics that are important to you. It includes procedures for the tasks you're most likely to perform from the beginning of the project-planning stage to project completion. Organized the way you work, this book will help you to quickly find the information you need to complete your project planning efficiently.

The following parts are included in *Managing Projects with Microsoft Project 98*.

Part 1: Your Project Takes Shape

A good project management strategy combined with a project management tool such as Microsoft Project can be a potent partnership for success. The trick is in knowing how best to apply the software to your strategy. To help you make the most effective use of Microsoft Project, Part 1 explains the project management process, the ways Microsoft Project helps you to manage projects, and how to begin a project by using Microsoft Project.

Part 2: Creating and Refining Your Project Plan

A project plan is the key to guiding a project to a successful conclusion. Thus, Part 2, which explains how to create and refine a project plan, is the heart of this book. In Part 2 you'll learn how to set project goals, create a task list, estimate how long each task will take, put tasks in a logical sequence, show dependencies between tasks, and assign people and other resources to tasks. Lastly, you find out how to refine your project plan so that it is as efficient and realistic as possible.

Part 3: Tracking Your Project and Updating Your Project Plan

After you create and refine your project plan, the project begins. That's when the power of your project plan really starts to show: By using your project plan to track actual project progress, you improve your ability to make the changes that keep your project on schedule and within budget. Part 3 explains how to track project progress, collect project data, and set up and use a workgroup communications system on an e-mail system, an intranet, or the World Wide Web. You use the workgroup communications system to request and confirm task assignments, send updated task assignment information to the workgroup manager, and incorporate updated information into the project plan.

Part 4: Viewing, Formatting, and Printing Project Information

Though Microsoft Project can store thousands of pieces of information, you're probably only interested in viewing a small subset of that information at a time. When you're viewing project information, you may want that information to look a certain way. Occasionally, you'll want to share a set of particularly useful—and well-formatted—project information with team members, upper management, or clients. Part 4 explains how to display exactly the project information you want, change the appearance of project information, and print project information.

Part 5: Exchanging Information with Other Projects, Other Programs, and the World Wide Web

Sharing project information is necessary in every part of your job. At the beginning of a project, discussions with team members help you to develop project goals and determine the tasks required to fulfill those goals. Later on, feedback enables you to track project progress. If you're managing several projects at the same time, you need to be able to collect and organize a great deal of project information to stay on top of each project. If project participants—supervisors, clients, or team member—require up-to-date project information, you need to be able to get them the information they need in a form they can use. Part 5 explains how to share project information between projects and between the different kinds of programs people use during a project.

Part 6: Customizing Microsoft Project Tools

Microsoft Project is like a desk filled with tools. Those tools help you perform the many detailed tasks required to manage projects and work with project files, such as menus and menu commands, toolbars and toolbar buttons, and forms and dialog boxes. Part 6 describes how to customize the tools that enable you to perform the detailed tasks of project management—menus, toolbar buttons, forms, and so on—so that you can work with Microsoft Project as efficiently as possible. It also explains how you can automate repetitive tasks that you perform with Microsoft Project.

Glossary

The Glossary contains a list of many of the important terms that appear in this book.

Index

The comprehensive Index helps you locate the information you want quickly and efficiently.

CONVENTIONS USED IN THIS BOOK

This section describes the common terms and other conventions used in the procedures in this book.

Terms used for mouse actions

Mouse term	Description
Point	Position the mouse pointer over the item.
Click	Point to an item and click the mouse button. If your mouse has more than one button, click the left button, unless told to use the right button.
Double-click	Click the mouse button twice rapidly.
Drag and drop	Position the mouse pointer at the starting point, press and hold down the mouse button, move the pointer to the new location, and then release the mouse button. Again, use the left button.

Selecting Project Information

To select	Keys	Mouse
One task or resource	Use arrow keys to move to the item.	Click the item.
Adjacent tasks or resources	Use SHIFT+arrow keys.	Drag over the items.
Nonadjacent tasks or resources	Press F8 and select the first group; press SHIFT+F8 and move to the next group; repeat the steps until all groups are selected.	Select the first group, and then hold down CTRL.

Where Did *OK* and *Close* Go?

The procedures in this book follow many of the conventions used in documentation for programs that work with the Windows operating system. One of those conventions is to leave out the "Click OK" or "Click Close" step at the very end of a procedure. Since this last step is so common and familiar, it's left out of this book also.

Part 1

Your Project Takes Shape

How well you manage a project has a direct effect on the outcome of the project. There are several parts in the project management equation, two of which are the project management steps and the tools you have to support these steps. Part 1 explains the project management process, the ways Microsoft Project helps you to manage projects successfully, and how to begin a project by using Microsoft Project.

Chapter 1 discusses how you can manage projects more effectively by using project planning methods in combination with project management software. It focuses on how Microsoft Project schedules your projects.

Chapter 2 explains the major ways that Microsoft Project assists you in each phase of your project.

Chapter 3 shows you how to use Microsoft Project to begin your project. It tells you exactly what information is essential to any project plan.

The Elements of Project Management

Project management means different things to different people. To some project managers, it means directing the troops ever forward until the project goal has been reached. To others, it means empowering the personnel who will perform the project tasks, mediating disputes, and keeping the project team informed. Between the centralized versus distributed approaches to project management lie a broad spectrum of intermediate approaches.

All of the approaches have these elements in common: They want to achieve project goals as efficiently as possible, they follow a set of steps to achieve project goals, and they prescribe ways to manage tasks, resources, and other important parts of a project.

This chapter describes those elements of project management shared by all or nearly all approaches to project management. It explains a tried-and-true four-phase project model as well as the main project components you need to manage to complete your project on time and within budget.

WHAT IS A PROJECT?

A *project* is a one-time set of activities that ends with a specific accomplishment. It originates when something out of the ordinary has to be accomplished. A project has the following characteristics:

- A set of non-routine tasks performed in a certain sequence leading to a goal.
- A distinct start and finish date.
- A limited set of resources that may be used on more than one project.

A project is not an ongoing process, such as preparing a weekly payroll or manufacturing a product on an assembly line. These processes have no real completion date, which is a requirement of a project, nor are they in any way unique. Rather, they are part of the everyday business.

WHAT IS PROJECT MANAGEMENT?

Project management is the defining, planning, scheduling, and controlling of the tasks that must be completed to achieve your project goals. *Defining* and *planning* are necessary so you know what you will do. *Scheduling* is important so you know when you will do it. And *controlling* is important because things never work out exactly as planned.

To meet your project goals, it's important that you be on top of changes. This means tracking and rescheduling as the project progresses. You're successful when you satisfy the requirements of your client or management, and meet your project goals on schedule and within your budget.

A FOUR-PHASE PROJECT MODEL

A *project model* represents the way real projects proceed in the real world. There are a number of project models in the realm of project management, and you may already use one that works for you. But if not, consider using the following project model, which consists of four phases that are part of nearly every project.

The four-phase project model consists of:

- Defining your project.
- Creating and refining your project plan.
- Tracking your project and updating your plan.
- Closing your project.

Defining Your Project

Defining your project means that you set project goals, scope, and assumptions. The project *goals* determine the purpose of the project. They tell you what it is you want to accomplish. For example, the project goal may be to build a new house.

The *scope* determines which tasks do and do not need to be performed to achieve the project goals. For example, if you build a house, you may decide to construct two stories but to leave out a second fireplace.

Assumptions are guesstimates of those factors that you think will come into play during the project. An example of an assumption you might make when you build a house is that it will rain no more than 15% of the time.

Creating and Refining Your Project Plan

A *project plan* is a model of your project that you use to predict and control project progress. It shows you what will get done, when it will get done, and by whom. You create a project plan before the project gets under way.

The most important part of your project plan is the task schedule, which you create in three steps. First, you specify *what* you are going to do by defining the tasks that must be completed to reach your goals. Then you specify *when* by scheduling the tasks. Then you specify *how* by assigning people, equipment, and costs to complete the tasks.

Of course, these steps are not independent. After seeing the first schedule, you'll probably evaluate your task and resource lists to ensure you're creating the best schedule to fit the situation. And you can't do this alone. You will have a better schedule and more support for the project if you involve the project team in the planning process.

You can use a project plan and its schedule to:

- Communicate to others in your organization what you're going to do.
- Get support from project team members.
- Gain approval for the project or justify the need to management.
- Show a customer how you'll deliver a product or service.
- Prove the need for additional staff and manage resource work loads.
- Determine cash flow needs.
- Keep a record of what happened on the project, to be compared to the original plan, and to be used as the basis of future schedules for similar projects.
- Use the project schedule as a baseline against which you check the progress of your project.

Having a plan helps everyone see who needs to do what and when they need to do it. It helps communication, makes everyone aware of deadlines, and reduces uncertainty. And by tracking the actual progress of the project and comparing it to your original schedule, you can see deviations from the plan, anticipate any problems, and correct any delays before they become severe. With a plan, there's a better chance of completing your project successfully.

Tracking Your Project and Updating Your Plan

To know what's really going on in your project—whether individual tasks and the project as a whole are on schedule—you need to track your project. Tracking means that you compare your original, estimated task start and finish dates, task durations, costs, and other values to actual values. Without a reference point, you can't track.

When you track project progress, you can pinpoint the parts of your schedule that are in trouble and devise a strategy for keeping your project on schedule. Tracking will tell you, for example, which tasks need more resources assigned to them, which tasks are under or over budget, and which resources are available to do more work.

You can track project progress only if you update your plan by adding actual values for task durations, start and finish dates, costs, and so on. Then you can compare your original values to the actual values to determine whether your project is on schedule and within budget.

Closing Your Project

After you've achieved your project goals, you can close the project. Closing a project may mean writing a memo to your supervisor to report that the project's ended, or it could mean much more.

For example, you might conduct an extensive post mortem to analyze what went right and what went wrong. You can record what you learn from the just-finished project and use that information to manage future projects more effectively. The close of one project can be just as important as the beginning of a new project.

THE THINGS YOU MANAGE: TASKS, RESOURCES, TIME, AND MONEY

The success of a project depends on how well you manage tasks, resources, time, and money, which are the primary objects of project management. In some projects, you may need to manage only one or two of these items. For example, the project budget may be someone else's concern; you need only concentrate on getting the job done.

Even if you don't need to concern yourself with all four items in every project you manage, you'll manage more effectively if you understand what they are.

Tasks are the specific actions that need to be carried out in order to achieve project goals. Examples of tasks required to build a house are digging the foundation, installing the plumbing, and painting the walls. You manage tasks by scheduling tasks, tracking task progress, and keeping tasks on schedule.

Resources are the people, equipment, and facilities (such as conference rooms, warehouses, and so on) that are required to perform the tasks. You manage resources by assigning them to tasks, making sure that their assigned work time matches their available work time, and tracking resource costs.

Time is how long it takes to complete an individual task or the project as a whole. You manage time by adjusting task scope or project scope, assigning more or fewer resources to a task, and adjusting the start or finish relationships between tasks.

Money is, well, we all know what money is. It's that thing we all want more of and want to spend less of. Money is what you need to cover the costs of tasks, resources, and materials. Without money (someone's money), there's no project. Even if all the labor, equipment, and facilities were donated to your project, someone would still be incurring costs (though you might not need to manage costs in that case). You manage money by keeping tasks on schedule, using the least expensive resources possible, adjusting task scope and project scope, and tracking costs.

At any point during your project, you may need to focus on only one of these items: either tasks, resources, time, or money. But you'll best keep your project under control when you understand the relationships between them.

A QUESTION OF BALANCE

The things you manage in a project—tasks, resources, time, and money—are interdependent. Rarely can you change one without affecting at least one other.

You manage a project effectively by keeping tasks, resources, time, and money in balance from the beginning to the end of the project. Typically, one of these quantities is fixed and the other three may vary.

For example, if you have an immovable deadline (time is fixed), and the project scope is large (that is, the project consists of many tasks or a small number of long, complex tasks), then you may need a large number of resources to complete the project on time. The more resources you add, the more the project will cost.

If, let's say, you have a fixed number of resources (or a fixed budget), you may need to decrease the project scope or increase the amount of time required to complete the project.

If you absolutely must complete each task in your project plan in order to achieve your project goals (scope is fixed), then you can adjust resources, time, or both. The quantity you choose to vary depends on whether you have more resources or more time available.

After a project gets under way, it's almost inevitable that the balance you so carefully established at the beginning of the project will totter to one side or the other. For example, if tasks take longer than expected, you may need to add more resources, lengthen the project deadline, or cut project scope. Or, upper management may decide to add a few more goals to the project, thus increasing scope, so you may need to add resources or extend the deadline.

Effective project management requires a constant watch over the balance between tasks, resources, time, and money. Maintaining the balance is the best way to ensure project success.

YOUR MAIN TASKS WHEN YOU MANAGE A PROJECT

Your overarching task when you manage a project is to achieve project goals on time and within budget. Your most important strategy for reaching project goals is to keep tasks, resources, time, and money in balance. The main tasks you need to perform to achieve project goals are:

- Define the project. Set the project's goals, scope, and assumptions. Make sure that the goals are measurable, and describe a definite end to the project.

- Create a project plan. List all the tasks required to achieve the project goals, put those tasks in a logical sequence, and establish start and finish relationships between tasks. You'll also need to set a start date and assign resources to tasks.

- Refine the project plan. Your first-draft plan may contain all the pieces, but then it's time to whittle them down, reorganize them, maybe delete or add a few. Remove unneeded tasks, make sure no resource is overworked, and check to see if the project can realistically finish on time and within budget.

- Track project progress. Compare actual project data to your original estimates. Make any adjustments to the schedule that are necessary to keep on track. Remember to keep tasks, resources, time, and money in balance.

- Close the project. Analyze the project and apply what you learn to the next project.

2

How Microsoft Project Helps You to Manage Projects

Why should you use Microsoft Project? Why, indeed, should you use any project management program at all?

You can probably manage a small project without using a project management program. But what determines project size? Here are some of the main factors that define a project's size and complexity:

- The number of people and other resources, such as equipment, involved in the project.
- The number of tasks required to achieve the project goals.
- The schedule length.
- The difficulty of meeting a tough project deadline.
- The size of the project budget.

These factors are inherently vague. A project that one person can keep track of in his or her head may completely overwhelm another person. It might have nothing to do with ability. The first person might be managing only one project at a time, and the second person, four or five.

As a rule of thumb, many project managers find that they need to use a project management program when a project involves more than 25 resources and 100 tasks and takes longer than 30 days.

In general, the bigger the project, the more details you need to keep track of. When the amount and complexity of project details overtax your head and common paper methods, you should use a project management program. Just about all project management programs excel at helping you to organize, store, analyze, and communicate project information. So why choose Microsoft Project over the other programs?

Microsoft Project provides the flexibility to help you manage a project your way. For example, if, as in many businesses today, you empower team members to be responsible for accomplishing their tasks, you can use Microsoft Project's workgroup feature to request and keep track of task assignments. Or, if you decide to track task progress and not costs incurred during the project, you can update task information only.

But Microsoft Project is more powerful than these few examples suggest. Microsoft Project:

- Provides essential assistance in nearly every phase of your project.
- Calculates your schedule and other project information.
- Fills in many fields as you enter or change information in your project plan.
- Stores and displays project information.
- Prints a variety of project information.
- Enables you to exchange task information with team members.
- Supplies the tools to share project information with other programs.

ASSISTS YOU IN MOST PROJECT PHASES

Most successful projects have four phases:

1 Define project goals.
2 Build the project plan.
3 Track the project.
4 Close the project.

While Microsoft Project can't provide much help with the first and fourth phases (nor can any other project management program, for that matter), it does most of the work for you in the second and third phases.

Define Project Goals

Your project goals determine the purpose of the project, what you want to accomplish. Though only you can define your project goals, Microsoft Project can store those goals with your project plan. You can refer to them at any time during the project to make sure your project stays on the right track.

Build the Project Plan

The project plan is a model of your project that tells what tasks are going to be done, by whom, and when. Like any model, it's only as accurate as the information you put into it. The most important part of the plan is the project schedule, which includes task and project start and finish dates. It might also include resource and cost information.

You figure out the best way to achieve your project goals. Then you enter project information, such as tasks, task durations, resources, and costs, into Microsoft Project. Using the information you enter, Microsoft Project creates your project schedule.

Track the Project

When you track project progress, you compare your original estimates to actual values to see if your project can achieve its goals within your original time and cost estimates. You can also identify problems early, before they affect your schedule. You compare original and actual values for task start and finish dates, task length, costs, and more.

Using Microsoft Project, you can save your original plan information so that you can compare it with actual data throughout the project lifetime. That way, you can make any adjustments necessary to complete your project goals on time.

Close the Project

During the final project phase, you gather and analyze information about the project to determine what went right and what went wrong. Then you use this information to help you in your next project.

If you save your original plan information in Microsoft Project, you can compare this information to the way the project actually progressed. You can store your project analysis with the plan, save the plan, and apply what you've learned to successive projects.

CALCULATES YOUR SCHEDULE AUTOMATICALLY

One of the most powerful and time-saving aspects of Microsoft Project is its ability to calculate a schedule. But it can't create a schedule out of thin air. You need to enter raw information first. The schedule Microsoft Project creates from your information provides important dates, helps you identify problems, and more.

You:

- Set the project start date, which is the earliest date tasks can begin.
- List all required tasks in the approximate order in which you expect to do them.
- Estimate the amount of time to do each task. Your time estimates are very important. The more accurate they are, the more accurate is the schedule calculated by Microsoft Project.
- Indicate task dependencies. For example, if one task can start only when a previous task finishes, you'd indicate a finish-to-start dependency between these tasks. Finish-to-start is the most common dependency between tasks.
- Assign resources to tasks. You tell Microsoft Project which resources will work on which tasks. You don't have to assign resources to tasks, but it's better if you do. That way, Microsoft Project can factor resources into your schedule and track costs.

Microsoft Project:

- Schedules tasks immediately as you enter project information.
- Calculates the task start and finish dates, durations, and other values.
- Calculates the project finish date.

Though Microsoft Project begins scheduling tasks as soon as you start entering task information, the schedule isn't finished until you've entered information about all tasks.

As you enter new information or change existing information, Microsoft Project recalculates task start and finish dates, durations, and so on. You see the impact of your changes immediately.

FILLS IN MANY FIELDS FOR YOU

This is the way it works:

As in a Microsoft Excel spreadsheet, you fill in some fields. Microsoft Project fills in others. For example, you can enter and edit task names. Microsoft Project calculates and enters task start and finish dates.

There are two types of fields filled in by Microsoft Project: editable and calculated. You can change the information in an editable field; you cannot change the information in a calculated field. An example of an editable field is the Duration field. An example of a calculated field is the Variance field, which displays the difference between an original estimated value and an actual value (such as the difference between an estimated and an actual cost).

DISPLAYS EXACTLY THE PROJECT INFORMATION YOU WANT

A project of almost any size is bound to generate hundreds, if not thousands, of pieces of information. There are start dates, finish dates, task durations, task dependencies, critical tasks, resource names, e–mail names, group names, working times, actual work, remaining work, baseline cost, fixed cost, cumulative cost, total cost, and total exhaustion—just to name a few.

Thrown together, these pieces of project information are just a meaningless pile of rubbish; they tell you nothing. But group the right pieces of project information together and present them in an organized format, and you can easily determine the status of your project. Microsoft Project enables you to view only the information you want by providing views, tables, and filters.

Views are the organized formats Microsoft Project uses to display project information. Each view displays just a portion of the total information stored in Microsoft Project. A view displays a particular set of information about tasks or resources in one of several kinds of familiar formats. There are chart views, graph views, form views, and sheet views, which are spreadsheetlike views whose information is arranged in columns. You enter, edit, and display project information in views.

Tables are interchangeable sets of information arranged in columns that you display in sheet views. To each sheet view, you can apply a number of tables, one at a time. For example, to view or edit cost information, you can apply a cost table to a sheet view. A cost table might consist of columns of information such as total cost, actual cost, and remaining cost. By applying a work table next, you replace (and hide) cost information with information such as total work, percent work completed, and remaining work.

Filters consist of a set of criteria that tasks or resources must match for them to be displayed or highlighted. Whereas a table displays a set of information for all tasks or resources, filters enable you to display only the particular tasks or resources that share a specific set of characteristics. For example, you can use one filter to view only completed tasks, another to view only incomplete tasks, and yet another to view only those tasks assigned to a particular resource. Like views and tables, filters don't delete any information. They only show certain information and hide the rest of the information stored in Microsoft Project.

PUBLISHES PROJECT INFORMATION TO SUIT A VARIETY OF NEEDS

A project manager once said that there's no project plan until the plan's been shared with others. After you complete your project plan and at regular intervals during the project, you'll probably need to share project information with team members, supervisors, clients, and contractors.

Microsoft Project provides a full palette of features for printing project information that suits the needs of any recipient. It enables you to print what you see on screen (views) as well as predefined reports. Just as in a view, each report contains a set of information about a specific aspect of your project. For example, there are task reports, resource reports, and cost reports. You can print the view or report that contains the information required by the recipient.

Not every recipient of project information needs the same level of detail. Supervisors and clients may need only overview information. But team members might require detailed task and resource information. Using Microsoft Project, you can tailor views to display just the level of detail you want or pick a report that already has the right amount of detail. If none of the predefined views or reports meets your requirements, you can easily create a custom view or report.

After you've decided on the right view or report, you can make it shine. Microsoft Project enables you to adjust page layouts, add headers and footers, change the appearance of text (for example, by making it bold or italic), customize various page elements, and much more. You can publish effective project documents with ease.

PUTS YOU AT THE HUB OF A PROJECT COMMUNICATIONS NETWORK

Communicating project information efficiently among team members is essential to achieving your project goals. Whether your team members are at the same location or dispersed around the world, Microsoft Project can be the center of your project communications network.

Linked within a communications systems based on e–mail, the World Wide Web, or an internal network that resembles the World Wide Web called an *internal network* or an *intranet*, Microsoft Project becomes a versatile communications hub. It enables you to assign tasks over a network, receive task updates, and incorporate up-to-date task information into your project plan without typing it. You can coordinate many of your team's activities by sending (and receiving responses to) Microsoft Project messages that are specifically designed to exchange task information.

SHARES PROJECT INFORMATION WITH OTHER PROGRAMS

In a number of projects, Microsoft Project might not be the only program you and your team need to use to store, edit, display, or print project information. For example, you or your accounting department might use Microsoft Excel to calculate project costs in detail. In addition, clients and contractors who need to see or work on project information in electronic form might not even have Microsoft Project. Perhaps the only program they have for viewing project information is a rudimentary word-processing program.

In these situations and many others Microsoft Project extends a friendly hand by providing the capability to share project information with different kinds of programs. These include word-processing programs, spreadsheet programs, database programs, earlier versions of Microsoft Project, and other project management programs.

You can exchange information between Microsoft Project and other programs in several ways, choosing the way that best suits your needs as well as the requirements of the other program. You can copy and paste, link and embed, and import and export project information. The information can be text or graphics.

3

Starting a Project

When you start a project, your first and most important step is to set project goals. This means deciding what you want to accomplish, when it has to be finished, and how much money you can spend. Well-defined goals help the project team and clients grasp the project's purpose and enable you to determine when the project is complete.

As you list the project goals, be sure to consider the project scope and your assumptions about the project. The scope defines the project's limits. For example, you may decide to build a one-story house instead of a two-story house. Assumptions are your expectations of how various factors will affect the project. For example, you might assume that certain items will cost the same throughout the project.

Goals, scope, and assumptions are interdependent. For instance, if an assumption proves wrong—let's say, the price of certain essential building materials skyrockets shortly after house construction begins—you may need to adjust your goals by building a smaller house than originally planned. Or, if the client wants another story added to the house, you may need to increase scope by adding tasks and resources in order to achieve the expanded goals.

To ensure that you, your project team, upper management, and clients pull together from the beginning of the project to the end, you should set project goals, define the scope, and develop assumptions as early in the project-planning process as possible. You'll probably want to work with project team leaders to analyze and define the project, refine your assumptions, and ensure that the goals and scope are realistic. By including others in the planning, you solidify their commitment to the project, and you end up with a more accurate plan.

Once you've determined project goals, scope, and assumptions, you can enter some general information about your project into Microsoft Project. For example, you can record the project start date, project title, company name, project manager, and notes about the project, including the goals, scope, and assumptions.

Setting Clear Project Goals, Scope, and Assumptions

When you set goals, make sure they state clearly what you're trying to accomplish. There are several ways you can analyze your goals as you develop them:

- Think about what you want to achieve or where you want to be at the end of the project. What is the end product?
- State the goal in user or client terms. What does this person want?
- Decide how you'll know when you're finished.
- Analyze your goals to determine if there are more appropriate goals.
- Think of other ways to state your goals to be sure you're pinpointing the project's purpose.

Once you've determined your goals, test them by answering the following questions:

- Are the goals measurable and specific in terms of time, cost, quality, quantity, and the end result?
- Are the goals realistic and achievable?
- Are the goals stated clearly so they are understandable and unambiguous to everyone working on the project?

If the answer to any of these questions is no, restate the goals so that they pass the test.

Defining the Project Scope

By defining scope, you define the work that needs to be done as well as the work that shouldn't be done. Explicitly stating the scope helps you and your team focus on the project's purpose and the steps necessary to complete the project. As the project progresses, any changes in scope will be easy to identify and justify. Even if you're not sure of the scope, getting your best guess down on paper gives you a starting point.

You define scope by stating what is and what is not part of the project. For example, you could decide that a house you're building will have one story and not two. If it's later decided that the house should have two stories, it will be obvious that the scope has changed, and that the original budget, resource requirements, and schedule no longer match the scope.

Defining scope is especially important when working with outside contractors. If you don't accurately define scope, the work they do may be either inadequate or overdone and can adversely affect your schedule and budget. If you assumed a contractor understood the scope, you may be charged for work you considered part of the project but the contractor considered extra.

Making Assumptions About the Project

When you plan a project, you need to make assumptions. Stating your assumptions at the beginning of the project-planning process helps you to later identify when conditions affecting your project have changed—and which assumptions must change to keep the project on track. It's important to state assumptions clearly and concisely so everyone knows the premises on which your goals and the schedule are based.

Some of your assumptions may turn out to be inaccurate. What's more important than the accuracy of your assumptions, though, is that you're aware of the assumptions you make. By stating them clearly, you'll be able to zero in on changes when they occur.

Suppose, for example, you're assuming that an outside contractor will be available to install the house's electrical wiring. You state this up front, so everyone understands that achieving your goals depends on this assumption being true. If the contractor isn't available, your assumption becomes false, requiring a change in the plan.

If incorrect assumptions could dramatically affect your schedule, be sure to put together a contingency plan. For example, if your outside contractor is not available to install the electrical wiring, what will you do instead? If you plan for this contingency before the project begins, you'll know exactly what to do if it occurs, and you'll lose the least amount of time in the schedule.

How do you decide which assumptions to make? Use the following questions as a guide.

- What are you assuming will have been done before you start?

- What external factors, outside of your control, can have a major impact on your schedule? The weather? Materials that must come from an outside vendor? Inflation, which may drive your costs over budget?

- What are you expecting to happen at the end? Do you consider, for example, that the project will be finished when the house's yard has been landscaped?

After you've prepared your goals, scope, and assumptions, share them with other members of your team. You may end up repeating the goal-setting process several times until you have the agreement and support of both your management and the rest of the project team. But in the long run, taking the time to get this agreement will save time and ensure success later.

ENTERING BASIC PROJECT INFORMATION IN YOUR PROJECT FILE

If you could keep your project's goals, scope, and assumptions near at hand as you develop your project plan, you'd have a better chance of building a realistic plan that meets your requirements. Microsoft Project allows you to do just that. In the first step to creating your project plan, you can enter your goals, scope, and assumptions directly into the plan. At the same time, you can also enter information such as the project title, a brief description of the project, the name of the company conducting the project, and the project manager's name. Most importantly, this is the time to enter the project start date and other date information.

Start a New Project File and Enter Project Date Information

A project file is the place where all of the information for a project plan is entered, stored, calculated, and edited. Before you can create your project plan, you need to start a new project file. You can start a new project file only if you've installed Microsoft Project on your computer and Microsoft Project is displayed on your computer screen.

Before Microsoft Project can schedule individual tasks or the entire project, you need to provide it with a reference point. Usually, this reference point is the *project start date*, which is the date on which you want your project to begin. Microsoft Project schedules tasks from that date forward only; it can't schedule tasks to begin before that date.

Enter a project start date when you want Microsoft Project to schedule tasks forward from a particular date. As you enter tasks, Microsoft Project schedules them to begin on the project start date by default. As you enter more information about each task, such as dependencies on other tasks or date constraints, Microsoft Project calculates new task start dates.

The other possible reference point you can specify is the *project finish date*, which is the latest date on which you want your project to end. If you enter a project finish date, Microsoft Project schedules backwards from this finish date, with each task finishing as late as possible to make the finish date.

Specify a project finish date if you want Microsoft Project to calculate the latest possible date that you can start and still make the schedule or if you want to know the latest possible start date for your project after you have entered all task information.

Typically, you enter a project start date, which enables Microsoft Project to schedule tasks flexibly from that date forward. If you enter a project finish date, you lock in the finish date and limit Microsoft Project's ability to schedule tasks flexibly. It's usually better to enter a project start date, add tasks, let Microsoft Project schedule the tasks, and then see if the end date calculated by Microsoft Project meets your needs. If it doesn't, you can edit the schedule (reduce the scope, shorten task durations, add more resources, and so on). Unless you know that the project must definitely end by an absolutely fixed deadline, you should avoid entering a project finish date.

➤ **To start a new project file and enter a project start date or finish date**

1   Click **New** 🗋.

The Project Information dialog box appears in front of a blank project file.

If you don't enter a date, Microsoft Project inserts the current date as the project start date.

2   Enter a project start date or a project finish date.

To enter a start date, enter the date on which you want to start your project in the **Start date** box.

To enter a finish date, click **Project Finish Date** in the **Schedule from** box, and then enter the finish date from which to schedule your project in the **Finish date** box.

To accept the default start date (the current date) and to have Microsoft Project schedule tasks from the project start date (which is the default method), click **OK**.

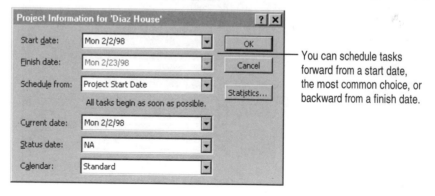

You can schedule tasks forward from a start date, the most common choice, or backward from a finish date.

After you click OK in the Project Information dialog box, an empty project file appears. By default, the Gantt Chart view is displayed.

To change your project information at any time, you can click **Project Information** on the **Project** menu.

Enter Project Goals, Scope, and Assumptions

Once you've determined your project goals, scope, and assumptions, you can add them directly to your project plan. Incorporating them into the plan helps keep you focused as you develop the plan. Then after your project has begun, you can easily refer back to your original goals, scope, and assumptions should you need to reevaluate them.

➤ **To enter project goals, scope, and assumptions**

1   On the **File** menu, click **Properties**, and then click the **Summary** tab.

2   In the **Comments** box, type your goals, scope, and assumptions.

   You can enter any other project notes here as well.

To find a project file, you can enter keywords in the **Text or Property** box of the **File Open** dialog box.

3   Fill in other boxes, as appropriate, such as the **Title**, **Manager**, **Company**, and **Keyword** boxes, and then click **OK**.

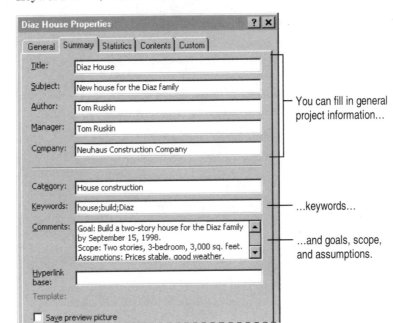

You can fill in general project information...

...keywords...

...and goals, scope, and assumptions.

Save Your Project File

When working on a project file, it's always smart to save your work frequently.

> ### To save your project file

- Click **Save** 💾.

  If this is the first time you've saved the project file, the **File Save** dialog box appears. Type a name for the project in the **File Name** box, and then click **Save**.

  If you haven't set a baseline for your project, the Planning Wizard dialog box appears, prompting you to save a baseline. A baseline is a set of original, planned project information that you can save and compare with actual information as your project progresses. The Planning Wizard continuously monitors your actions as you work and makes suggestions. Typically, you don't set a baseline until you've completed and refined your project plan, so select **Save without a baseline**.

Part 2

Creating and Refining Your Project Plan

In Part 2, you learn the basic steps for gathering project information and entering that information into Microsoft Project. You find out how to:

- Set your project goals.
- Create a task list.
- Estimate how long each task will take.
- Put tasks into a logical order.
- Show the dependency between one task and another, if any.
- Assign people, equipment, and costs to tasks.

In following these steps, you and your planning team spend the majority of your time gathering and analyzing information about project goals, tasks, resources, and costs. You enter this information into your project plan—and then you'll see the power of Microsoft Project as it helps you to create and refine your project model.

Each of the five chapters in Part 2 (chapters 4 to 8) describes a discrete step. In reality, each step depends on the others. You may find it easier to do all your planning at once, and then enter all the information into Microsoft Project. Or you may want to do one step at a time as you go through each chapter.

4

Breaking Your Project into Phases, Tasks, and Milestones

After you've determined your project goals, scope, and assumptions, your next step is to create a list of all those tasks that must be accomplished to meet your goals. Creating a comprehensive task list is essential, because if a required task is missing from the list, you may not achieve all your goals.

As you develop your task list, you should include phases and milestones, as well as tasks. A *task* is one of a number of specific activities that must be completed to achieve your project goals. A *phase* is a group of tasks that represents a distinct time period, intermediate goal, or some other logical division within a project. A *milestone* is a task that you use to indicate important events in your schedule, such as the completion of a project phase, and which has zero duration.

CREATING A TASK LIST

The task list is the heart of your project plan. Microsoft Project uses the task list you enter into a project file to schedule tasks, perhaps your primary reason for using project management software in the first place. Also, after you enter a task list, you can add task information, such as your estimates for task durations, costs, and the resources that should perform each task. Then, once the project begins, you can use your task list to keep track of task progress.

The main tasks you need to perform to create an effective task list are:

- Enter the tasks in the order they'll likely be performed, including milestones.
- Estimate and enter the amount of time required to complete each task.
- Group tasks into phases.

If your project consists of relatively few tasks, you may not want to group them into phases. Though for larger projects, phases can visually break a long task list into fewer, more manageable chunks and give you an overview of the major steps you need to take to reach your project goals.

Milestones are also optional, but by including them you in effect include a built-in check list of the most important events in your project. Milestones make it easier for you to tell when you've completed a major step and whether your project is progressing on schedule.

Phases First or Tasks First? Two Approaches to Creating a Task List

To create your list of tasks and milestones, you can use two basic methods, the top-down method or the bottom-up method.

Using the *top-down method*, you identify and enter the major phases first, and then you enter the tasks and milestones within each phase. You continue breaking tasks into smaller and smaller units until you reach the level of detail you want.

One advantage of this approach is that you have a version of the plan, although not very detailed, as soon as you decide the major phases. Once you determine this top-level schedule, you can distribute the major phases to the appropriate managers and have them work with their teams to create the detailed schedules.

For example, suppose your project is to build a house. The major phases might be "Lay the Foundation," "Put up the Frame," "Construct Outer Walls and Roof," and so on. The manager in charge of each phase can then work with the appropriate team members to create the individual task lists for each phase.

Using the *bottom-up method*, you list all possible tasks first, and then you group them into phases. For example, you could identify all tasks that would be performed by each department, such as all marketing department tasks to market a new product, all manufacturing tasks to manufacture a new product, and all procurement tasks to procure materials for a new product.

Since it may not be easy to know how the tasks from different departments are interrelated, the bottom-up method works best when you create a task list for smaller projects that involve only one department.

Whether you use the top-down or the bottom-up method, there are several ways you can generate your task list. For example, you can brainstorm with team members to identify major phases or detailed tasks. You can begin with the the goal or purpose of the project and then work backward to the start of the project, identifying the required tasks at each stage, or start at the beginning of the project and work forward to the goal.

Guidelines for Determining Your Tasks and Milestones

Since tasks and milestones provide the basis for the rest of your plan and for tracking the progress of your project, it's important that the task list be detailed and clear. You want tasks and milestones to be clearly worded and unambiguous so those using the plan know exactly what's expected to be accomplished by each task.

How do you determine which tasks and milestones to include in your project? The best way is to have each person who will do or manage the work submit a list of the tasks and milestones for which he or she is responsible. Once you have your task list, you enter it into Microsoft Project.

Guidelines for Determining Tasks

A task has an identifiable start and end; it usually requires people or equipment to complete it; and it's specific enough to permit both intermittent progress and the final result to be measured. For example, the task "Pour the concrete" calls for one or more people to do the work. Progress on the task can be measured by comparing the foundation sections that have been poured with the total number of sections. When you've poured all the sections, you're done.

Use the following guidelines to identify the tasks you should include in your project plan.

- Identify tasks as precisely as possible. Each task should be short compared to the overall project duration. For example, if you plan to put up a frame house, you may want to break the "Put up the Frame" task into three or more tasks, one for each part of the house (outer walls, inner walls, roof). This helps you make a more reliable estimate for the time and resources required to complete the task.

- Tasks must also be significant enough to be included in the plan. Insignificant or nonschedule–related tasks only clutter your project task list. For example, in the "Pour the concrete" task, mixing the concrete may be important in completing the task, but it may not be significant enough to include as a separate task if it doesn't affect how the tasks are scheduled.

- The level of detail in your list of tasks should be appropriate to the amount of planning and control you want. For example, if you're hiring an outside consultant to do a study, you're interested in when the consultant starts and when the study will be in your hands, but you aren't interested in the detailed tasks performed by the consultant. In your list of tasks, you'd include one task for the study, showing the duration for the whole, rather than many tasks indicating each step in the study.

- But if you're doing the study yourself, the separate steps in completing the study are crucial to you. Your list of tasks would include every step necessary to do the study.

- When you list your tasks and milestones, you must be aware of the scope of the tasks and the assumptions on which the tasks and milestones are based. This helps you to identify changes and measure progress.

- Be complete. Remember to include reports, reviews, and coordination activities in your list of tasks. And remember to include tasks for anticipated rework or modifications after a task has been completed, such as revising a manual or reworking and retesting a new product.

- Name a task using a verb and noun, such as "Pour the concrete," "Build the outer-wall frame," and "Shingle the roof." Make the names as explicit as possible, and keep the style of the names consistent throughout. This consistency will help others understand each task in your schedule.

Guidelines for Determining Milestones

A milestone is a task that indicates the end of a phase or the completion of an interim goal. It requires no work and has a duration and cost of zero. For example, if an interim goal of your project is to lay the foundation for a house, the actual tasks might include "Dig the foundation" and "Pour the concrete," and the milestone might be "Foundation complete."

By placing your milestones appropriately, they can help you measure the progress of your project and increase the motivation and productivity of team members by providing short-term goals. A missed milestone date can provide early warning that your project may not finish on time.

Use the following guidelines to identify the milestones you should include in your project plan.

- Put a milestone at the start and end of a series of tasks so it stresses the importance of starting and completing the tasks by a certain time. For example, at the beginning of "Lay the Foundation," you could include the milestone "Foundation phase begins" and at the end, "Foundation phase complete."

- Since milestones serve as checkpoints to help you track the schedule throughout the project, include milestones only down to the level of detail you want to monitor. If it's not important to you when the foundation phase starts, don't include the milestone.

- Be sure that milestones are related to tasks so you know when the milestone is achieved. For example, the milestone "Foundation phase complete" is directly related to the completion of the tasks preceding it. It will be obvious when you reach the milestone, because the tasks in the foundation phase will be complete.

- Include milestones that represent events outside your control if they influence your schedule. For example, include a milestone showing when you must have a bank loan to be able to proceed with a building project. As you approach the milestone, you can check on the loan to assure it will be in your hands when it's needed.

- Name a milestone in a way that it is clear when the milestone is reached. Use a noun and a verb, such as "Walls complete," "Funding request due," or "Loans approved." Make the names as clear as possible. The style of the names should be consistent throughout. This consistency will help others understand each item in your schedule.

Enter a Task

After you decide which tasks need to be accomplished in order to achieve your project goals, you enter those tasks into your project plan. Entering tasks is the first and most important step in creating a project plan. Later, after you enter information about each task, Microsoft Project uses that information to calculate task start and finish dates as well as the project finish date.

By default, Microsoft Project gives each task a duration of 1 day and a start date that's the same as the project start date.

❶	Task Name	Duration	Feb 1, '98
			T F S S M T W
1	Lay the Foundation	1 day	▓ — The default duration: 1 day.

> **To enter a task**

1 On the **View Bar**, click **Gantt Chart**.

2 In the **Task Name** field, type a task name.

   Use a verb and a noun to name tasks (for example, "Wire the outlets").

3 Click **Enter** or press ENTER.

If you already have a list of tasks created in a spreadsheet or database program, such as Microsoft Excel or Microsoft Access, you can import this list into Microsoft Project. For more information about importing project information, see Chapter 15, "Sharing Project Information with Other Programs and Projects."

Estimate the Time to Do a Task

All tasks, except milestones, will take some time to accomplish. The amount of time required to complete a task is called the task *duration*. When you include each task's duration in your project plan, Microsoft Project can calculate your project schedule. In the simple case, each task begins as soon as another one ends, and Microsoft Project adds only the individual task durations to calculate the project length (which, in turn, determines the project deadline).

But in a more realistic—and more common—project scenario, two or more tasks may be worked on at the same time or there may be a delay between the finish of one task and the start of the next one. In that case, Microsoft Project includes not only task durations but also other factors (such as delay, overlap, and task dependencies) when it calculates the project length, though task durations remain the most important factor.

Because of the importance of task durations, Microsoft Project's calculation of the project length will only be as accurate as your duration estimates. To estimate a duration as accurately as possible, you need to analyze the task and gather evidence to support your estimate. You can also estimate a duration based on three estimates: an optimistic estimate, a pessimistic estimate, and an expected estimate.

You can use the following sources to determine a task duration accurately:

- Look at how long similar tasks took on past projects. When you use historical data, note any differences between the new task and similar tasks in the past. Take these differences into account when you estimate the duration for the current task.

- Estimate the duration based on how long you'd take to do the task. If you're experienced, assume it would take an average worker longer. If you're not experienced, assume an average worker could do it faster.

- Let those who will actually do the work estimate how long the task will take. In the end, there's nothing like input from someone who's had hands-on experience with the task or a similar task.

For many projects, you can make a single duration estimate for each task and wind up with an accurate schedule. But if you want a greater degree of confidence in your duration estimates and you want to see how optimistic, pessimistic, and expected task durations each affect the resulting schedule, you can perform a PERT analysis (also known as what-if analysis). PERT analysis has nothing to do with the PERT Chart view. In fact, in Microsoft Project, you carry out PERT analysis using predefined variations of the Gantt Chart view and the PERT analysis toolbar. For more information on using PERT analysis, see Chapter 8, "Reviewing and Fine-Tuning Your Project Plan."

Microsoft Project doesn't include nonworking time, such as weekends and the time between the end of one workday and the beginning of the next workday, in a task's duration. For example, a 2-day task scheduled to begin on a Friday will occur on Friday and Monday.

If you want a task duration to span a continuous period of time, including any nonworking time, you can specify an *elapsed duration*. If you use an elapsed duration, then a 2-day task that begins on a Friday will occur on Friday and Saturday. For example, you can use an elapsed duration to indicate the drying time of a concrete wall.

Enter a Task Duration

After you enter a task name in the Task Name field (for instance, in the Gantt Chart view), Microsoft Project enters a duration of 1 day by default. If your estimate for the task's duration is different than 1 day, you can change the duration.

You can specify a duration in the following time units: minutes, hours, days, or weeks. To allow Microsoft Project to calculate a task's start and finish dates for you, enter a duration only; do not enter the start and finish dates yourself. By entering a duration only, you enable Microsoft Project to schedule tasks flexibly and calculate the most efficient overall schedule possible. If you also enter the start and finish dates for a task, you may pin the task to certain fixed dates and prevent Microsoft Project from scheduling tasks in a realistic sequence.

➢ **To change a task duration**

1   On the **View Bar**, click **Gantt Chart**.

2   In the **Duration** field for the task duration you want to change, type the duration you want.

To specify elapsed duration, precede the time unit with the letter "e" (for example, eday for elapsed days).

3   Press ENTER.

Enter a Milestone

In many projects, some events will be more significant than others. The completion of a major phase, the deadline for distributing an important project report, and the date of a crucial meeting with clients and upper management are examples of significant events. To visually distinguish significant events from regular tasks in your project schedule, you can turn those events into milestones.

In the Gantt Chart view, a milestone is listed along with other tasks in the task list. But, since the purpose of a milestone is to indicate a significant event and not work that needs to be accomplished, you give the milestone a duration of zero. Microsoft Project represents any zero-duration task by a diamond-shaped symbol instead of a Gantt bar in the bar chart portion of the view. By scanning for diamond shapes, you can quickly identify milestone events.

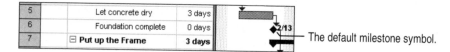
— The default milestone symbol.

If you use milestones to mark the completion of project phases, they can help you keep track of project progress. A milestone reachd on its scheduled date can give you confidence that you're on schedule. A milestone reached after its scheduled date can warn you that the project end date is threatened before it's too late to take corrective action.

➢ **To change a task to a milestone**

1   On the **View Bar**, click **Gantt Chart**.

2   In the **Duration** field of the task you want to change, type **0 days**.

3   Press ENTER.

Although milestones usually have zero duration, there may be times when you want to use a regular task, one with a nonzero duration, as a milestone marker. In Microsoft Project, you can make any task a milestone, even one with a nonzero duration.

➢ **To change a task with a nonzero duration to a milestone**

1   On the **View Bar**, click **Gantt Chart**.

2   In the **Task Name** field, select the task you want to change, and then click the **Information** button.

3   Select the **Advanced** tab, and then select the **Mark task as milestone** check box.

Enter a Recurring Task

Some tasks may occur repeatedly throughout a project. Printing a monthly status report is a typical example. Tasks that occur repeatedly are called *recurring tasks*. To reduce the amount of time it takes to add a recurring task to your project plan, you need only enter information about the recurring task once—information such as the task name and the frequency of occurrence. Then, Microsoft Project adds all occurrences of the task to the project plan at the frequency you specify.

➢ **To enter a recurring task**

1   On the **View Bar**, click **Gantt Chart**.

2   In the **Task Name** field, select the row above which you want to insert the recurring task.

3   On the **Insert** menu, click **Recurring Task**.

4   In the **Name** box, type the task name.

5   In the **Duration** box, type the duration of a single occurrence of the task.

6   Under **This occurs**, click the interval at which the task will recur.

   The interval you click determines whether the **Daily**, **Weekly**, **Monthly**, or **Yearly** options are displayed to the right of the interval list. By default, Weekly is selected and the Weekly options are displayed.

7   Under **Daily**, **Weekly**, **Monthly**, or **Yearly**, specify the task frequency.

   For example, if you clicked **Daily** under **This occurs**, you might specify every third workday. Or, if you clicked **Monthly**, you might specify the last Friday of every other month

8   Under **Length**, enter the start date for the recurring task in the **From** box and the finish date in the **To** box. Or, instead of entering the finish date in the **To** box, you can enter the number of times the task will occur in the **For occurrences** box.

   If you don't enter a date in the **From** box, the project start date is used.

Delete a Task

There are a number of reasons why you might want to delete a task from your project plan. Maybe you decided that the task isn't significant enough, or that it's too broad and needs to be broken down into smaller tasks. Perhaps you need to cut costs, eliminate some project goals, or reduce the project scope, each of which could result in some tasks no longer being necessary.

> ➤ **To delete a task**
> 1   On the **View Bar**, click **Gantt Chart**.
> 2   In the **Task Name** field, select the task you want to delete.
> 3   On the **Edit** menu, click **Delete Task**.

Change the Default Start Date for New Tasks

After you add a task to your project plan, Microsoft Project gives the task a start date that's the same as the project start date, by default. You can, however, change the default start date for new tasks to the current date (the only other option). After you change the default to the current date, tasks that you entered before you made the change aren't affected (their default start date is still the project start date). The same holds true if you change the default start date for tasks back to the project start date: Any tasks you entered while the default was the current date won't be affected by the change.

> ➤ **To change the default start date for new tasks**
> 1   On the **Tools** menu, click **Options**, and then click the **Schedule** tab.
> 2   In the **New tasks start on** box, click **Current Date**.

ORGANIZING YOUR TASK LIST

If you list ten or fifteen tasks in a logical order, your team members will be able to understand the purpose of the tasks and the relationships among them without much problem. But if your list contains dozens or perhaps hundreds of tasks, you'll need to structure your list to show relationship and hierarchy. In Microsoft Project, the main way to structure your task list is by outlining it. You can use outlining to:

- Group your tasks into phases, to make it easier to track progress.
- Reorganize your task list by moving tasks from one part of the list to another part.
- Collapse and expand your task list to see different levels of detail.
- Make your task list easier to read.

An outline consists of subtasks and summary tasks. A *subtask* is a step in a major task. You have to complete all of the subtasks to accomplish the major task.

A *summary task* includes several subtasks and often represents a major task or phase. An example of a summary task is "Dig the foundation," which includes the subtasks "Mark the digging area" and "Dig the hole." A summary task can include other summary tasks as well as subtasks.

As its name suggests, a summary task summarizes the information of its subtasks. For example, the duration of a summary task is the total time between the earliest start date and the latest finish date of its subtasks.

In Microsoft Project, a summary task appears bold and its subtasks are indented beneath it.

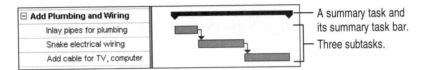

A summary task and its summary task bar.
Three subtasks.

You create an outline the same way you create a task list: by using either the top-down method or the bottom-up method. You can list the major phases first—summary tasks—and then add the detailed tasks required to fulfill the goals of those phases, or you can list the detailed tasks first and then group them under summary tasks.

When you want to share information about the project, you can share as much detail as required by the recipient of the information. For example, with top management, you might share the main phases; with the construction manager, you might share the main phases, plus all the tasks in those phases in which the construction crew is involved, such as "Put up the Frame" and "Construct the Outer Walls and Roof."

Indent and Outdent Tasks to Create an Outline

By outlining tasks, you convey useful information about those tasks. For example, you can show which group of tasks need to be performed to complete a project phase. You can also show hierarchy by using summary tasks to represent phases and subphases that are intermediate steps on the way to achieving your major project goals.

In Microsoft Project, the way to outline your task list is by indenting and outdenting tasks. When you indent a task one level with respect to a preceding task, the preceding task appears bold, indicating that it has become a summary task. The indented task becomes a subtask.

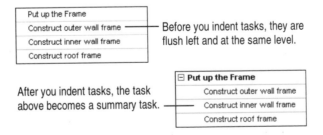

Before you indent tasks, they are flush left and at the same level.

After you indent tasks, the task above becomes a summary task.

You can outline tasks on the Gantt Chart view or on the Task Sheet view.

> ➤ **To indent or outdent tasks to create an outline**
>
> 1   On the **View Bar**, click **Gantt Chart**.
>
> 2   In the **Task Name** field, select the task you want to indent or outdent.
>
> 3   Click **Indent** [➡] to indent the task or **Outdent** [⬅] to outdent the task.

What to Do If the Outline Buttons Don't Work

The outline buttons, which are located on the Standard toolbar, work only when the Gantt Chart or Task Sheet is the active view. So first, make sure you're using one of these views. If you're using the Gantt Chart view or the Task Sheet view and the outline buttons still don't work, try doing one of the following:

*   On the **Tools** menu, click **Options**, and then click the **View** tab. In the **Outline options** box, make sure the **Show summary tasks** check box is checked.

*   On the **Project** menu, point to **Sort**, and then click **Sort by**. If the task list is not sorted by ID, either select **ID** in the **Sort by** box or select the **Keep outline structure** check box to maintain the outline structure in the sorted project. Click the **Sort** button.

Reorganize Your Outline

Your outline may not be perfect the first time around. You might, for instance, decide that a task belongs to a different phase, or that you don't need some tasks after all. The main ways to reorganize your outline are to move tasks and delete tasks.

You can move and delete summary tasks and subtasks. When you move a summary task, all of its subtasks go with it. When you delete a summary task, all of its subtasks are deleted too.

> ➤ **To move a task**
>
> 1   On the **View Bar**, click **Gantt Chart**.
>
> 2   On the left side of the task row, click the ID number of the task you want to move.
>
>   The entire task row is selected, which is necessary if you want to move a task and all of the information about that task.
>
> 3   On the **Edit** menu, click **Cut Task**.
>
>   The Cut Task command appears on the Edit menu only if an entire task row is selected (for example, by clicking the ID number of a task).
>
> 4   Select any part of the row where you want to insert the task.
>
> 5   On the **Edit** menu, click **Paste**.

Show and Hide Subtasks

In your outline, you can show or hide the subtasks of one summary task or show or hide the subtasks of all summary tasks. For example, you may want to hide all subtasks to display only the highest-level summary tasks and then print that view in a summary report. Or you may want to display every subtask so that team members can see a comprehensive list of their tasks.

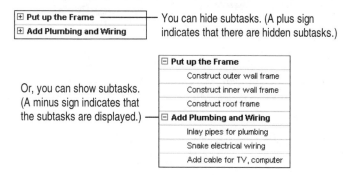

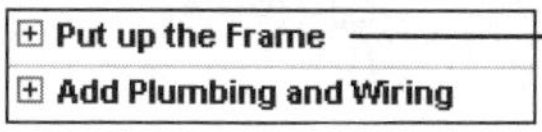
Put up the Frame
Add Plumbing and Wiring

You can hide subtasks. (A plus sign indicates that there are hidden subtasks.)

Or, you can show subtasks. (A minus sign indicates that the subtasks are displayed.)

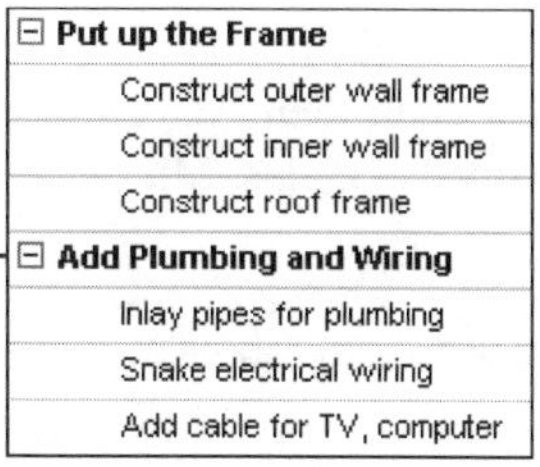
Put up the Frame
Construct outer wall frame
Construct inner wall frame
Construct roof frame
Add Plumbing and Wiring
Inlay pipes for plumbing
Snake electrical wiring
Add cable for TV, computer

> **To show and hide subtasks**

1 On the **View Bar**, click **Gantt Chart**.

2 In the **Task Name** field, select the summary task containing the subtasks you want to show or hide.

You can also click the plus or minus sign next to a summary task name to show or hide subtasks.

3 Click **Show Subtasks**  to show the subtasks or click **Hide Subtasks**  to hide the subtasks.

To show all subtasks, click **Show All Subtasks** 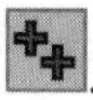.

Show Outline Symbols and Numbers

Outline symbols are tiny squares that contain either a plus sign or a minus sign. They are displayed next to summary tasks only (on the Gantt Chart view and the Task Sheet view), and indicate whether the subtasks of a summary task are hidden (plus sign) or displayed (minus sign). By clicking on an outline symbol, you can quickly show or hide subtasks.

Outline numbers indicate the level of a task in an outline. For example, 1, 1.1, and 1.1.1 indicate tasks of the highest level, the second-highest level, and the third-highest level, respectively. These numbers also show that task 1.1 is grouped under task 1 and task 1.1.1 is grouped under task 1.1. To help you keep track of a task's place in the outline hierarchy, you can use outline numbers.

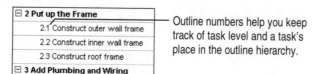

Outline numbers help you keep track of task level and a task's place in the outline hierarchy.

Outline numbers are updated automatically when you move a task in your schedule. You cannot edit them. If you want to use a work breakdown structure but don't add your own WBS codes, Microsoft Project uses the outline numbers as the default WBS codes.

➢ **To show outline symbols and numbers**

1 On the **View Bar**, click **Gantt Chart**.

2 On the **Tools** menu, click **Options**, and then click the **View** tab.

3 To show outline symbols: Under **Outline** options, click the **Show outline symbol** check box.

To show outline numbers: Under **Outline** options, click the **Show outline number** check box.

USING A WORK BREAKDOWN STRUCTURE

Most people managing most projects can organize their task lists by outlining them. But some project managers are required by their organizations or clients to organize project tasks by using a work breakdown structure.(When you create an outline, Microsoft Project also creates a WBS for you.) If you need to organize tasks in a work breakdown structure, then you should read this section.

A *work breakdown structure*, or WBS, is a tree-type of structure that includes every task and every result. It looks like an organizational chart for your company but is task-oriented instead of people-oriented. Each level of the WBS depicts the project at a different level of detail; the higher the level on the WBS, the less detailed are the tasks. Usually, there are three to five levels, depending on the project.

At the bottom or lowest level of a WBS is a *work package*, which is where the actual work is done and the resources are assigned. The characteristics of a work package are similar to those of a task.

Each task is given a code number. This number shows the level of the task and where the task fits in the hierarchy. You can use these codes for sorting and filtering tasks to look at a limited part of the project information. For example, if a department code is part of the WBS code, you could filter the task list to display only those tasks that include a certain department code.

When you create a WBS, you start with the project goals and then divide and redivide tasks until you get to the level of detail you need. This assures that all required tasks are logically identified and grouped. In the previous illustration, the first divisions are by project phases, but they could be by work units (engineers, programmers, production line, and so on), financial cost codes, departments (marketing, accounting, lab, and so on), or major units of the product (if you are building a car, for example, the major units might be engine, transmission, body, suspension, and so on).

Create a Work Breakdown Structure

In some organizations, it's necessary to keep track of tasks using a coding system called a work breakdown structure (WBS). When you use a WBS, each task is given its own code, such as a number. A task's code can indicate its place in the overall task hierarchy, the department responsible for completing the task, and so on.

By default, Microsoft Project uses outline numbers as the WBS coding system. If you want to organize your tasks in a WBS, you can use the outline numbers or add your own numbering system to the tasks in your schedule by changing the default outline numbers to custom WBS codes in the WBS field. Microsoft Project still retains the outline numbers it assigned to the tasks.

WBS codes differ from outline numbers in the following ways:

- Microsoft Project doesn't automatically calculate WBS codes. You'll need to enter a code for each individual task.

- Microsoft Project doesn't automatically update WBS codes when you add, move, delete, or rearrange tasks. You'll have to adjust your WBS codes manually.

➢ **To create a work breakdown structure**

1   On the **View Bar**, click **Gantt Chart**.

2   In the **Task Name** field, select the task to which you want to assign a WBS code.

3   Click the **Task Information** button.

4   Click the **Advanced** tab.

5   In the **WBS Code** box, type the code you want to assign to your task.

   To show outline numbers: On the **Tools** menu, click **Options**, and then click the **View** tab. Under **Outline options**, click the **Show outline number** check box.

You can also enter WBS codes for your tasks by adding the WBS field to the Task Sheet. Type the WBS code in the WBS field as you enter your tasks.

You don't have to create an outline to use a WBS coding system. However, if you want to use outlining features, such as showing and hiding subtasks, the hierarchy in your WBS coding system should match the outline hierarchy. Despite the WBS number you enter, the tasks must be entered at the appropriate level in the outline. All tasks at the same level in the WBS should be entered at one level in the outline.

You can use the WBS code to sort and filter tasks. For example, you can filter the task list to display only those tasks that have a WBS code for a certain department, or, if your coding system indicates processes, filter the tasks to see all tasks associated with one process.

5

Making Tasks Happen in the Right Order and at the Right Time

When you first enter tasks, Microsoft Project starts each task on the project start date, by default. But tasks usually occur in a logical sequence. For example, you dig a hole and then pour the foundation for a house.

To schedule your tasks so that they occur in the right order and at the right time, you first need to determine the task sequence and the type of task dependency one task has on another. The *task sequence* is the order in which your project tasks are worked on. A *task dependency* is the logical or causal connection between two tasks. In most cases, one task can't begin until the previous task is completed (the hole must be dug before the foundation is poured). But tasks can also start or finish at the same time. For example, you can shingle the roof at the same time that someone else is putting up the outer walls.

A task whose start or finish depends directly on the start or finish of another task is called a *successor* task. The task that a successor task depends on is called a *predecessor* task. For example, pouring the foundation is the successor task to digging a hole.

You specify dependencies between tasks by linking them. A *link* specifies the type of dependency that exists between two tasks. The most common type of dependency is one in which one task can't start until its predecessor has been completed.

Once two tasks are linked, the start and finish dates of the successor are contingent upon the start and finish dates of the predecessor task. For example, if the successor task can't begin until the predecessor task is completed, then the start date of the successor task will slip by 1 day for each day the predecessor task slips. By linking tasks, you let Microsoft Project calculate (and, if necessary, recalculate) the start and finish dates of tasks as well as the project finish date.

A predecessor task is a task that
a successor task depends on.

A line that shows a link, or
dependency, between two tasks.

A successor task's start or finish dates depend
on the start or finish dates of its predecessor task.

It's strongly recommended that you enter durations only and then link tasks. Doing so lets Microsoft Project calculate your schedule, so that you don't have to manually enter task start and finish dates. If you enter task dates manually, you may prevent Microsoft Project from automatically moving task dates forward or backward in time in response to changes in the schedule. You'd have to change the task dates yourself.

Sometimes, however, a task link alone might not be enough to show the complex dependency between two tasks. You may, for example, want the work on two tasks to overlap. Or, you may want one task to start several days after its predecessor task has been completed, and not immediately after. For example, after pouring the foundation, you may want to let the concrete dry for 3 days before you start putting up the house frame. The overlap between two tasks is called *lead time*. The delay between two tasks is called *lag time*.

In rare circumstances, you may really want a task to begin or end on or near a specific date, regardless of how dates for other tasks may change. An example of such a task is a conference to discuss project progress with a client. No matter how late or early tasks preceding the conference may be, you may want the conference date to remain fixed. A condition that tethers a task to a specific date is a *constraint*.

In real life, a task might not be worked on continuously from its start to its completion. Work on a task might be interrupted by sickness, vacation, or unplanned tasks that take priority. Microsoft Project enables you to model the pauses that occur during a task's lifetime by splitting tasks. When you *split tasks*, you show not only the overall start and finish dates for a task, but also the dates when work stops and resumes, as well as the time gaps that represent interruptions.

By using links, you specify the dependencies between tasks and the time frame within which each task will occur. By using lead time, lag time, constraints, and task-splitting, you can fine-tune your schedule so that tasks occur at exactly the right time.

DECIDE THE SEQUENCE OF YOUR TASKS

You should determine the general task sequence before you link tasks. To decide task sequence, answer the following questions for each task or group of related tasks:

- Does this task depend on another task? Most likely it does, but not all tasks do. For example, making a copy of the house blueprint to save in your files is something you can do at any point in the project.
- Which tasks does this task depend on? For example, which tasks must start or finish before this task can start?
- Which tasks depend on this task? For example, which tasks cannot start or finish until this task starts or finishes?

When you identify the predecessor tasks for a task, list only those tasks that the task depends on directly. For example, because you must build walls before you can paint them, building walls is a predecessor to painting walls. But, although the house frame must be built before the walls can be painted, building the frame is not an immediate predecessor to painting.

LET TASK DEPENDENCIES ESTABLISH THE BACKBONE OF YOUR SCHEDULE

Dependencies do not nail down task start and finish dates. Instead, they form a flexible time framework that indicates when each linked task should start or finish relative to the start or finish date of another task. Dependencies allow tasks to be scheduled flexibly. Microsoft Project can recalculate task dates as you enter actual start and finish dates for tasks that have started or finished earlier or later than your original estimates. You see the effects of schedule changes immediately.

For example, one kind of task dependency says, "Begin this task immediately after its predecessor task is completed." After you finish your project plan (but before the project starts), let's say that Microsoft Project calculates a task's finish date to be February 10, so that according to the dependency rule, the successor task's start date is February 11. But suppose the predecessor task actually takes one day longer than you estimated. After you enter the task's actual duration, Microsoft Project recalculates a finish date of February 11 for the predecessor task and, subsequently, a start date of February 12 for the successor task.

To develop most project schedules, you should start by linking tasks. This framework of linked, dependent tasks should form the backbone of your schedule. Once this backbone is in place, you can modify portions of it, if necessary, by adding lead or lag time, applying constraints, or splitting tasks.

The Types of Task Dependencies

The most common type of task dependency, the one you're likely to use the most, is one that specifies that a task can begin only when its predecessor has been completed. One task follows another sequentially. But tasks need not follow one another sequentially. In fact, if you linked all tasks so that one task could begin only after its predecessor was completed, you'd be guaranteed to have an unnecessarily long schedule. Sometimes, for instance, two tasks can start at the same time, a project-shortening dependency.

After you decide task sequence, you can link tasks. Each link can specify one of the four kinds of dependencies described in the following table.

Finish-to-start (FS) is the most commonly used task dependency.

To specify	Link the tasks with this task dependency type	How it looks on the Gantt Chart
A task starts after its predecessor is completed	Finish-to-start (FS)	
A task starts at the same time as its predecessor starts	Start-to start (SS)	
A task must be completed at the same time as its predecessor is completed	Finish-to-finish (FF)	
A task is completed after its predecessor starts	Start-to-finish (SF) (seldom used, but included in the program so that every possible dependency is available)	

By default, Microsoft Project applies a finish-to-start (FS) link to tasks, but you can choose the type of link that most accurately reflects the way one task depends on another.

Create a Task Link

After you've determined how the start or finish date of one task depends on the start or finish date of another task, you can link those tasks.

You can link tasks in two ways. For most projects, the finish-to-start (FS) link will be the most common link used. Therefore, Microsoft Project provides you with a way to quickly link two or more tasks with an FS link. If you want to link tasks with other than an FS link, you can use a different method. Whichever method you use, you can change a link from one type to another.

You can create an FS link between summary tasks as well as between subtasks. When you create an FS link between summary tasks, the start of one group of tasks depends on the completion of another group.

➤ **To link tasks in a finish-to-start (FS) dependency**

1   On the **View Bar**, click **Gantt Chart**.

Select nonadjacent tasks by holding down the CTRL key while you select the task.

2   In the **Task Name** field, select two or more tasks you want to link.

3   Click **Link Tasks** 🔗 .

A link line appears in the Gantt Chart view, connecting the two tasks. When you use the Link Tasks button, Microsoft Project automatically creates an FS link between the selected tasks.

➤ **To link tasks in a start-to-start (SS), finish-to-finish (FF), or a start-to-finish (SF) dependency**

1   On the **View Bar**, click **Gantt Chart**.

2   In the **Task Name** field, double-click the task you want to link.

The Task Information dialog box appears.

3   Click the **Predecessors** tab.

4   In the **ID** field, type the ID number of the predecessor task.

As you enter tasks, they are numbered sequentially. This number is called the ID.

5   In the **Type** box, click the row containing the ID number of the predecessor task.

6   Select the link type you want.

Change and Remove a Task Link

If the link between tasks doesn't accurately reflect the dependency between those tasks, you can easily change the type of link that connects them. If you later decide that you don't want a link between particular tasks, you can remove that link.

> **To change a task link**

1 On the **View Bar**, click **Gantt Chart**.

2 Double-click the link line of the tasks you want to change.

The Task Dependency dialog box appears. If the Bar Styles dialog box appears, you didn't click precisely on the task link line. Close this dialog box and click on the task link line again.

3 In the **Type** box, click the task link you want.

> **To remove a task link**

1 On the **View Bar**, click **Gantt Chart**.

2 Double-click the link line you want to remove.

The Task Dependency dialog box appears.

3 Click **Delete**.

FINE-TUNE TASK START AND FINISH DATES

When you link tasks, you accomplish two main goals. First, you create a dependency between each predecessor task and its successor task. For each kind of dependency, the successor task starts or finishes immediately after the start or finish date of its predecessor task.

For example, if a task that's completed at the end of the workday on February 10 is linked to its successor task with a finish-to-start link, the successor task will be scheduled to start at the beginning of the workday on February 11. If these tasks were linked with a finish-to-finish link, then the successor task would be scheduled to be completed exactly at the end of the workday on February 10, the same time as its predecessor task.

Second, by linking tasks you establish a flexible time framework in which one task starts or finishes relative to the start or finish date of a predecessor task. If a task starts earlier or later than planned, all the succeeding linked tasks start earlier or later.

For many linked tasks, the link alone sufficiently specifies the entire relationship between two tasks. Often, for instance, you probably do want one task to start immediately after its predecessor is completed. But what if the predecessor task is "Paint the walls" and the successor task is "Put up molding"? You'd probably want to delay putting up the molding until a few days after the walls have been painted, so that they can dry first.

Or, what if the painter, a part-time contractor who works only on Monday, Wednesday, and Friday, can't finish painting all the walls in one continuous time period? By default, Microsoft Project schedules each task to be worked on over consecutive time periods.

It might also turn out that the painter, who happens to be the best in town and very much in demand, can fit your job in only between specific dates. To make sure you get the best painter to do the job, you'd probably want to fix the "Paint the walls" task to a specific date so that it couldn't move even if preceding tasks finished earlier or later than planned.

For situations when linking alone doesn't specify the complete relationship between two tasks, you can:

- Overlap or delay tasks, by adding lead time or lag time, respectively.
- Indicate interruptions to a task as time gaps in a Gantt bar by splitting the task.
- Constrain a task to begin or end on or near a specific date.

The following topics describe these schedule fine-tuning methods in detail.

Overlap or Delay Tasks

When task links alone don't indicate accurately when a task should start or finish, you can add *lead time* or *lag time*. By using lag time, you can specify a waiting period, or delay, between the finish of a predecessor task and the start of a successor task. For example, if you need a three-day delay between painting walls and putting up molding, you can link these tasks with a finish-to-start dependency and then specify a three-day lag time.

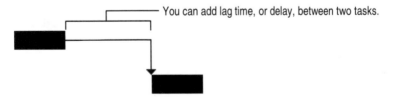

You can add lag time, or delay, between two tasks.

By using lead time, you can specify an overlap between linked tasks. For example, if you can start painting the walls after half the walls have been put up, you can specify a finish-to-start dependency with a lead time of 50 percent for the successor task.

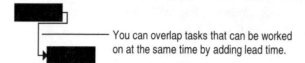

You can overlap tasks that can be worked on at the same time by adding lead time.

➤ **To overlap or delay linked tasks**

1   On the **View Bar**, click **Gantt Chart**.

2   In the **Task Name** field, select the task you want, and then click **Task Information** ▦.

3   Click the **Predecessors** tab.

Quickly add lead or lag time by double-clicking the link line.

4   In the **Lag** field, type the lead time or lag time you want, as a duration or as a percentage of the predecessor task duration.

Type lead time as a negative number or as a negative percentage, and type lag time as a positive number or as a positive percentage.

Interrupt Work on a Task (Split a Task)

If you know that work on a task will be interrupted when you initially enter the task, or if a task is interrupted during the course of the project, you can indicate the interruptions by splitting the task. For example, the person working on a task may have left on vacation and won't return for a week.

When you split a task, you show time gaps between portions of a task bar on the Gantt Chart. If the interruption occurs after a task has started, you can split it and use the split to show when work will continue on the remaining portion.

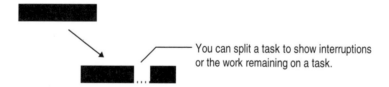

You can split a task to show interruptions or the work remaining on a task.

➢ **To split a task**

1   On the **View Bar**, click **Gantt Chart**.

To make multiple splits, double-click **Split Task**, make the splits, then single-click **Split Task**.

2   Click **Split Task** .

3   Move the pointer over the task bar you would like to split, and then click on the task bar where you want the split to occur.

You can create a longer split by clicking and dragging the task bar to the right.

➢ **To remove a task split**

1   On the **View Bar**, click **Gantt Chart**.

2   Drag a portion of a split task so that it touches another portion.

Note that dragging the leftmost portion of a split task moves the entire task.

Starting and Finishing Tasks On or Near Specific Dates

The most effective way to create a schedule is to enter tasks in a logical order, enter task durations, link the tasks, and then let Microsoft Project calculate the start and finish dates for you. This approach allows Microsoft Project to recalculate task start and finish dates if you enter changes to the schedule.

By default, Microsoft Project schedules tasks to start as soon as possible. That means, it schedules a task to begin as soon as the schedule allows. For instance, if a task starts 2 days earlier than planned and it's linked to a successor task with a finish-to-start link, Microsoft Project reschedules the successor to start "as soon as possible." In this case, that means 2 days earlier also.

A task that's scheduled to start as soon as possible is flexible: its start and finish date can change if other tasks start or finish earlier or later than planned. But sometimes you may want a task to start or finish on a particular date or no later than or no earlier than a particular date. When that's the case, you can apply a constraint to the task. A *constraint* is a condition that governs a task's start or finish date.

There are two categories of constraints, flexible constraints and inflexible constraints. A *flexible constraint* allows a task's dates to change as the schedule changes. The default constraint, As Soon As Possible, is an example of a flexible constraint. An *inflexible constraint* either ties a task to specific date or allows a task's dates to change until a specified date is reached. The Must Start On and Finish No Later Than constraints are examples of inflexible constraints.

To emphasize: By entering tasks and task durations and then linking tasks, you give your schedule maximum flexibility. You allow Microsoft Project to automatically recalculate task start and finish dates as the schedule changes. Only when you definitely need to model a real-world constraint on a task should you apply a constraint.

Types of Task Constraints

All tasks in Microsoft Project have a constraint applied to them. By default, the As Soon As Possible constraint is applied to a task. You can, however, specify any of the eight constraint types provided by Microsoft Project. These eight constraint types are described in the following table.

Constraint	Description
As Soon As Possible (ASAP)	Starts a task as soon as links and other factors in the schedule allow.
As Late As Possible (ALAP)	Starts a task as late as possible, without delaying the project finish date.
Start No Earlier Than (SNET)	Starts a task on or after the date you enter. Microsoft Project automatically assigns this constraint when you enter a task start date.
Finish No Earlier Than (FNET)	Finishes a task on or after the date you enter. Microsoft Project automatically assigns this constraint when you enter a task finish date.
Start No Later Than (SNLT)	Starts a task on or before the date you enter.
Finish No Later Than (FNLT)	Finishes a task on or before the date you enter.
Must Start On (MSO)	Starts a task on the date you enter.
Must Finish On (MFO)	Finishes a task on the date you enter.

Constrain a Task to Start or Finish on or Near a Specific Date

Sometimes, linking tasks and adding lag time or lead time may not cause a task to start or finish when you want it to. Then you might want to add a constraint to a task.

If you add a flexible constraint to a task, such as As Soon As Possible or As Late As Possible, then Microsoft Project can recalculate the task's start and finish dates if the schedule changes. If you add an inflexible constraint to a task, such as Must Start On or Start No Later Than, then Microsoft Project either won't be able to recalculate the task's dates (Must Start On) or it will only be able to recalculate the task's dates until a specified date is reached (Start No Later Than).

➤ **To constrain a task to start or finish on or near a specific date**

1   On the **View Bar**, click **Gantt Chart**.

2   In the **Task Name** field, select the task you want, and then click **Task Information** 📇.

The Task Information dialog box appears.

3   Click the **Advanced** tab.

4   In the **Type** box, click a constraint type.

If you selected a constraint other than As Late As Possible or As Soon As Possible, type a constraint date in the **Date** box.

If you type a start date for a task or drag a Gantt bar to change the start date, Microsoft Project sets a Start No Earlier Than (SNET) constraint based on the new start date. If you type a finish date for a task, Microsoft Project automatically assigns a Finish No Earlier Than (FNET) constraint.

6

Assigning Resources to Tasks

Resources are the people and equipment required to accomplish project tasks and goals. Each resource works on the task or tasks you assign to it. Often, a task has only one resource assigned to it. But you can assign several resources to the same task. Typically, the more resources you assign to a task, the shorter the task duration. For example, if 2 painters take 4 days to paint a house, then you can cut the length to 2 days by assigning a total of 4 painters.

You can assign any resource to any task, but you want to be sure that a resource has the skills required to accomplish the assignment. At any time, you can change resource assignments.

Although resources are the engine of every project, a project plan that contains just tasks provides enough information to enable you to manage your project and accomplish your goals. But by including resources in your project plan, you can:

- See who is working on which task and when.

- Fine-tune task duration by assigning more or fewer resources to a task. Microsoft Project calculates a task's duration based on the number of resources assigned to it and whether they're working on the task full-time or part-time.

- Identify resources who are overworked or underworked, and then distribute the workload more evenly.

- Track how much each resource is costing throughout the project.

- Keep project scope, time, and resources in balance. For example, if the project scope increases because your client wants to add three rooms to the house but still want the house completed by the original deadline, you can compensate by adding more resources to the project.

To use resources effectively in your project plan, you need to create a *resource list*, which contains the name of the resources that are available to your project, assign those resources to tasks, and set the working and nonworking days and hours for your resources.

You set working and nonworking days and hours in a *project calendar*, which shows the working days and hours for your entire plan. You can also create a *base calendar*, which shows the working days and hours for a group of resources (such as a department or a shift) as well as a *resource calendar*, which shows the working days and hours for an individual resource only.

Microsoft Project uses the information from these *working times calendars* to calculate task schedules and durations. For example, suppose an 8-hour task is scheduled to begin first thing Monday morning. If Joe, a part-timer whose resource calendar indicates he works 4 hours per day, is assigned to the task, the task will have a duration of 2 days and a finish date of Tuesday. But if Mary, scheduled to work 8 hours per day, is given the assignment, the task will have a duration of 1 day and finish end-of-day on Monday.

ASSEMBLING YOUR RESOURCES

When you use resources in your project plan, you need to consider the needs of the individual tasks as well as the needs of the project. To satisfy the needs of an individual task, you want to assign a resource that has the ability to accomplish the task swiftly and skillfully. You do this by matching resource skills to task requirements.

To satisfy the needs of the project as a whole, you need to assign enough resources to accomplish your project goals on time. The number of resources you require to complete the project on schedule may change as the project progresses.

As you determine your resource needs and create a resource list, you may want to create sets of resources that perform the same function, with the intention of assigning all or part of the set to individual tasks. You could, for instance, group all 4 painters under the resource name "Painters," and then assign 1, 2, 3, or all 4 painters to the same task all at once.

Estimating Resource Needs

How many resources does your project require, and what skills do those resources need? The best way to answer these questions is by estimating the resource needs of each task. One way to analyze the resource requirements of a task is to check similar tasks from past projects. Another way is to have the resource who's most knowledgeable about a task estimate the task's resource needs.

Whether you or someone else estimates resource needs, the following questions should be asked:

- What skills are required to accomplish the task?
- What level of skill is required to achieve the desired level of quality?
- How many resources are needed to accomplish the task in the time allotted?
- Can a resource work on more than one task, or perhaps more than one kind of task?

As you estimate resource needs, you may find that breaking a task into smaller tasks improves your ability to predict the resources and work for the task. If so, repeat the steps to enter the new tasks, estimate duration, and add the appropriate relationships with other tasks so the new tasks fit into the schedule.

Create a Resource List for Your Project

After you've determined which resources you need, you can add them to your project plan by creating a resource list. A resource list tells you who is on your project team.

Although Microsoft Project enables you to add resources to your plan one at a time as you assign them to tasks, it will take less time if you add all resources to your plan at once, and then assign them. In addition, you'll be able to see a list of all of your resources before assigning them, making it easy to pick the most qualified resource for each task.

Your resource list should include the name of the resource, which can be a person, a piece of equipment, or a group of interchangeable resources, such as painters, as well as the maximum amount of time per day a resource is available to work.

If resources with the same skills are going to work together on the same task, you can group them into a resource set, and then give this set a name that represents all resources in the set. For example, "Painters" could represent two or more painters.

➤ **To create a resource list**

1 On the **View Bar**, click **Resource Sheet**.

2 On the **View** menu, point to **Table**, and then click **Entry**.

3 In the **Resource Name** field, type a resource name.

4 If you want to designate a resource group, type a name in the **Group** field.

5 If necessary, type the number of resource units available for this resource in the **Max. Units** field, as a percentage.

By default, Microsoft Project enters 100% into this field, the correct value for an individual, full-time resource. For a resource that represents a set of full-time resources, enter a multiple of 100%. For example, type 200% to indicate two full-time units of a particular resource.

6 Change the default information in the remaining fields as appropriate.

7 Repeat steps 3 to 6 for each resource.

To use the workgroup features of Microsoft Project, you must enter e-mail names for resources. The workgroup features enable you and your team members to exchange task assignment messages over an e-mail or web-related network, such as an *intranet* or the World Wide Web. For more information about workgroup, see Chapter 10, "Updating Task Information by Using E-Mail and the Web."

As you work in the Gantt Chart or other task sheet views, you can enter additional resource names.

➤ **To enter additional resources on your resource list**

1 Click **Assign Resources** .

The Assign Resources dialog box appears.

2 In the **Name** field, type a resource name.

You can also click **Address**, and then select a resource from your e-mail address book.

Add a Resource to a Group

A resource *group* is any combination of individual resources and/or resource sets that can be logically grouped, typically to track costs. An example of a resource group is a department within an organization.

➢ **To add a resource to a group**

1   On the **View Bar**, click **Resource Sheet**.

2   On the **View** menu, point to **Table**, and then click **Entry**.

3   For those resources you want to assign to a group, type a name for the group in the **Group** field.

Resource groups cannot be assigned to tasks.

ASSIGNING RESOURCES TO TASKS

By assigning resources to tasks, you gain a high degree of control over your project. For instance, you can:

- Adjust a task duration with great precision by adding more or fewer resources to the task.
- Know at a glance who's responsible for a task.
- Make sure the workload is evenly distributed among resources.
- Monitor how much work has been done by the resources assigned to tasks.
- Keep track of resource costs.

If you use Microsoft Project's default scheduling method, called *effort-driven scheduling*, then the number of resources assigned to the task affect the task duration. If you assign resources and you've entered cost information, Microsoft Project calculates the costs for your resources and tasks. If a task has a fixed duration, Microsoft Project ignores the resource work when scheduling that task. For example, "paint drying" can be a fixed-duration task because it takes the same amount of time no matter how much work is performed.

You can assign a resource to work full-time or part-time on a task. For example, suppose that a full-time resource works 8 hours per day. If you assign that resource to work half-time on a 20-hour task, then the resource will work on the task for 4 hours per day and accomplish the task in 5 days.

To adjust task schedules, durations, and costs (if you entered cost information), you can assign resources in the following ways:

- Assign an individual resource or a set or interchangeable resources to a task.
- Assign several resources to a task.
- Assign a resource to work part-time on a task.
- Control the order in which multiple resources work on the same task.
- Remove a resource from a task.
- Replace one resource with another resource.

About Resource Units

Units indicate the percentage of time a resource will spend working on a task. For example, if you assign a resource to work full-time on a task, you'd assign that resource at 100% units. (If the resource works a full, 8-hour day, then 100% units equals 8 hours.) If you want that resource to spend only half of its available time on the task, you'd assign that resource at 50% units (which Microsoft Project calculates to be 4 hours for this resource).

When you assign a set of resources to a task, 100% units means you've assigned one resource from that set to work on the task full-time, 200% means you've assigned two resources from the set, and so on.

Assign One or More Resources to a Task

When you assign resources to tasks, you allow Microsoft Project to adjust task durations based on the number of resources assigned, keep track of task assignments, calculate task and resource costs, and more. Assigning resources gives you added control while adding little to your management overhead.

You can assign more than one resource to a task and specify whether a resource works full-time or part-time on the task by using resource units. By default, Microsoft Project assigns each resource at 100% units. If a resource represents a set of resources, then you may want to change the units to reflect the number resources you're assigning from the set.

When you assign a resource to a task, the name of the resource appears next to the Gantt bar (on the Gantt Chart) that represents that task.

➢ **To assign a resource to a task**

1 On the **View Bar**, click **Gantt Chart**.

2 In the **Task Name** field, select the task to which you want to assign a resource, and then click **Assign Resources** .

3 In the **Name** field, select the resource you want to assign to the task or click **Address** to select a resource from your e-mail address book.

   To assign a resource part-time, type a percentage less than 100 in the **Units** field to represent the percentage of working time you want the resource to spend on the task.

   To assign several different resources, select them.

   To assign more than one of the same resource (such as two painters), type a percentage amount greater than 100% in the **Units** field.

   If necessary, type the name of a new resource in the **Name** field.

4   Click **Assign**.

A check mark to the left of the Name field indicates that the resource is assigned to the selected task.

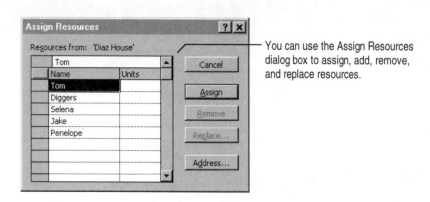

You can use the Assign Resources dialog box to assign, add, remove, and replace resources.

To assign resources as you complete other work on your schedule, you can continue to display the Assign Resources dialog box while you work with the Gantt Chart and other Microsoft Project views.

Remove a Resource from a Task

Resources can get sick, leave the project, or be reassigned to more urgent tasks before they've completed their assignments. If a resource is a piece of equipment, it can break down. When any of these and similar circumstances occur, you can remove a resource from a task.

Removing assigned resources from tasks can change the durations for those tasks. The work assigned to the removed resources will be redistributed to the remaining assigned resources. If you don't want this to happen for some tasks, turn off effort-driven scheduling for those tasks.

➢ **To remove a resource from a task**

1   On the **View Bar**, click **Gantt Chart**.

2   In the **Task Name** field, select a task, and then click **Assign Resources** .

3   Select the resource you want to remove.

4   Click **Remove**.

Assign Part-Time Resources to a Task

Some resources may work on more than one task at the same time, and others may only be working part-time on the project. If you assign a resource full-time to concurrent tasks, Microsoft Project will indicate that the resource is overallocated. That is, you've scheduled the resource to work more than a full workday. To take into account resources who don't work full-time and to avoid overloading resources who work on several tasks concurrently, you can assign resources part-time.

For example, if a resource works on two tasks concurrently, you can assign that resource at 50% units on each task, or at 30% on one task and 70% on the other, and so on, as long as you keep the total at or below 100%. (Assigning a resource at more than 100% units means that you've assigned the resource to work more hours than the resource is normally available.)

➤ **To assign a resource to a task part-time**

1 On the **View Bar**, click **Gantt Chart**.

2 In the **Task Name** field, select a task, and then click **Assign Resources** .

3 In the **Name** field, type the name of a resource or select an existing resource.

4 Type a percentage less than 100 in the **Units** field.

5 Click **Assign**.

Control When a Resource Works on a Task

When several resources are assigned to a task, each resource may not be required to work on the entire task from beginning to end. For example, a supervisor may work at the beginning of a task to help the team get started and then again at the end of the task to review the results. To fine-tune exactly when a resource "jumps in" on a task, you can delay the starting time of one or more resources.

By specifying more than one delay for a resource, you can, in effect, assign the same resource several times to the same task. For instance, suppose a task is 40 hours long. Selena is assigned to do 6 hours of work and 3 hours of work on the task, with these assignments delayed 10 hours and 27 hours after the task's start time, respectively. That means, 10 hours after the task has begun, Selena will do 6 hours of work and then stop. Then, 27 hours after the task has started, Selena will perform 3 more hours of work on the task, completing her involvement with that task.

You can assign one or more resources to a task as many times as necessary to control when work occurs. When you delay a resource's start on a task, Microsoft Project recalculates the start date and times for the resource's work on the task.

➤ **To control when a resource works on a task**

1   On the **View Bar**, click **Task Usage**.

2   In the **Task Name** field, select the resource you want to change.

3   Click **Assignment Information** 📋, and then click the **General** tab.

4   In the **Start** box or the **Finish** box, type the date you want the resource to start or finish.

Replace a Resource in One Step

Occasionally, a piece of equipment might break down. Or, maybe you can reduce costs by replacing an expensive resource with a less-expensive one. In these and other situations, you may need to replace a resource.

With Microsoft Project, you can replace a resource with another resource on your resource list in one step. Rather than removing the assigned resource and then assigning another resource in a separate action, you can simply replace one resource with another.

➤ **To replace a resource with another resource**

1   On the **View Bar**, click **Gantt Chart**.

2   In the **Task Name** field, select a task with a resource you want to replace.

3   Click **Assign Resources** 🖼.

4   Select the resource you want to replace, and then click **Replace**.

5   Select one or more resources to assign to the task.

Setting Working Times for Resources

Assigning resources to tasks affects the way Microsoft Project calculates task start and finish dates and task durations. For example, if you assign one full-time resource to a task and then at a later time assign a second full-time resource, Microsoft Project will, by default, reduce the task duration by half. To calculate the durations of tasks to which resources are assigned, Microsoft Project needs to know what "full-time" means. You define "full-time" and "part-time" by setting a working times calendars.

A *working times calendar* supplies the resource working and nonworking days and hours required to calculate task schedules. It specifies the number of hours in a full working day, workdays, vacations, holidays, and other days off.

For most projects and resources, you won't need to create a working times calendar; you can use the default working times calendar, Standard. You don't need to assign Standard to your resources, because Microsoft Project does that for you automatically. Standard defines an 8-hour working day that begins at 8:00 A.M. and ends at 5:00 P.M., with a 1-hour break. You'll probably need to modify Standard, though, because it doesn't include vacations and holidays and it defines all Saturdays and Sundays as nonworking days.

There are two kinds of working times calendars, base calendars and resource calendars. A *base calendar* specifies the working and nonworking time of a group of resources. You can have several base calendars, one for each different set of working times. For example, you can have one base calendar each for a day shift, a swing shift, and a night shift. A base calendar that applies to all resources in a project is called the *project calendar*. An example of a project calendar is the default calendar, Standard.

A *resource calendar* specifies the working and nonworking time of an individual resource. You can use a resource calendar to specify a resource's vacation days, personal days, sick days, and so on.

Exceptions in base and resource calendar take precedence over the corresponding times and days in the project calendar. For example, the project calendar may designate February 10 to be a workday, but Tom's resource calendar shows that he's taking a vacation day on February 10. If Tom is assigned to a 2-day task that begins on February 9, then Microsoft Project schedules the task to be completed on February 11, not on February 10. Microsoft Project doesn't schedule work on a task during nonworking time. If you don't modify base and resource calendars, they will be identical to the project calendar, which is usually a modified version of Standard.

Change Your Project's Working Days and Hours

Microsoft Project automatically attaches the Standard calendar to your plan, which is your default project calendar. According to the Standard calendar, a full working day is 8 hours long, lasting from 8:00 A.M. to 5:00 P.M. with a 1-hour break from 12:00 P.M. to 1:00 P.M. Each Monday, Tuesday, Wednesday, Thursday, and Friday is a working day, and each Saturday and Sunday is a nonworking day. Standard doesn't include holidays and vacations. At a minimum, you need to modify Standard to show all holidays and vacation time shared by your team members (if team members take vacation at the same time).

The settings in Standard affect all of your project resources. You can modify these settings to reflect the actual working times of your resources. Because the project calendar (or any base calendar) acts as the "parent" calendar, the changes you make to it will be reflected in the resource calendars that are based on it.

If your resources don't work specific shifts, make sure that the workday start and finish hours equal the total number of hours they work each day. For instance, if a resource works 10 hours per day, you might specify start and finish times of 7:00 A.M. and 6:00 P.M., with a 1-hour break.

➢ **To change the project calendar**

1   On the **Tools** menu, click **Change Working Time**.

2   Select a date on the calendar.

   To change a day of the week for the entire calendar, select the day at the top of the calendar.

3   Click **Use default**, **Nonworking time**, or **Working time**.

4   If you clicked **Working time** in step 3, type the times you want work to start in the **From** boxes and the times you want work to end in the **To** boxes.

You can use the Change Working Time dialog box to change the working times of a single resource, a specific group of resources, or all resources. You can also use it to create base calendars.

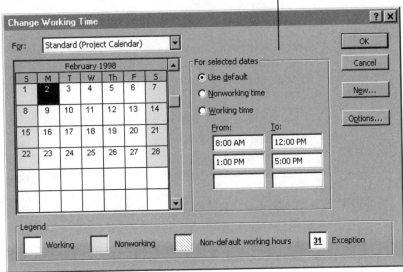

Create a Base Calendar

For each resource in your project plan, Microsoft Project automatically creates a resource calendar based on the Standard calendar. In some projects, though, different groups of resources may work at different times. For example, some resources may work the day shift and other resources, the night shift. When different groups of resources have different schedules, you can create a base calendar for each resource group. Then, you base each resource calendar on a new base calendar.

Just as with the Standard calendar, when you make a change in a base calendar, that change is transmitted to the resource calendars that are based on it. For example, suppose Rosemarie's and Tom's calendars are based on the Electricians calendar. If you set March 15 to a working day in the Electricians calendar, then March 15 also becomes a working day in Rosemarie's and Tom's individual resource calendars.

➢ **To create a base calendar**

1 On the **Tools** menu, click **Change Working Time**.

2 Click **New**.

3 In the **Name** box, type a name for your new base calendar.

   If you want to begin with a default calendar, click **Create new base calendar**.

   If you want to create a new calendar based on an existing calendar, click **Make a copy of**, and then click the calendar name in the calendar box.

4 Click **OK**.

5 On the calendar, select the days you want to change.

   To change a day of the week for the entire calendar, select the day at the top of the calendar.

6 Click **Use default**, **Nonworking time**, or **Working time**.

7 If you clicked **Working time** in step 6, type the times you want work to start in the **From** boxes and the times you want work to end in the **To** boxes.

➢ **To quickly remove all the changes you've made to a calendar**

• Select all of the days on the calendar, and then click **Use default**.

Assign a project or base calendar to a resource

Each resource in your plan is, by default, assigned to the project calendar, which in most cases is the default calendar, Standard. If you create a new project calendar or a new base calendar, you'll need to assign the new calendar to some or all of your resources.

➢ **To assign a project or base calendar to a resource**

1   On the **View Bar**, click **Resource Sheet**.

2   In the **Resource Name** field, select the resource to which you want to assign a calendar.

3   Click **Resource Information** , and then click the **Working Time** tab.

4   In the **Base Calendar** box, click the calendar you want for the resource.

Change Working Times for a Resource

Resources on a project often share the same working days, nonworking days, and holidays. So that you don't have to specify these shared working and nonworking days for each resource, each resource calendar inherits the same set of working and nonworking days from the base calendar its based on.

But, in many projects, one resource's working days and hours may differ from the working times of other resources in the group. For example, the resources might take vacations at different times. When resources have different schedules, you can modify the working times in each resource calendar.

➢ **To change working times for a resource**

1   On the **Tools** menu, click **Change Working Time**.

2   In the **For** box, click the resource whose calendar you want to change.

3   On the calendar, select the days you want to change.

To change a day of the week for the entire calendar, select the day at the top of the calendar.

4   Click **Use default**, **Nonworking time**, or **Working time**.

5   If you clicked **Working time** in step 4, type the times you want work to start in the **From** boxes and the times you want work to end in the **To** boxes.

Night and Swing Shift Calendars

You can create a night-shift or swing-shift base calendar and assign it to a group of resources or set the working hours for each resource individually.

To create night shifts, you enter the working times for each of the 2 days that the shift spans. For example, if a resource works from 11:00 P.M. Thursday to 8:00 A.M. Friday, you would enter shifts for each day: Thursday: From 11:00 P.M. to 12:00 A.M. Friday: From 12:00 A.M. to 8:00 A.M.

The first day of the work week has the evening hours only. The last day has the morning hours only.

7

How to Assign and Manage Costs

In many projects, cost management helps project managers control not only costs but the schedule as well. For example, costs can help you decide how quickly tasks should be performed: Should you add more resources now to accomplish tasks sooner (and bring in the schedule) or wait until the budget is approved for the next fiscal year? Although you can manage your project effectively by working with tasks and resources only, you'll be better able to factor costs into your key decisions if you add cost information to your project plan.

By estimating costs and assigning them to tasks and resources in your project plan, you can:

- Develop a project budget based on estimated task and resource costs so you can know when and where your money is spent.
- View the cost to date of tasks or of the project as a whole so you can make the adjustments necessary to stay within your budget.
- Control when task and resource costs are accrued.
- View the component costs per task, such as resource and materials costs.
- Estimate the cost required to complete a task by viewing remaining cost.
- Determine how closely the final project costs match their budget or baseline costs.
- Generate more accurate bid proposals by estimating project costs, and then reducing those costs to realistic levels.
- Plan budgets for future projects.

In most projects, the effort required to accomplish tasks takes the largest bite out of the project budget. The cost of a task can be broken down into a resource cost and a materials cost, with the resource cost usually being the larger of the two. (Here, "materials" is broadly defined to include anything from silicon to steel, and from carpeting to computers.)

Costs can be fixed or variable. A *fixed cost* remains constant regardless of the amount of time required to accomplish a task or the number of hours resources spend on the task. For example, contractors often bid a fixed price for a job, so the contractor cost stays the same even if the job takes more or less time than planned. The cost of a piece of equipment or of the materials required to accomplish a task are also examples of fixed costs.

A *variable cost* typically increases over time. For example, if a resource is paid hourly, the longer the resource spends on a task, the greater will be the resource cost for that task.

ASSIGNING COSTS

A project budget doesn't materialize out of thin air. It's the sum of task costs, resource costs, and other project costs. One of the best ways to determine the total project cost, and thus the size of the budget you require, is to assign a cost to each task, resource, and material in your project plan and then let Microsoft Project calculate the total cost for you. Of course, the initial costs you enter may be estimates, but as you enter actual costs during the project, Microsoft Project recalculates task and resource costs as well as overall project costs.

The key to monitoring costs effectively is to assign rates to resources. You can assign hourly rates to some resources and *per-use* costs to others. A per-use cost is a flat usage charge you incur each time, and only each time, you use a resource. For example, the fee for renting a tractor might be $100 per use.

With Microsoft Project, you can:

- Assign a rate to a resource, to monitor resource costs and let Microsoft Project calculate task costs by multiplying resource rates by task durations.

- Assign different rates to a resource over time, to specify pay increases (or decreases) that go into effect at a particular time.

- Assign a different rate for each kind of task performed by the same resource.

- Assign fixed costs to a task, to keep track of one-time-only or set costs.

- Assign a unit-based material cost to a task, to enter material costs based on a unit price.

- Change the standard and overtime default rates, to save time specifying the rates of newly added resources.

- Assign overtime work to apply overtime rates to tasks.

Assign a Rate to a Resource

When you decide to track costs, probably the most important factor to consider is the cost of resources. That's because resource costs usually make up the largest portion of task costs, and thus of overall project costs. Mainly, you'll want to monitor how the cost of each task depends on the amount of time its resources spend on it. Typically, as resources spend more time on a task, the task cost increases.

To keep track of the resource contribution to the cost of a task, you need to do two things: assign at least one resource to the task and assign a rate to each resource. While you can track costs without including resources in your project plan (for example, by assigning a fixed cost to each task that includes an estimate for the resource cost), your task costs can more closely reflect reality if you assign resources to tasks and then assign rates to resources.

You can assign hourly or fixed rates to resources. For hourly rates, you can assign a standard rate, which is the rate you pay a resource during normal working hours. To resources you anticipate working longer than the normal working hours, you can assign also an overtime rate. To resources who charge a flat amount to do a job, you can assign a fixed cost per use. You can also assign both an hourly rate and a fixed-cost-per-use rate to the same resource. For example, you might pay a $100 setup charge for each computer you rent, plus an hourly rate to the personnel who set up the computers.

➤ **To assign a rate to a resource**
1 On the **View Bar**, click **Resource Sheet**.
2 In the **Std. Rate**, **Ovt. Rate**, and **Cost/Use** fields for the resource, type the rates that apply, and then press ENTER.

Assign Different Pay Rates Over Time to a Resource

The initial pay rate you assign to a resource might be applicable for only a portion of the time that the resource works on the project. For instance, a resource's pay rate may change due to pay increases or decreases. You can allow Microsoft Project to apply new resource rates to cost calculations automatically by assigning different rate values to be applied at times you specify. You can assign up to 25 different rate levels and decide the date each rate will take effect.

> ➤ **To assign different pay rates over time to a resource**

    1   On the **View Bar**, click **Resource Sheet**.

    2   In the **Resource Name** field, select the resource for which you want to enter different rates.

    3   Click **Resource Information** 📋, and then click the **Costs** tab.

        The default cost rate table, A, is on top. If you don't specify which of a resource's cost rate tables to use for a task, Microsoft Project uses cost rate table A by default.

    4   In the **Cost rate tables**, type the effective date and the new standard, overtime, or per-use cost rate in the corresponding fields of the first blank row.

        You can enter rate increases or decreases by entering a new rate or a percentage. For example, you can enter +8% or –8%. When you enter a percentage, Microsoft Project will calculate the new rate for you.

    You can enter up to 25 different resource rates in each of the five cost rate tables to support increases or decreases for different initial resource rates.

Assign a Different Rate for Each Kind of Task Performed by the Same Resource

A resource may have several skills, each of which can be applied to a different type of task in your project. For example, an individual resource may be both an electrician and a painter, skills that usually command different pay rates. If you assign a multitalented resource to tasks that require different pay rates, you can enter different rates into that resource's rate tables.

For each resource, you can specify rates for up to five different kinds of tasks. To automatically apply pay increases or decreases, you can specify up to 25 rates for each kind of task as well as the date each rate goes into effect, so that you can select the correct rate for each task assignment.

> ➤ **To assign a different rate for each kind of task performed by a resource**

    1   On the **View Bar**, click **Resource Sheet**.

    2   In the **Resource Name** field, select a resource, and then click **Resource Information** 📋.

    3   Click the **Costs** tab.

        The default cost rate table, A, is on top. If you don't specify which of a resource's cost rate tables to use for a task, Microsoft Project uses cost rate table A by default.

4   In the **Standard Rate**, **Overtime Rate**, and **Per Use Cost** fields, type the rates for one of the kinds of tasks performed by the resource.

To take account of pay increases or decreases, you can specify up to 25 rates for each kind of task as well as the date on which each rate becomes effective.

5   To specify the rates for another kind of task performed by the resource, click another cost rate tab, and then repeat step 4.

To Apply a Different Rate for Each Kind of Task Performed by the Same Resource

By default, Microsoft Project applies the standard pay rate specified in cost rate table A or the Std. Rate column of the Resource Sheet view to each of a resource's task assignments, even if the assignments require different kinds of work. (By default, Microsoft Project assigns the resource rates you enter in the Resource Sheet view to cost rate table A). For example, if you enter $20.00 per hour for Jake in the Std. Rate column of the Resource Sheet view and then assign Jake to the tasks "Compact the soil" and "Construct the outer walls," Microsoft Project applies the $20.00 per hour rate to each task.

But suppose the standard pay rates for compacting soil and constructing walls are $20.00 per hour and $30.00 per hour, respectively. For the wall-construction assignment, you can replace the default $20.00 per hour rate with the $30.00 per hour rate. To do so, you specify $30.00 per hour in one of Jake's other cost rate tables (for example, cost rate table B), and then apply this rate to the wall-construction assignment.

➢   **To apply a different rate for each kind of task performed by the same resource**

1   On the **View Bar**, click **Task Usage**.

2   In the **Task Name** field, select the resource whose pay rate you want to change for the associated task assignment.

3   Click **Assignment Information** .

4   Click the **General** tab.

5   In the **Cost rate table** box, click the rate table you want to use for this resource on this task.

Assign a Fixed Cost to a Task

In many projects, the most common type of task cost is a rate-based cost, a cost based on an amount of money spent per unit of time (for example, the hourly rate paid to a resource). But there's often a fixed cost associated with a task, such as the cost of materials or equipment used to accomplish the task. Such costs are fixed because they remain constant even if a task takes much longer than planned.

Moreover, if you aren't assigning resources to tasks, a fixed cost could be the total cost of a task, an estimate that includes both resource and materials costs. If you know the cost of materials or you're not going to assign a resource to a task, you can enter a fixed cost. If a task has both a fixed cost and rate-based costs associated with it, Microsoft Project will add the fixed cost to the rate-based costs to determine the total cost of the task.

➢ **To assign a fixed cost to a task**

1   On the **View Bar**, click **Gantt Chart**.

2   On the **View** menu, point to **Table**, and then click **Cost**.

3   In the **Fixed Cost** field for the task, type the cost.

4   Press ENTER.

In the Cost table, you can also specify when the fixed cost is accrued by selecting an accrual method in the Fixed Cost Accrual field.

Assign a Fixed Resource Cost to a Task

A resource cost can be fixed for a task. For example, a contractor may charge a flat rate to do a job, no matter how long it takes to complete. A resource cost can also be a combination of fixed costs and rate-based costs. For example, a computer consultant may charge a flat fee for installing computers plus an hourly rate for service and repair. In either kind of situation, you can enter a fixed cost for the resource assignment.

A fixed resource cost is added to other resource costs when Microsoft Project calculates the total cost of a task, but it does not depend on the time a resource spends working on the task.

➤ **To assign a fixed resource cost to a task**

1   On the **View Bar**, click **Gantt Chart**.

2   In the **Task Name** field, select a task.

3   On the **Window** menu, click **Split**.

4   In the **Resource Name** field in the bottom pane, select the resource name.

    For a new resource, type the resource name in the **Resource Name** field.

5   On the **Format** menu, point to **Details**, and then click **Resource Cost**.

6   In the **Task type** box, click **Fixed Duration**.

7   In the **Units** field for the resource, type **0**, and then click **OK**.

    If a resource costs a fixed amount to perform a task, the number of units worked by the resource doesn't matter. When you set units to zero, however, Microsoft Project calculates the amount of work performed by the resource to be zero. If you didn't change the task type to Fixed Duration (step 6) and the fixed-cost resource were the only resource assigned to the task, then the duration of the task would also be recalculated to be zero.

    If the fixed-cost resource is the only resource assigned to the task, the task bar is replaced by a series of dots (because the task has a fixed duration but no work assigned to it). If at least one non-fixed-cost resource is also assigned to the task, the task bar retains its usual appearance.

8   In the **Cost** field, type the fixed resource cost.

Assign a Unit-based Material Cost to a Task

Materials and supplies often have a unit-based price associated with them. To enter materials costs that are based on a unit price, you can assign a per-use cost to a material resource. You specify the number of units you'll use, and Microsoft Project calculates the total material cost by multiplying the base unit price you enter by the number or percentage of units you specified.

For example, you may need cement to build the foundation as well as the walls of a house. For the resource "Cement," you can enter a price per pound of, let's say, 2 dollars, in the Cost/Use field of the Resource Sheet view. If you require 1,000 pounds of cement for the foundation, you can assign the cement at 100,000% units. If you require 400 pounds for the walls, you can assign the cement at 40,000% units.

Before you perform the following procedure, you must enter a unit cost for the material resource in the Cost/Use field of the Resource Sheet view.

➤ **To assign a unit-based materials cost to a task**

1 On the **View Bar**, click **Gantt Chart**.

2 In the **Task Name** field, select a task.

3 On the **Window** menu, click **Split**.

4 In the **Resource Name** field in the bottom pane, select the material resource to which you assigned a per-use cost.

5 On the **Format** menu, point to **Details**, and then click **Resource Cost**.

6 In the **Units** field for the resource, type the percentage you want, and then click **OK**.

By default, the maximum number of units at which you can assign a resource is 100%. After you assign a resource at more than this amount within a given time period, Microsoft Project displays the resource name in red to indicate that the resource is overallocated. For example, let's say you specify a price per pound for cement of 2 dollars in the Cost/Use field of the Resource Sheet view. If you assign 10 pounds (1,000% units) of cement to a task, the cement will appear as an overallocated resource.

You can choose to ignore the overallocation, keeping in mind the reason cement appears overallocated. Or, you can specify the maximum possible number of units that this resource can be available within a particular time period in the Max. Units field of the Resource Sheet view. (The largest number you can enter in this field is 1,000,000%.) For example, if you know that you might use up to 1,000 pounds of cement in your project at the same time, you can specify 100,000% in the Max. Units field. That way, cement won't appear overallocated unless you use more than this amount.

If you're going to use more than 1,000,000% units of a unit-priced materials resource at the same time, you can enter a cost in the Cost/Use field for a larger unit of the resource. For example, you can enter the cost per ton (the cost per 2,000 pounds) rather than the cost per pound for cement. So, instead of assigning 1,000 pounds of cement by specifying 100,000% units (if you entered the per-pound cost in the Cost/Use field), you can specify 50% units (if you entered the per-ton cost in the Cost/Use field).

Change the Standard and Overtime Default Rates for New Resources

When you add resources to your project plan, you often think of, and add, one group of related resources at a time. For example, you may add all the painters, then all the electricians, and so on. Frequently, each resource in a related group gets paid the same hourly rate.

If each resource you're about to add to your project plan gets paid the same hourly rate, you can save time by specifying the rate as the default rate, and then letting Microsoft Project enter this rate automatically. You can specify both standard and overtime default rates.

These default pay rates apply only to the resources you've added after you enter the rate, not to resources that are already in your project plan. You can change the default pay rates before you add each new group of resources (providing that the individuals in each group get paid the same hourly rate).

➤ **To change the default standard or overtime rate for resources**

1   On the **Tools** menu, click **Options**, and then click the **General** tab.

2   In the **Default standard rate** box, enter the new rate.

3   In the **Default overtime rate** box, enter the new rate.

4   Click **Set as Default**.

5   To change the default currency symbol and number of decimal digits, click the **View** tab, and then change the information under **Currency**.

VIEWING COSTS

You include cost information in your schedule when task and project costs are important for you to monitor and control. Microsoft Project provides a number of ways to examine those costs closely on a regular basis. For example, you can:

- View the cost per task, to see what portion of the total cost is due to resource costs and what portion is due to fixed costs.
- View the cost per resource, to see how much you're spending on regular work, overtime work, and per-use resources.
- View the total project cost, to see if your project is staying within budget.

View the Cost per Task

The sum of the individual task costs make up most, if not all of, the total project cost. If the total project cost exceeds your budget, you can view the total cost of each individual task in detail to see where you can pare task costs.

➤ **To view the cost per task**

1   On the **View Bar**, click **Gantt Chart**.

2   On the **View** menu, click **Table**, and then choose **Cost**.

3   Scroll right to view the **Total Cost** field.

View the Cost per Resource

Because resource costs usually make up the largest portion of task costs, and therefore of the overall project cost, you'll need to monitor resource costs if you're going to keep costs under control. By viewing a resource cost in detail, you can see exactly how much of the overall cost is due to standard, overtime, and per-use costs.

➤ **To view the cost per resource**

1 On the **View Bar**, click **Resource Sheet**.

2 On the **View** menu, point to **Table**, and then click **Cost**.

The cost you see for each resource is the total cost of that resource for all the tasks the resource is assigned to.

You can view the cost of each resource, broken down by the time period you specify, in the Resource Usage view.

➤ **To view a resource cost in greater detail**

1 On the **View Bar**, click **Resource Usage**.

2 On the **Format** menu, point to **Details**, and then click **Cost**.

You can view resource costs graphically in the Resource Graph view.

➤ **To view resource cost totals graphically**

1 On the **View Bar**, click **Resource Graph**.

2 On the **Format** menu, point to **Details**, and then click **Cost** or **Cumulative Cost**.

View Total Project Costs

In some projects, it's imperative to stay within budget. In fact, sometimes the success of a project is determined by whether the project goals are accomplished without exceeding the budget. If accomplishing your project goals by staying within a budget is important to you, you can view your project's current, baseline, actual, and remaining costs. You can then compare the project costs in your plan with your budget to determine whether you'll meet your budget or not.

➤ **To view total project costs**

1 On the **Project** menu, click **Project Information**.

2 Click **Statistics**.

Project costs are displayed in the Cost column.

If you've combined several projects into one project file, you can view the total cost of each individual project. For information about combined projects, see Chapter 14, "Working with Multiple Projects."

➢ **To view the total cost of a project that's combined with other projects in one project file**

1   On the **View Bar**, click **Task Usage**.

2   Select the summary task that represents the project whose total cost you want to see.

3   On the **Format** menu, point to **Details**, and then click **Cost**.

View How Costs Are Distributed Over a Task's Duration

Often, the cost of a task accumulates over time; it doesn't just occur all at once. For example, if a resource who's assigned to a 2-day (16-hour) task is paid $20 per hour, then the task will cost $160 on the first day and $160 on the second day. If the resources assigned to a task are paid an hourly rate or a fixed rate that is prorated, you can view how the cost of the task breaks down on a day-by-day (or week-by-week, month-by-month, and so on) basis.

➢ **To view how costs are distributed over a task's duration**

1   On the **View Bar**, click **Task Usage** or **Resource Usage**.

2   On the **Format** menu, point to **Details**, and then click **Cost**.

MANAGING COSTS AND CASH FLOW

The main goal of managing costs and cash flow is to know how much money you're spending and when you're spending it. You can use Microsoft Project to monitor the cash flow of your project. For example, you can:

- Control how resource costs are accrued, to incur hourly resource charges all at once or gradually, over time.

- Control how fixed costs are accrued.

- Change how costs are calculated, either automatically by Microsoft Project or manually.

Control How Resource Costs Are Accrued

You can incur the charges for a resource as soon as the resource starts working on a task or as soon as the resource finishes the task. These are the different options you have of accruing costs. When you *accrue* a cost, you incur the entire cost all at once. You can also prorate a resource cost. When you *prorate* a cost, you incur a portion of the cost at a time, as the task progresses.

When the cash flow in your project is important, you can change how costs are accrued on individual tasks so that the costs of a task occur when you have the cash to pay for them. Except for resource per-use costs, which always accrue at the start of a task, Microsoft Project prorates costs by default. However, you can also accrue the cost of a task when it starts if you have to pay a lump-sum amount before any work begins. Or, you can accrue the cost of a task when it ends if you're holding payment until the work is finished.

➢ **To select a method for accruing resource costs**

1 On the **View Bar**, click **Resource Sheet**.

2 In the **Resource Name** field, select a resource, and then click **Resource Information** 📇.

3 Click the **Costs** tab.

4 In the **Cost accrual** box, click an accrual method.

To accrue the cost when the task begins, click **Start**.

To accrue the cost based on the completion percentage of the task, click **Prorated**.

To accrue the cost when the task is completed, click **End**.

The cost accrual method you select will be applied to all the rates on each cost rate table. You cannot select a different cost accrual method for each rate or for each cost rate table.

Control How Fixed Costs Are Accrued

By default, Microsoft Project prorates fixed costs. Their accrual is based on the percentage of completion of the task and distributed over its duration. You can, however, change the default accrual method for fixed costs so that charges are incurred either at that start or finish of a task instead.

➢ **To control how fixed costs are accrued**

1 On the **Tools** menu, click **Options**, and then the **Calculation** tab.

2 In the **Default fixed costs accrual** box, click the accrual method you want.

Change How Costs Are Calculated

Usually, Microsoft Project calculates task costs for you, based on the resource costs and fixed costs associated with a task. You can, however, enter your own cost values rather than having them calculated by Microsoft Project. By default, Microsoft Project is set to calculate task costs automatically. If you want to enter your own cost values, you need to set the cost-calculation option to manual.

➤ **To change how costs are calculated**

1   On the **Tools** menu, click **Options**, and then the **Calculation** tab.

2   In the **Calculation** box, click **Manual**.

➤ **To enter actual cost values manually**

1   On the **Tools** menu, click **Options**, and then the **Calculation** tab.

2   Clear the **Actual costs are always calculated by Microsoft Project** check box.

If you turn on the automatic calculation settings again, Microsoft Project will recalculate all cost values, overwriting the values you entered manually.

8

Reviewing and Fine-Tuning Your Project Plan

When you construct a project plan, you're really creating a "first draft." You add tasks that are required to meet your project goals, sequence those tasks logically, link tasks, and, perhaps, add resource, assignment, and cost information as well.

The big pieces are there, pretty much the way you want them. But if you take two more important steps, you can have a project plan that models project reality even more closely than your first-draft plan and helps you achieve your project goals as efficiently as possible. Those two steps are to review and fine-tune your project plan.

The main goals of reviewing and fine-tuning your project plan are to:

- Shorten the schedule, to meet the project deadline.
- Distribute the workload evenly, by resolving resource overallocations, so that no resources are overworked.
- Reduce costs to a minimum, to save money and complete the project within your budget.

You should also look for information that's missing, unessential, and erroneous. For example, some tasks may be in the wrong order, or you may have assigned the wrong resource to a task.

When you review your plan, you identify parts of the plan that can be made more efficient or that may cause problems during the project. For example, you may find an unnecessary 2-day delay that's been added between critical tasks. Or, you may discover a day when a resource has been assigned to 12 hours of work instead of the usual 8 hours.

When you fine-tune your plan, you adjust tasks, resources, and costs in a way that resolves the problems you discovered during your review. For example, by removing the 2-day delay, you might be able to bring in the project finish date. By reducing the resource's workload from 12 hours to 8 hours, you make sure the resource works only as many hours as he or she has available on that day.

It's best to review and fine-tune your plan before the project starts. That way, you can pinpoint and resolve problems before they occur. You'll also know that your plan represents your most accurate prediction of what will occur during the project: how long tasks will take, how much tasks will cost, and so on. It will provide a valid basis for comparing actual data to estimated data. A deviation from a well-honed plan is significant; a deviation from a "rough" plan may mean nothing.

You can also review and fine-tune your plan periodically after the project begins. If you track progress, the actual data you collect may show that tasks are taking longer than planned or you're spending money faster than planned. An evaluation of your plan may show you where you can trim time and costs. Most of the procedures discussed in this chapter apply to reviewing and fine-tuning your plan before the project starts as well as to tracking and adjusting your plan after the project starts.

TOOLS FOR ANALYZING YOUR SCHEDULE

Whether your project plan includes tasks only or resources and costs as well, you'll probably want to analyze and adjust the most important part of that plan: the schedule. By adjusting the schedule, you can, for instance, schedule a task to start and finish sooner, bring in the project finish date, shrink task durations, and distribute the workload more evenly.

But before you adjust your schedule, you need to know how Microsoft Project calculates the schedule, so you can predict the effects of the adjustments you make. You need to know, for example, how Microsoft Project calculates the length of your project or how it responds when you add an additional resource to a task.

This section describes:

- Effort-driven scheduling, which is the default scheduling method available in Microsoft Project.
- The role of duration, work, and resource units in determining a task's schedule.
- How task types can change the way duration, work, and resource units affect a task's schedule.
- The critical path and its central role in helping you to shorten your schedule.

- Ways to identify slack in your schedule, which may be making your schedule longer than it needs to be.
- A way to calculate more accurate task duration estimates and generate schedule scenarios based on optimistic, pessimistic, and expected task duration estimates.
- The effects of calculating your schedule automatically versus calculating your schedule manually.

The Basics of How a Task is Scheduled

Before you can analyze and adjust a task's schedule, you need to know what factors affect its schedule. The main factors that affect how Microsoft Project determines a task's start and finish dates are:

- **Placement in the task list.**   In a logically ordered set of tasks, the tasks are usually performed in the order in which they appear in the task list. For instance, a task near the top of the list occurs near the beginning of the project, a task in the middle of the list occurs in the middle of the project, and a task near the bottom of the list occurs toward the end of the project. You can change a task's schedule by moving it to another part of the task list.

- **Duration.**   Several factors affect task duration, but in general, the longer the duration you enter, the later a task finishes. Changing the duration may change the task finish date.

- **Task dependencies (or links).**   The type of link you establish between two tasks determines whether the successor task starts after the predecessor task is completed (finish-to-start), starts at the same time the predecessor starts (start-to-start), finishes at the same time the predecessor task finishes (finish-to-finish), or, rarely, finishes when the predecessor task starts (start-to-finish). By replacing one type of link with another, you can change a task's start and finish dates and, perhaps, the project end date.

- **Overlap and delay (or lead and lag time).**   The overlap, or lead time, you add between two tasks causes the successor task to begin earlier. The delay, or lag time, you add between two tasks causes the successor task to begin later. If the nature of the task allows it, you can change the task start date by changing or removing lead time or lag time.

- **Constraints.**   You can force a task to start or finish on or near a date you specify by entering a start or finish date yourself (Microsoft Project automatically applies the constraint Finish No Earlier Than to the entered finish date). Or, you can change the default constraint, As Soon As Possible, to an inflexible constraint such as Must Start On or Finish No Later Than. (You shouldn't, however, replace the default constraint unless it's absolutely necessary. It's better to let Microsoft Project calculate—and, if the schedule changes, recalculate—task start and finish dates.)

- **Assigned resources.** When you assign resources to a task, the task duration can change. Generally, the more resources, and resource units, you assign to a task, the more you decrease its duration (and bring in the task's finish date).

- **Work.** If you assign resources to a task, then by default Microsoft Project calculates a task duration based on the amount of work required to complete the task, the number of resource units assigned to it, and the working times and work assigned to those resources. By changing the amount of work required to accomplish a task, you can change the task duration, and thus its finish date.

- **The scheduling method.** By default, Microsoft Project calculates a task's schedule based on the method known as effort-driven scheduling. You can turn this method off for individual tasks.

- **Task type.** By default, each task is a fixed-units task. That means, with effort-driven scheduling on, when you assign additional resources to a task, the task duration decreases. You can change the task type to fixed-duration or fixed-work.

Other factors that affect how a task is scheduled are the project start date, the day on which the work week starts, and whether you split a task into portions, with an interruption between each portion.

Effort-Driven Scheduling and Task Types

Before you assign a resource to a task, the task has the duration you specify but no work associated with it. Only after you assign a resource to the task does Microsoft Project calculate the amount of work required to accomplish it. For example, if you specify a duration of 2 days and then assign a resource to the task, Microsoft Project will calculate 16 hours of work (assuming the resource's full working day is 8 hours long). If you assign a second resource to the task, also full-time, Microsoft Project will calculate a new duration of 1 day, but the number of hours of work required to perform the task will remain the same, 16 hours.

By default, Microsoft Project's initial calculation of the total work required to perform a task stays the same, regardless of the number of additional resources you assign to it. Adding or removing resources can decrease or increase the task duration, but the work remains constant. The method Microsoft Project uses to calculate a new task duration when resources are added or removed, while holding the amount of work constant, is called the *effort-driven scheduling* method. This method is on by default for each task. There's no other scheduling method available, but you do have the option of turning effort-driven scheduling off for particular tasks or for all new tasks.

The calculation for the total work on a task is based on the initial assignment of resources made at the same time. It's only after the initial assignment that effort-driven calculations come into play. For example, a task has a duration of 3 days. If you assign 2 resources initially at the same time (that is, you select both at the same time in the Assign Resources dialog box, and then click the Assign button), Microsoft Project assumes that there's 24 hours of work for each resource, and so calculates 48 hours of work (with the duration remaining at 3 days). The amount of work is now fixed. If you then assign a third resource, the amount of work remains constant at 48 hours, but Microsoft Project calculates a new duration of 2 days.

A major factor that affects how the effort-driven scheduling method calculates duration, work, and resource units is the task type. A *task type* is a way of keeping constant either the duration, work, or resource units associated with a task. When you select a task type, you fix one of these quantities, allowing Microsoft Project to recalculate only the two unfixed quantities (for example, when you assign additional resources).

With effort-driven scheduling turned on, work remains constant, regardless of the task type you select for a task. Otherwise, the three task types work like this when you assign additional resources:

- If the task type is *fixed units*, the default task type, you'll shorten the duration of the task. The resource units for each resource remain constant.

- If the task type is *fixed duration*, you'll decrease the individual unit values for resources. The task duration remains constant.

- If the task type is *fixed work*, you'll shorten the duration of the task. The total work and the resource units for each resource remain constant.

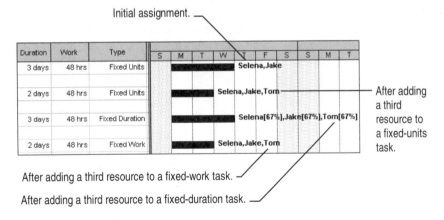

Initial assignment.

Duration	Work	Type	S	M	T	W	T	F	S	S	M	T
3 days	48 hrs	Fixed Units					Selena,Jake					
2 days	48 hrs	Fixed Units					Selena,Jake,Tom					
3 days	48 hrs	Fixed Duration					Selena[67%],Jake[67%],Tom[67%]					
2 days	48 hrs	Fixed Work					Selena,Jake,Tom					

After adding a third resource to a fixed-units task.

After adding a third resource to a fixed-work task.

After adding a third resource to a fixed-duration task.

When effort-driven scheduling is turned off and you assign additional resources to a task, the total work increases but the resource units and duration remain constant when the task type is fixed units or fixed duration. If the task type is fixed work, the calculations occur exactly as they do when effort-driven scheduling is turned on.

To Turn Off Effort-Driven Scheduling for a Task

By default, Microsoft Project decreases or increases the duration of a task as you assign or remove people from the task, but the total work on the task remains constant. This situation occurs when effort-driven scheduling is turned on.

For some tasks, however, the reality may be that the total work should increase as you assign more resources. To see this occur, you can turn off effort-driven scheduling for a task.

➤ **To turn off effort-driven scheduling for an individual task**

1   On the **View Bar**, click **Gantt Chart**.

2   In the **Task Name** field, select the tasks for which you want to turn off effort-driven scheduling.

3   Click **Task Information** 📧 , and then click the **Advanced** tab.

4   Clear the **Effort driven** check box.

➤ **To turn off effort-driven scheduling for all new tasks you add to your schedule**

1   On the **Tools** menu, click **Options**, and then click the **Schedule** tab.

2   Clear the **New tasks are effort driven** check box.

Critical Tasks

In nearly every project, there are tasks that can delay the project if they're not completed on time and tasks that can be completed after their original finish date without affecting the project finish date. Tasks that can delay a project are *critical tasks*. Tasks that can be delayed or accomplished at any time before the project finish date without delaying the project finish are *noncritical tasks*.

The critical tasks make up a special task sequence known as the critical path. The *critical path* is the sequence of tasks that ends on the latest finish date. The finish date of the last task in the critical path is the project finish date. When you want to shorten your schedule, you begin by shortening the critical path.

Most often, the critical path is the longest sequence of linked tasks in your project. But the critical path can also consist of a single critical task. For example, a lone, unlinked task that's constrained to finish later than any other task can be the only critical task in your project.

By default, a critical task has zero total slack time, which is the amount of time a task's finish date can slip before it delays the project finish date. If any critical task slips, the project finish date will probably be delayed.

A noncritical task can be an unlinked task whose finish date is earlier than the project finish date. It can also be a task that's linked in a task sequence that finishes earlier than another task sequence in the same schedule. (You can, for instance, have a separate sequence of linked tasks for each project phase, if there's overlap between the phases.) Noncritical tasks have slack time. Therefore, increasing the duration of a noncritical task less than its slack time or decreasing its duration has no effect on the project finish date.

Critical tasks can become noncritical tasks and vice versa. Whenever you change data that affects a task's schedule (such as assigning resources, changing links, adding or removing constraints, or changing a duration), Microsoft Project recalculates the critical path.

Identify the Critical Path

Before you can adjust critical tasks, you need to identify them. In several views, Microsoft Project graphically distinguishes critical tasks from noncritical ones.

➤ **To identify the critical path**

1   On the **View Bar**, click **More Views**.

2   On the **Views** list, select **Detail Gantt** or **Tracking Gantt**, and then click **Apply**.

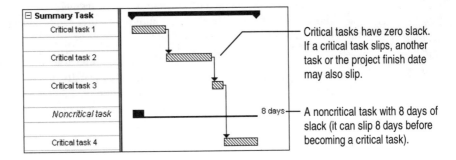

Critical tasks have zero slack. If a critical task slips, another task or the project finish date may also slip.

A noncritical task with 8 days of slack (it can slip 8 days before becoming a critical task).

Sort Critical Tasks by Duration

The longest critical tasks have the biggest effect on project length. Therefore, when you need to bring in the project finish date, you'll want to shorten the critical tasks with the longest duration first. Filtering for critical tasks (to display critical tasks only) and then sorting them by duration is the easiest way to do this.

➤ **To sort critical tasks by duration**

1   On the **View Bar**, click **Gantt Chart**.

2   On the **Project** menu, point to **Filtered for**, and then click **Critical**.

3   On the **Project** menu, point to **Sort**, and then click **Sort by**.

4   In the **Sort by** box, click **Duration**, and then click **Descending**.

5   Click **Sort**.

Summary tasks are sorted from the longest to the shortest. The tasks under each summary task are also sorted from the longest to the shortest.

Find Slack in Your Schedule

When you need to shorten a task duration and the only way to do it is to "borrow" a resource from another task, or you need to replace an overworked resource with another resource, you should first look to tasks that have slack time.

Only noncritical tasks have slack time. They can have total slack and/or free slack. *Total slack* is the amount of time a task can be delayed without delaying the project finish date. *Free slack* is the amount of time a task can be delayed without delaying the finish date of another task.

You can think of each noncritical task's slack time as an individual "time account" from which you can "withdraw" without interest or penalty, but only up to the amount of available slack time. For instance, if you withdraw all of a noncritical task's total slack time (that is, its total slack time becomes zero), the task becomes a critical task. The tasks dependent on this task also lose their slack and become critical. If you withdraw more than the available total slack time, you pay a penalty: the project finish date is pushed out.

When and how do you withdraw slack time from a noncritical task? You do this mainly when you want to shorten critical tasks, in order to bring in the project finish date. You might also do this when you need to resolve resource overallocations.

For example, to shorten a critical task, you may decide it's best to remove a resource from a noncritical task and assign it to the critical task. When you remove the resource from the noncritical task, the duration of the noncritical task may increase. If the duration increases by an amount that is less than the initial total slack time, the task remains a noncritical task. Then by reassigning the resource to the critical task, you shorten that task's duration. In effect, you shift time from tasks that have an excess of time (noncritical tasks) to tasks that have a time-deficit (critical tasks that are too long).

Before you try to shorten the durations of critical tasks or resolve resource allocations, you should look to tasks with slack for time that you can redistribute to where you need it most.

➢ **To find slack in your schedule**

1   On the **View Bar**, click **More Views**.

2   In the **Views** list, click **Detail Gantt**, and then click **Apply**.

Slack on a task appears graphically as thin slack bars adjoining the regular Gantt bars.

3   Drag the divider bar to the right to view the **Free Slack** and **Total Slack** fields.

By default, a zero duration in the Total Slack field indicates a critical task. A negative value in the Total Slack field indicates that there's a scheduling conflict. In many cases, the conflict results from a predecessor task that has a finish-to-start dependency with a successor task that has a Must Start On constraint date that's earlier than the finish date of the predecessor task. (This situation could occur if the predecessor task start and finish dates are pushed out by schedule changes.) If the finish-to-start dependency is true, then it must be impossible for the successor task to start before the predecessor task is completed.

The default amount of slack time that defines a critical task is zero slack time. You can, however, change this amount. For example, if you specify the default to be 2 days, then all tasks with 2 days of slack time or less will be critical tasks.

➢ **To change the default slack time for critical tasks**

1   On the **Tools** menu, click **Options**, and then click the **Calculation** tab.

2   In the **Tasks are critical if slack is less than or equal to** box, enter the amount of slack time.

Estimate Durations and Generate Schedule Scenarios by Using PERT Analysis

How will variations from your estimated task durations affect the project length? What, for example, will the schedule look like if tasks take longer than you expect? What will it look like if tasks take less time than you expect? You can create and look at three scenarios, one based on expected duration estimates, another on optimistic duration estimates, and a third on pessimistic duration estimates, by using Microsoft Project's PERT analysis tools. The PERT analysis tools not only enable you to generate three schedule scenarios but they also provide you with a sophisticated way to calculate a single duration that's based on your expected, optimistic, and pessimistic estimates.

To use the PERT analysis tools, you enter the expected, optimistic, and pessimistic durations of the tasks in your schedule. After you specify how much weight to give to each of the three durations, Microsoft Project calculates a single duration estimate from the weighted average of the three durations.

➢ **To estimate durations by using PERT analysis**

1   On the **View** menu, point to **Toolbars**, and then click **PERT Analysis**.

2   Click **PERT Entry Sheet** 🔲 on the **PERT Analysis** toolbar.

3   For each task, enter the optimistic, expected, and pessimistic durations in the **Opt Dur**, **Exp Dur**, and **Pes Dur** fields.

   If there's a task duration that you don't want Microsoft Project to calculate, enter the same duration in all three fields.

4   To calculate the estimated durations, click **Calculate PERT** 🔲.

   Microsoft Project calculates a single duration estimate based on a weighted average of the three duration values and enters this duration in the Duration field.

By default, Microsoft Project gives the optimistic duration estimate a weight of 1, the pessimistic duration estimate a weight of 1, and the expected duration estimate a weight of 4 (the weights must always add up to 6). If you have reason to believe that the three durations should be weighted differently, you can change their weights.

➤ **To change the weights given to the expected, optimistic, and pessimistic duration estimates**

1   On the **View** menu, point to **Toolbars**, and then click **PERT Analysis**.

2   Click **PERT Weights** ⚖️ on the **PERT Analysis** toolbar.

3   Enter new weight values for the three duration estimates.

The three values must add up to 6. Because the default weight values represent standard deviations for PERT probabilities, changing the defaults may make the estimated duration less accurate.

4   To calculate the new durations, click **Calculate PERT** 🖩.

After Microsoft Project calculates your estimated task durations, you can view the optimistic, pessimistic, and expected durations—and the resulting schedules.

➤ **To view the three schedules resulting from the optimistic, pessimistic, and expected duration estimates**

- Click **Optimistic Gantt** 🔲, **Pessimistic Gantt** 🔲, and **Expected Gantt** 🔲 on the **PERT Analysis** toolbar.

On each view, you can, in turn, see an optimistic, a pessimistic, and an expected schedule and project finish date.

Turn Off Automatic Schedule Calculation

Each time Microsoft Project recalculates your schedule, it takes some time. By default, Microsoft Project recalculates your schedule automatically after each change you enter into the schedule. When you're making many changes to your schedule, that can be annoying and time-consuming. To enter your changes more quickly, you can turn off automatic schedule calculation and have Microsoft Project calculate the schedule only when you want it to.

➤ **To turn off automatic schedule calculation**

1   On the **Tools** menu, click **Options**, and then click the **Calculation** tab.

2   Under **Calculation**, click **Manual**.

Microsoft Project will only recalculate the schedule when you click **Calculate All Projects** or **Calculate Project**.

SHORTENING YOUR SCHEDULE

One of the most common problems project managers encounter after they complete the first draft of their project plan is that the schedule is too long. The schedule as configured—with the existing task durations, resource assignments, task dependencies, constraints, and so on—just won't meet the required deadline. When that's the case, you need to shorten your schedule.

The most effective way to shorten your schedule is to adjust tasks that lie on the critical path. Adjusting noncritical tasks will not shorten the schedule (though you might reassign resources from noncritical tasks to critical tasks).

The actions you can take to shorten your schedule fall into two categories:

- **Shorten task durations.** For example, you can decrease a task duration directly, decrease a task duration by decreasing the total work on a task, assign more resources to a task, assign overtime work, and increase a resource's work schedule.
- **"Compress" the schedule by making tasks start sooner.** For example, you can delete or combine tasks, break down a task into noncritical subtasks, add lead time to a task, change the task dependency, change the constraint type, and change the task type.

You can use each method individually or in combination with other schedule-shortening methods. The methods you use depend on whether your project is limited by budget, resources, and the flexibility of the tasks in your schedule.

Decrease the Duration of a Critical Task

Because project length is determined by the tasks on the critical path, decreasing the duration of critical tasks can bring in the project end date.

➤ **To decrease the duration of a task**
1. On the **View Bar**, click **Gantt Chart**.
2. In the **Duration** field, type a new duration for the task.

Decrease Task Duration by Decreasing Total Work on a Critical Task

By default, Microsoft Project calculates a task duration based on the amount of work required to complete the task. For example, if you assign 1 full-time resource to a 2-day task, Microsoft Project calculates the total work to be 16 hours. If you assign a second full-time resource to the task, Microsoft Project holds the work constant and recalculates the task duration to be 1 day.

If you decrease the total work in a task, then Microsoft Project decreases the task duration accordingly. For example, if you change the total work from 16 hours to 8 hours and then assign 2 full-time resources to it successively, Microsoft Project will calculate a duration of a half day.

➤ **To decrease task duration by decreasing total work on a task**

1   On the **View Bar**, click **Task Usage**.

2   In the **Work** field, reduce the total amount of work for the task you want to shorten.

Assign More Resources

With effort-driven scheduling turned on (which it is, by default), assigning additional resources to a task decreases its duration. The more resources you assign, the more the duration decreases.

When you assign more resources to a task, use resources that have available working hours on the days you assign them, reassign resources from noncritical tasks to critical tasks so you don't inadvertently lengthen the schedule, or hire new resources. You can also assign additional resource units of the same resource.

➤ **To assign more resources to a task**

1   On the **View Bar**, click **Gantt Chart**.

2   In the **Task Name** field, select the task for which you want to assign more resources.

3   Click **Assign Resources** .

4   In the **Name** field, select the resource you want to assign to the task.

To assign a single resource, enter a number in the **Units** field to indicate the percentage of working time you want the resource to spend on the task. To assign the resource full-time, enter 100%; for part-time, enter a smaller number.

To assign several different resources, select the resources (CTRL+click).

To assign more than one resource from the same set of resources, enter the number of units in the **Units** field. For example, if you assign 2 painters from the Painters set, choose 200%.

If necessary, type the name of a new resource in the **Name** field.

5   Click **Assign**.

A check mark to the left of the Name field indicates that the resource is assigned to the selected task.

> ### To increase the resource units assigned to a task

1   On the **View Bar**, click **Gantt Chart**.

2   In the **Task Name** field, select the task for which you want to increase resource units.

3   Click **Assign Resources** .

4   In the **Units** field for the resource, enter the number of resource units you want, and then click **Assign**.

Assign Overtime Work

If you can't decrease the total work in tasks, and all of your resources are working to their maximum availability, and you can't hire new resources, then you can assign overtime work to resources in order to decrease task durations.

When you assign a resource to work overtime, in many cases you'll have to pay that resource an overtime rate, which can be costly. Microsoft Project calculates task costs based on the overtime rate you specified for that resource.

> ### To assign overtime work to a task

1   On the **View Bar**, click **Gantt Chart**.

2   On the **Window** menu, click **Split**.

3   Click anywhere in the bottom pane.

4   On the **Format** menu, point to **Details**, and then click **Resource Work**.

5   In the top pane, select the task for which you want to assign overtime work in the **Task Name** field.

6   In the bottom pane, type the number of hours in the **Ovt. Work** field for each resource.

Increase a Resource's Work Schedule

In many projects, the normal working day for a resource is 8-hours long, which is the default work-day length in the Standard project calendar. If you can't get additional resources for a project but you need to shorten task durations, you can increase the number of working hours of already assigned resources. You increase a resource's working hours on his or her resource calendar.

A task duration is based partly on the number of working hours of assigned resources. For example, if a resource with an 8-hour working day is assigned to a 3-day task, the task will take the resource 3 days to complete. If you increase the resource's work day to 12 hours, then the resource will complete the task in 2 days.

➢ **To increase a resource's work schedule**

1   On the **Tools** menu, click **Change Working Time**.

2   In the **For** box, click the resource whose calendar you want to change.

3   On the calendar, select the days you want to change.

To change a day of the week for the entire calendar, select the day at the top of the calendar.

4   Click **Use default** or **Working time**.

5   To change working time hours, type the new times in the **From** and **To** boxes.

Delete or Combine Critical Tasks

Because critical tasks make up the critical path that determines project length, there's no surer way to bring in the project end date than to delete critical tasks or to combine two critical tasks into one critical task whose duration is less than the sum of the durations of the separate tasks.

When you delete a critical task that's linked to both its predecessor and successor tasks with finish-to-start (FS) links, Microsoft Project automatically re-links its predecessor task to its successor task with an FS link by default. If you delete a task with any other type of link, after you delete the task, you'll need to link its predecessor to its successor manually.

➢ **To delete a critical task**

1   On the **View Bar**, click **Gantt Chart**.

2   In the **Task Name** field, select the task you want to delete.

3   On the **Edit** menu, click **Delete Task**.

To combine two critical tasks, you first delete one of the tasks. Then, you can change the name of the remaining task and, if necessary, adjust its duration or assign to it some of the resources that had been assigned to the deleted task.

Break Down a Critical Task into Noncritical Subtasks

Some of the tasks on the critical path may actually "hide" smaller tasks. If you need to shorten the schedule, you can break down these large critical tasks into subtasks.

Breaking down a critical task into subtasks can shorten the schedule in two ways. Perhaps the work on at least some of the subtasks can overlap (for example, either with lead time or by being linked with a start-to-start dependency). Or, perhaps some of the subtasks can be made noncritical tasks, if they don't need to be completed in sequence.

➢ **To break a large task into a summary task and subtasks**

1 On the **View Bar**, click **More Views**.

2 On the **Views** list, select **Detail Gantt** or **Tracking Gantt**, and then click **Apply**.

3 In the **Task Name** field, select a single task on the critical path that could be completed in several steps.

4 Click **Unlink Tasks** 🔗.

5 Remove the resources assigned to this task.

6 Select the task beneath the task you want to change, and then click **New Task** on the **Insert** menu.

7 Repeat step 6 for each subtask you want to add.

Microsoft Project schedules these new unlinked subtasks to begin on the start date for the summary task.

8 For each new task, type a name in the **Task Name** field and a duration in the **Duration** field.

9 In the **Task Name** field, select all the new tasks, and then click **Indent** 🔲 to make them subtasks of the original task.

The original task becomes a summary task. The subtasks will be on the critical path.

10 Click **Link Tasks** 🔗.

You may also need to link the last new task to a successor task.

Add Lead Time to Critical Tasks

In many projects, the most common link between dependent tasks is the finish-to-start (FS) link, the link that gives Microsoft Project the greatest flexibility when scheduling tasks. But by not allowing a successor task to start until its predecessor is completed, the FS link can make your schedule longer than it needs to be.

If the FS link represents the true dependency between tasks, you shouldn't change it to another dependency type. Instead, you can determine if the successor task can start before the predecessor task is completed. If it can, you can add lead time to the successor task so that it begins on an earlier date and overlaps the predecessor task, thus allowing the project to end on an earlier date. If the tasks can overlap so much that they can begin on the same start date, you may want to replace the FS link with a start-to-start (SS) link instead of adding lead time.

➤ **To add lead time**

1 On the **View Bar**, click **Gantt Chart**.

2 In the **Task Name** field, select the successor task you want, and then click **Task Information** 📋.

3 Click the **Predecessors** tab.

4 In the **Lag** field, type the lead time you want as a duration (type a negative number) or as a percentage of the predecessor task duration (type the negative percentage complete).

For example, if the predecessor task has a duration of 2 days and you want the successor to begin 1 day before the predecessor task is completed, type -50% in the Lag field.

Lead time units are minute, hour, day, and week. To specify elapsed duration, precede the time unit with the letter e (for example, edays for elapsed days). Elapsed days include weekends and other nonworking days.

Change a Task Dependency

Tasks linked with start-to-start (SS) and finish-to-finish (FF) links automatically overlap predecessor and successor tasks, which tends to bring in the project finish date. One way to shorten your schedule, then, is to replace finish-to-start (FS) links with either SS or FF links. Look for FS-linked critical tasks in your project whose dependency is better represented by an SS or FF link.

➤ **To change a task dependency**

1 On the **View Bar**, click **Gantt Chart**.

2 Double-click the link line you want to view or change.

3 In the **Type** box, check the task dependency.

4 To change the task dependency, click the task link you want.

Change the Constraint Type

Inflexible constraints set on tasks, especially critical tasks, can limit Microsoft Project's ability to recalculate and flexibly reschedule tasks. For example, suppose two critical tasks are linked with a finish-to-start (FS) link, and the successor task has a Must Start On constraint. If you decrease the duration of the predecessor task, the start date of the successor task remains unchanged. Neither the successor task nor any task that depends on it starts any earlier. As a result, decreasing the duration of the critical task doesn't shorten the schedule.

One way to avoid a situation where an inflexibly constrained task prevents the project end date from being recalculated is to replace an inflexible constraint with a flexible constraint, such as As Soon As Possible or As Late As Possible. Of course, you should apply the constraint that best represents the scheduling reality for a task. But use inflexible constraints cautiously (if at all).

For information about why you should use constraints cautiously, see Chapter 6, "Making Tasks Happen in the Right Order and at the Right Time."

➢ **To examine constraints on tasks**

1   On the **View Bar**, click **Gantt Chart**.

2   On the **View** menu, point to **Table**, and then click **More Tables**.

3   In the **Tables** list, click **Constraint Dates**, and then click **Apply**.

4   Scroll to the right to display the **Constraint Type** and **Constraint Date** fields.

   For each task with a constraint other than As Soon As Possible, look at the predecessor tasks and successor tasks on the Gantt Chart to determine if the constraint is necessary.

➢ **To change a constraint**

1   On the **View Bar**, click **Gantt Chart**.

2   In the **Task Name** field, select the task for which you want to change the constraint, and then click **Task Information** 📋.

3   Click the **Advanced** tab, and then, under **Constrain Task**, click a constraint in the **Type** box.

4   If the constraint requires a date, type or select a constraint date in the **Date** box.

   If you don't type or select a date, Microsoft Project uses the current date as the constraint date.

   Microsoft Project recalculates the start and finish dates of all tasks affected by the change.

Change the Task Type

If you assign resources, Microsoft Project uses the following formula to calculate duration:

duration = work/resource units

By default, Microsoft Project holds work and resource units constant, and recalculates duration only. For example, suppose the task duration you enter is 2 days and you assign a resource to the task full-time, at 100% resource units (where 100% = 8 available working hours per day). Microsoft Project calculates the total work to be 16 hours. If you assign another resource full-time to the task, Microsoft Project calculates a new duration of 1 day. (Work remains constant at 16 hours, and for each resource the resource units remain constant at 100%).

This example shows how Microsoft Project calculates duration, work, and resource units when the task type is set to fixed units, which is the default. But you can also make sure that a task's duration or its total work remain constant by changing the task type to fixed duration or fixed work.

When you select fixed duration for a task, Microsoft Project keeps the duration at the value you entered and recalculates resource units as you change resource assignments. For example, suppose you want the wiring for a new house to be installed in exactly 2 days. Initially, you assign 2 electricians to the job at 100% resource units each. Then you assign 2 more electricians to the job. Microsoft Project calculates the resource units to be 50% for each of the 4 electricians, because 4 electricians need work only half-time to complete the wiring in 2 days.

When you select fixed work for a task, Microsoft Project holds the work constant. As you assign more or fewer resources, Microsoft Project calculates duration. For example, if you assign 2 electricians full-time to wire a new house in 2 days, and then you assign 2 more electricians to the task, Microsoft Project calculates a new duration of 1 day.

> ### To change a task type
>
> 1   On the **View Bar**, click **Gantt Chart**.
>
> 2   In the **Task Name** field, select the task whose task type you want to change.
>
> 3   Click **Task Information** [icon], and then click the **Advanced** tab.
>
> 4   In the **Task type** box, click the task type you want to set.

RESOLVING RESOURCE OVERALLOCATIONS

When you're assigning resources to tasks, it's easy to mistakenly assign a resource to two or more tasks that occur during the same time period. If the resource is assigned to work more hours than it has available within a specified time period, the resource is said to be *overallocated*. (By default, Microsoft Project looks for resource overallocations on a day-by-day basis.) It's best to resolve overallocated resources before your project starts and whenever a change in resource assignments may cause an overallocation.

Your goal when you resolve resource overallocations is to distribute the workload evenly among resources. Each resource should be working at just about maximum capacity—each available work hour is filled by a task—but no more.

For example, Tom is available to work 8 hours per day (as defined in his resource calendar). You assign Tom to shingle the roof on Monday and Tuesday, full-time. Later, forgetting on which days you've assigned Tom to the shingling task, you assign him to construct the outer walls on Tuesday and Wednesday, also full-time. On Monday and Wednesday, Tom is assigned to work the same number of hours, 8, as he has available on those days. But on Tuesday, you've assigned him to 2 tasks full-time, for a total of 16 hours of work, twice the number of hours he's available to work on that day. Microsoft Project indicates that Tom is overallocated on Tuesday by a total of 8 hours.

There are a number of ways Microsoft Project helps you to resolve resource overallocations, including:

- Decrease the amount of work assigned to an overallocated resource on a particular task.

- Reassign a resource to work part-time on a task.

- Reschedule a task with an overallocated resource to occur when the resource is available.

- Contour work assignments.

- Use resource leveling to automatically resolve overallocations.

- Level resources yourself.

- Assign more resources to a task, to reduce the number of hours that the overallocated resource must work on the task. For more information about assigning more resources to a task, see the topic "Assign More Resources" earlier in this chapter.

- Change the resource calendar of an overallocated resource so that more work hours are available. For more information on changing a resource calendar, see Chapter 6, "Assigning Resources to Tasks."

- Split a task assigned to a resource so that a resource can work on the same task at a later time. For more information about splitting a task, see Chapter 5, "Making Tasks Happen in the Right Order and at the Right Time."

Remember that no matter what you do, some overwork and underwork may be unavoidable.

Be aware that there are trade-offs when you resolve resource overallocations. For example, when you resolve an overallocation, you may increase a task duration or push out the project finish date.

Check Resource Workload

Before you can resolve resource overallocations, you need to find out which resources are overallocated, when they're overallocated, and what tasks they're assigned to during the time periods they're overallocated. You'll also want to know which resources are underallocated or unassigned and which tasks have no work assigned to them. You can do all of this by checking the resource workload.

➢ **To check resource workload**

- On the **View Bar**, click **Resource Usage**.

On the timescale portion of the Resource Usage view, you see the total hours each resource is working, the number of hours the resource is working on each task, and the hours worked per time period. The names of overallocated resources are in red. In the Indicators column of each overallocated resource is a leveling indicator.

Resources that aren't assigned to any tasks do not have tasks listed underneath their names.

Tasks with no resources assigned are located under Unassigned in the Resource Name field.

Decrease a Resource's Work on a Task

Sometimes your options for resolving a resource overallocation are limited: You can't reschedule or remove some of the resource's tasks, and you can't allow the duration of the tasks to increase. You may, however, be able to decrease the amount of work required of an overallocated resource on a task that's contributing to the overallocation.

When you decrease a resource's work on a task, you also decrease the total amount of work on the task. Therefore, by default, Microsoft Project decreases the duration of the task.

➢ **To decrease the amount of work assigned to a resource**

1   On the **View Bar**, click **Resource Usage**.

Tasks are listed underneath the resources to which they are assigned. Overallocated resources are highlighted in red and displayed with an icon in the Indicators field.

2   In the **Work** fields for the tasks to which the overallocated resource is assigned, type a lesser value until the overallocation is removed (the resource name is no longer red).

On the timescale portion of the Resource Usage view, you see the total hours each resource is working, the number of hours the resource is working on each task, and the hours worked per time period.

To see a graphical representation of overallocated resources, display the Resource Graph view.

When you decrease the total work on a task, Microsoft Project decreases the duration of the task, by default. You can, however, choose to have the duration remain the same.

➤ **To keep the duration of a task constant after you decrease the amount of work assigned to a resource**

1   On the **View Bar**, click **Gantt Chart**.

2   In the **Task Name** field, select the task whose duration you want unchanged, and then click **Task Information** .

3   Click the **Advanced** tab, and then click **Fixed Duration** under **Task type**.

Reassign a Resource to Work Part-Time on a Task

Suppose Tom is assigned full-time to 2 tasks on the same day. Microsoft Project indicates that he's assigned to 16 hours of work on that day, an overallocation of 8 hours (assuming Tom's full working day is 8-hours long). One fairly simple way to reduce this overallocation is by assigning Tom part-time to each task, so that the sum of his allocations on the 2 tasks is no more than 100% resource units. (When Tom is assigned to 2 tasks full-time on the same day, he's allocated at 200% resource units on that day.)

For example, if you assign Tom at 25% resource units (which is equal to 2 hours of work) to one task and at 75% resource units (which is equal to 6 hours of work) on the other task, Tom will no longer be overallocated.

➤ **To reassign a resource to work part-time on a task**

1   On the **View Bar**, click **Gantt Chart**.

2   In the **Task Name** field, select a task.

3   Click **Assign Resources** .

4   In the **Name** field, select the resource.

5   In the **Units** field, enter the percentage of time the resource is assigned to work on the task.

For example, if you want the resource to work 25 percent of the time on the task, type 25.

6   Press ENTER.

Note that when you decrease the number of resource units on a task, Microsoft Project increases the task duration, by default. To prevent this, you can change the task type to fixed duration.

Delay a Task with an Overallocated Resource

Many resource overallocations occur because a resource is assigned to work on two or more tasks at the same time; the tasks overlap. One easy way to resolve such an overallocation is to delay a task until the resource can work on it without being overallocated. Frequently, this means adding enough delay to a task so that it no longer overlaps a predecessor task. You add delay to a task by adding lag time. You add some lag time, check to see if the overallocation is resolved, and then add more lag time, if necessary.

When you add lag time to a task, you'll delay the task as well as its successor tasks. You might even delay the project finish date. Therefore, it's best to delay noncritical tasks first, and then only by an amount less than or equal to their free slack.

For information about delaying tasks by adding lag time, see Chapter 5, "Making Tasks Happen in the Right Order and at the Right Time."

Work Contours

When you assign a resource to a task, Microsoft Project assigns the same number of work hours per day to the resource for each day the resource works on the task. For example, if you assign a resource full-time (8 hours/day) to a 3-day task, then Microsoft Project assigns the resource to work on the task 8 hours on each day.

But if you know that a resource will not be working a "flat" amount of hours per day, you can specify a work-hour pattern, or *work contour*, that more closely matches the number of hours per day (week, month, and so on) that the resource will actually work on the task.

For example, a resource may be finishing up one task as he or she begins work on another. The resource may "step up" its work hours gradually before working full-time on the new task, and then gradually taper off toward the end of the task. This kind of work contour is called the bell.

You can apply the following preset work contours:

- Flat, which is the default work contour.

- Back loaded, which you apply when the resource's work peaks at the end of the task duration.

- Front loaded, which you apply when the resource's work peaks at the beginning of the task duration and gradually declines to a minimum at the end of the task duration.

- Double peak, which you apply when the resource's work peaks twice in the middle of the task duration.

- Early peak, which you apply when the resource's work peaks before the middle of the task duration.

- Late peak, which you apply when the resource's work peaks after the middle of the task duration.

- Bell, which you apply when the resource's work peaks once in the middle of the task duration.

- Turtle, which you apply when the resource's work gradually increases, reaches a plateau, and then gradually declines.

You apply a specific work contour to a specific task. You display work contours on the Resource Usage and Task Usage views.

When you apply a work contour to a task, be aware that the contour obeys the following rules:

- Changing the start date of a task automatically causes the contour to shift and be reapplied to include the new start date. The work values within the task duration change to preserve the pattern of the original contour.

- If you add new total work values to the task, Microsoft Project automatically reapplies the preset work contour pattern, distributes the new task work values across the affected duration, and assigns new work values to the assigned resources.

- If you increase the duration of a task, Microsoft Project stretches the contour to include the added duration.

- When you edit a work value, the contour is removed from the assignment. You can, however, reapply the contour.

Contour a Work Assignment

If you know that a resource's work on a task will follow a specific work-hour pattern throughout the task's duration, you can apply a preset work contour to the assignment.

➤ **To apply a contour to an assignment**

1 On the **View Bar**, click **Task Usage**.

Resources are grouped under the tasks to which they are assigned.

2 In the **Task Name** field, select a resource for which you want to apply a preset work contour.

3 Click **Assignment Information** 📋 , and then click the **General** tab.

4 In the **Work contour** box, click a contour pattern.

An icon representing the contour pattern appears in the Indicators field.

5 To change the start and finish dates for the resource's work on the task, click dates in the **Start** and **Finish** boxes.

Use Resource Leveling to Automatically Resolve Overallocations

When you have a large project that contains many resource overallocations, you can resolve them all at once by having Microsoft Project level them. Microsoft Project levels overallocations by delaying or splitting tasks until the resources assigned to them are no longer overallocated. Even if you need to adjust tasks afterward, using automatic leveling may still be faster than adding delay to one task at a time.

Before you level overallocations automatically, you should refine your schedule yourself as much as possible. The results of automatic leveling can improve if your schedule is as "clean" and "lean" as possible (for example, no unnecessary inflexible constraints). In addition, you can prioritize tasks by specifying which tasks should be delayed first and which should not be delayed at all. You can also level all resources or only selected resources. You can even specify whether automatic leveling can delay the project finish date or not.

Because Microsoft Project follows only a limited set of rules when it levels, you should check the changes that result from automatic leveling, in the Leveling Gantt view. Immediately after automatic leveling, you can undo all of the changes. Of course, you can adjust or remove individual changes at any time.

➢ **To delay tasks automatically to level overallocated resources**

1 On the **Tools** menu, click **Resource Leveling**.

2 Click **Manual** to level resources only when you click the **Level Now** button.

3 In the **Look for overallocations on a basis** box, click a time period to determine the sensitivity with which leveling will recognize overallocations.

Leveling will occur only if a resource is scheduled to do more work than it has the capacity for in the specified period.

4 Under **Leveling range for**, select whether you want the entire project leveled or only those tasks falling within a specific time range.

5 In the **Leveling order** box, click one of the following leveling orders:

Click **ID Only** to have Microsoft Project check those tasks in the ascending order of their ID numbers before considering other leveling criteria to determine which tasks to level.

Click **Standard** to have Microsoft Project check tasks in the order of their predecessor dependencies, slack, dates, priority, and then task constraints.

Click **Priority, Standard** to have Microsoft Project check tasks' priorities to be leveled before considering predecessor dependencies, slack, dates, and then task constraints.

6 To prevent the finish date of your project from being moved out, select the **Level only within available slack** check box.

7 To have leveling adjust when a resource works on a task independent of other resources working on the same task, select the **Leveling can adjust individual assignments on a task** check box.

When the task's priority is set to **Do Not Level**, Microsoft Project will skip the task.

8 To interrupt tasks by creating splits in the remaining work on tasks or resource assignments, select the **Leveling can create splits in remaining work** check box.

9 Click **Level Now**.

Immediately after leveling your project, you can undo the changes if you don't get the results you want.

➢ **To immediately undo the effects of leveling**

• On the **Edit** menu, click **Undo Leveling**.

Although earlier versions of Microsoft Project didn't allow leveling for projects scheduled from a finish date, this new version does. When you automatically level overallocations in a project scheduled from the finish date, Microsoft Project applies a negative delay value to the affected tasks.

Level Resource Overallocations Yourself

If you have just a few overallocated resources, you may consider leveling them by adding delay to tasks yourself. When you add delay yourself, you can add delay to noncritical tasks only, if that works out, and avoid adding delay to critical tasks (which automatic leveling may do), which can delay the project finish date.

When you add a delay to a task yourself, first delay tasks that won't delay the project finish date, noncritical tasks with total slack. If you add delay time only up to the amount of total slack time for each task, you won't delay the project finish date.

Delay time is always given in elapsed time (nonworking time is included in the delay time).

➢ **To delay a task with an overallocated resource**

1   On the **View Bar**, click **More Views**.

2   In the **Views** list, click **Resource Allocation**, and then click **Apply**.

3   On the **View** menu, point to **Toolbars**, and then click **Resource Management**.

    In the Resource Usage view in the top pane, overallocated resources are highlighted in red and displayed with an icon in the Indicators field.

4   In the top pane, select an overallocated resource in the **Resource Name** field.

5   In the bottom pane, select a task in the **Task Name** field that is assigned to the resource during the time the resource is overallocated.

6   In the **Leveling Delay** field, enter the amount of time you want to delay a task that occurs during the time of overallocation.

    To avoid delaying successor tasks and the finish date of the schedule, type a value that is not greater than the total slack for that task. You can see the total slack for a task by inserting the Total Slack column into the Leveling Gantt view in the bottom pane.

7   Press ENTER.

    A task's slack is displayed as a bar to help you decide how much you can move a task before successor tasks or the end date of the project is affected.

8   If the resource is still overallocated, increase the delay value.

REDUCING COSTS

On some projects, costs may be someone else's concern. You only need to focus on achieving project goals as effectively as possible. But if you're responsible for costs and a review of your project plan shows that your project costs exceed your budget, you'll need to reduce costs.

In many projects, resources contribute to costs more than any other single factor. If this is the case in your project, then minimizing resource costs should be your main goal. But the size of a project can play a role, too. Often, the bigger the project, the more it costs.

Some of the ways you can reduce costs are to:

- Replace expensive resources with less costly ones.
- Reducing the scope of the project or individual tasks.

For more information about how to manage costs, see Chapter 7, "How to Assign and Manage Costs."

You can also reduce the number of resources assigned to a task, reduce the amount of work on a task, and combine or delete tasks. For more information about these strategies, see the appropriate topics in the "Shortening Your Schedule" and "Resolving Resource Overallocations" sections earlier in this chapter.

The Kinds of Cost Information You Can Display

A good strategy for cutting costs is to focus on reducing the cost of the factors that cost the most. You can determine which factors cost the most by displaying the cost of each factor in your project. For example, you can display:

- The total project cost, which is the cost of all the tasks, resources, assignments, and materials in your project.
- The total cost of an individual task, which is the cost of the resources and materials used to accomplish the task.
- The total cost of a resource, which is based on hourly and fixed costs.
- Costs distributed over a task's duration, which can be a baseline cost, cumulative cost, or actual cost that's apportioned over time.

For information about displaying costs, see Chapter 7, "How to Assign and Manage Costs."

Replace Expensive Resources with Less Costly Ones

Not all resources of the same type are created equal in regard to quality and cost. Some resources produce better results than others, and some resources cost more than others, even though they perform the same job. If a less-expensive resource can achieve the same level of quality as a more-expensive one, then you should consider replacing the more-expensive resource.

The less-expensive resource needs to be not only qualified, but available and able to accomplish the task without increasing the task duration. If you're strapped for resources, you can consider assigning the more-expensive resource to fewer tasks.

> ➤ **To replace an expensive resource with a less costly one**

To compare resource costs, display the Resource Sheet view.

1   On the **View Bar**, click **Gantt Chart**.

2   In the **Task Name** field, select the task for which you want to replace a resource.

3   Click **Assign Resources** .

4   In the **Name** field, select the resource you want to replace on the task.

5   Click **Replace**.

6   In the **Name** field, select the resource you now want to assign to the task, and then click **OK**.

Cut the Scope of the Project or Individual Tasks

When it comes to costs, the size of the project, the project scope, usually matters. Often, the size of the project is directly related to the number of tasks. You cut scope by reducing your project goals, and then deleting those tasks that are no longer required.

By deleting tasks, you cut the costs associated with those tasks: resource costs, materials costs, and so on. The more tasks you can delete, the more you can reduce the overall cost of your project. Of course, you shouldn't delete tasks that are required to achieve your project goals.

For more information about deleting tasks, see "Delete or Combine Critical Tasks" earlier in this chapter.

Part 3

Tracking Your Project and Updating Your Project Plan

The power of your project plan is that it can help you to both predict your project's course and keep it on course. Your original, refined plan represents your best estimate of how your project will proceed. It includes estimates of task durations, project length, costs, and more.

But once a project starts, reality sets in: A task starts later than planned. A flu epidemic among your team members threatens to blow the project deadline. An unexpected rise in the price of an essential material strains your budget. By using your project plan to track actual project progress, you improve your ability to make the changes that keep your project on schedule and within budget.

To track project progress, you need to collect project data. One of the best ways to collect and incorporate actual project data is to use Microsoft Project's predefined *workgroup* messages. Workgroup messages are used to request and confirm task assignments, send updated task assignment information to the workgroup manager, and incorporate updated information into the project plan. They can be exchanged across an e-mail system, an intranet, or the World Wide Web.

For more information about using workgroup messages, see Chapter 10, "Updating Task Information by Using E-mail and the Web."

9

Keeping Your Project on Track

Your project plan is your blueprint for achieving your project goals. But how do you know if your project is proceeding according to plan? You can identify deviations from your plan by tracking the progress of your project.

When you track progress, you compare how your project is really going with how your plan says it should be going. To track progress, you need to save key progress-indicating information after you fine-tune your project plan and before the project begins. This information is the *baseline* against which you compare actual progress. You also need to periodically collect *actual data* (or *actuals*)—data that shows what has actually occurred—enter the actual data into your project plan, and compare actual data to baseline data.

You can compare as many or as few details as you want. For example, you may decide to track only task start and finish dates and durations. Or, you may also track work, the percentage of each task that is completed, and costs.

By tracking progress, you can:

- Monitor the status of your project, which can include monitoring task completion dates, remaining work on tasks, costs, and the project finish date.

- Identify the sources of problems, such as the project finish date is being pushed out later than planned (or permitted) or costs are exceeding the budget.

- Determine solutions to any problems you discover and resolve them before they affect the desired project outcome.

- Develop a project history you can use to improve future project planning. For example, you can use the actual duration of a task in the next project plan that requires that task.

For some projects, you may want to know only whether your project is proceeding "well enough." To know that, you can compare actual data to baseline data and take no further action. But because projects are often limited by time, money, or resource availability, deviations from the project plan, even small ones, may require compensatory action on your part. For example, suppose a task that's taking longer than estimated pushes out a nonnegotiable project deadline. If you track your project, you'll be able to identify this problem readily. Then, going one step further, you can use Microsoft Project's scheduling tools to analyze the problem and determine the best way to get back on track.

A number of ways to identify scheduling problems and adjust your schedule to keep it on track are discussed in this chapter. But many of the procedures you need to adjust your schedule after the project begins are the same procedures you use to fine-tune your project plan before the project begins. You can find procedures for shortening your schedule, resolving resource overallocations, and reducing costs in Chapter 8, "Reviewing and Fine-Tuning Your Project Plan."

The value you get from tracking progress depends to some extent on how diligently you track. Your project plan will give you the most control over the project outcome if you update the plan at a set interval, say, every two weeks.

SETTING THE BASELINE

As your project progresses, some tasks may take longer than planned and others, shorter. Tasks or resources may cost more or less than you estimated. And some resources, who in the original, refined project plan were assigned the same number of work hours per day as they had available, may find themselves overworked or underworked. If you're tracking, you record actual durations, work, costs, and so on. But to know whether all the actuals mean you're ahead of schedule or behind, within your budget or exceeding it, you need to be able to compare your actual schedule to some reference point. That reference point is the *baseline*.

The baseline consists of key information, such as task start and finish dates, resource assignments, and costs, that represent your best estimates of how your project will progress and how much it will cost. Typically, you arrive at these best estimates after you fine-tune your project plan. (See Chapter 8, "Reviewing and Fine-Tuning Your Project Plan."). Then you set or "freeze" these estimates by saving baseline data before the project begins. After you save baseline data, it won't be overwritten when you adjust your project plan. The baseline data will always be available for you to compare with actual data.

When you freeze the baseline, Microsoft Project saves the baseline data as part of the project file. The baseline is not a separate file (although you can choose to save a copy of an entire project file as the baseline), nor is it a copy of all the data in your project plan. The baseline consists of key progress-indicating data, such as task start and finish dates, work, and costs, that Microsoft Project displays in baseline fields so that you can compare baseline data to actual data. You can, however, modify the baseline itself to accommodate changes in the project.

You can set a baseline for a project of any size and duration. But if a project has a very short duration or it isn't constrained by time, cost, or resource availability, you might not need to set a baseline.

Set and Save a Baseline

After you create and refine your project plan, you can set and save a baseline. When you set a baseline, Microsoft Project saves baseline information only and stores it in baseline fields. This information includes task start and finish dates, work, and costs, which you can display in the Baseline Start, Baseline Finish, Baseline Work, and Baseline Cost fields, respectively.

If the Planning Wizard appears when you save your project file, you can have it save a baseline for you. If not, you can use the following procedure.

➢ **To set a baseline**

1 On the **Tools** menu, point to **Tracking**, and then click **Save Baseline**.

2 Click **Save baseline**, and then click **Entire project**.

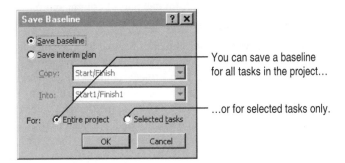

You can save a baseline for all tasks in the project...

...or for selected tasks only.

When you set a baseline, you don't create a separate baseline file that you can at some later time open and display. You can, however, create a backup copy of your project file that contains baseline information only, at the same time as you set a baseline.

> ➢ **To save a project file with baseline information only**

1 On the **File** menu, click **Save As**.

2 In the **File name** box, type a name that reminds you that this file is a backup of baseline information.

For example, you might type *<project name>* **baseline** *<today's date>*

3 Click **Save**.

Save an Interim Plan

As you begin updating your schedule, you may want to know how accurate your original scheduling estimates are. A good way to do this is to save an *interim plan*, which includes task start and finish dates only. By comparing the information in an interim plan with baseline information, you can determine the accuracy of your scheduling estimates as well as when your project began to deviate from the original project plan.

An interim plan is not a separate project file, but rather a set of task start and finish dates that are stored in columns and saved with a project file. When you save an interim plan, you specify the columns containing the set of task start and finish dates that you want to save and the pair of start and finish columns into which you want to copy and save them. For example, for the first interim plan, you might specify that you want to copy the dates from the Start and Finish columns into the Baseline Start and Baseline Finish columns. (When you save an interim plan, you can copy task start and finish dates from a predefined pair of columns, such as Start/Finish, into another predefined pair, such as BaselineStart/BaselineFinish, only.) By using the following procedure, you can copy the dates from one pair of columns into the other pair all at once, instead of manually copying and pasting one column at a time.

One way to use an interim plan is to save the current start and finish dates from a particular start/finish column pair before you overwrite those dates with new dates. For example, if changes in your project require you to change the dates in the Start and Finish columns, you can keep a record of those dates by copying them into the Start1 and Finish1 columns. Then, you can type the new dates over the old dates in the Start and Finish columns. Later on, if you again need to overwrite the dates in the Start and Finish columns, you can copy those dates into the Start2 and Finish2 columns.

You can copy the dates from any pair of start/finish columns into any other pair. For example, if you want to save the dates in the Start2 and Finish2 columns, you might copy those dates into the Start5 and Finish5 columns.

When you want to see the information stored in an interim plan, you can insert the appropriate columns into the Gantt Chart view or the Task Sheet view. For example, if your sixth interim plan is stored in the Start6 and Finish6 columns, you can insert those columns. You can save up to 10 interim plans for each schedule, at any time during the project.

➢ **To save an interim plan**

1   On the **Tools** menu, point to **Tracking**, and then click **Save Baseline**.

2   Click **Save interim plan**.

3   In the **Copy** box, click the plan name you want to save.

The predefined pairs of columns range from Start/Finish to Start10/Finish10. You can copy from any pair into any other pair.

4   In the **Into** box, click the name under which you want to save the plan.

5   Click **Entire project** or **Selected tasks** to save the portion of the schedule you want.

Add a Task to a Baseline or Interim Plan

As your project progresses, you may identify work that needs to be done, but there's no task in the project plan that takes care of this work. In that case, you'll probably add a task to your plan. To track the progress of the new task, you should also add this task to your baseline plan and an interim plan (if you created an interim plan).

➢ **To add a task to a baseline or interim plan**

1   In the **Task Name** field, select the task you want to add to the baseline or interim plan.

2   On the **Tools** menu, point to **Tracking**, and then click **Save Baseline**.

3   To add the task to the baseline plan, click **Save baseline**.

4   To add the task to the interim plan, click **Save interim plan**.

5   Click **Selected tasks**.

Change Baseline Information for One or More Tasks

If there are large, unexpected changes in your project, comparing your actual project data to baseline data may not be an effective tracking tool. Using baseline data as a reference point works best when the baseline reflects project realities fairly accurately.

For example, if after the project has begun upper management suddenly decides to cut project goals by half (and thus cut the project duration, costs, and so on by approximately half), it wouldn't be useful to compare actual data to the original baseline data. To track effectively, you'd need to change the baseline information.

➢ **To change baseline information for one or more tasks**

1 On the **View Bar**, click **Gantt Chart** or any other task view.

2 In the **Task Name** field, select the tasks whose baseline information you want to change.

3 On the **Tools** menu, point to **Tracking**, and then click **Save Baseline**.

4 Click **Save baseline**, and then click **Selected tasks**.

When you click **Selected tasks**, Microsoft Project updates the baseline data for the tasks you selected.

WHERE DO YOU GET ACTUAL INFORMATION?

There are several ways you can collect data on task progress:

- You can collect all the data yourself. This may be feasible in a small project where you can track everything.

- Have the supervisor or manager report on the tasks in their area.

- Have the individual responsible for each task provide a status report.

- Verify progress through inspection, quality control, or test data.

One other way to collect actual data is by exchanging Microsoft Project *workgroup* messages, which are electronic messages that are used to assign tasks, send updated task status information, and incorporate updated information into the project plan, without the workgroup manager (or project manager) needing to enter the information manually. For more information about using workgroup messages, see Chapter 10, "Updating Task Information by Using E-Mail and the World Wide Web."

The collected data should be based on some measurable physical progress, not just the time that has passed since that task started. Time from the start date to the present may not reflect the actual working time spent on the task nor progress made on the task; resources may not be actually working on the task as scheduled or actual progress may be faster or slower than planned. Measuring progress for physical tasks, such as laying pipe or erecting a building, is easier because you can measure the physical results; it is more difficult for "thinking" tasks, such as writing, designing, or programming. However, even in these areas, there is an end product that can be broken into measurable tasks.

Try to use objective data where possible. For what has happened, use sources such as time sheets, bills for materials and services from vendors, purchase orders, and other direct charges to projects. If a task involves using a certain quantity of a material, such as laying pipe or stringing wire, you can base progress on the quantity used to date versus expected total use, such as feet of pipe used versus the quantity needed for the completed task.

It's hard to be objective when estimating percent complete and remaining work or duration, but by using information from all your sources, you should be able to come up with data in which you have some confidence. Here, the judgment or experience of those responsible for the tasks will help when deciding just how far along a task is.

Agree on how you will measure progress, and how often, before you start the project. This should be discussed and settled in the planning stages. Those who will be collecting progress data should be involved in deciding how it will be measured.

WHICH INFORMATION SHOULD YOU UPDATE?

When you collect actual data, you are, first of all, interested in the tasks on which there is or should be activity. If you're going to track progress at all, you should at a minimum track actual start and finish dates of tasks. Tracking these dates will let you know whether your project will finish on time.

You can track and update:

- Task start dates
- Task finish dates
- Task duration
- The percentage of each task that is complete
- Task cost
- Work

You can collect information in task, resource, and assignment notes. For example, if a resource wasn't available as expected, you can explain the reason in a resource note. Or, if some problem has occurred in carrying out a task, you can describe the problem in a task note.

Enter Actual Start and Finish Dates for a Task

The project finish date is most affected by the schedules of the individual tasks, especially critical tasks. If tasks start and finish on time, it's likely the project will finish on time. If tasks start and finish late, it's likely the project will finish late. Therefore, if meeting the planned project deadline is important, you'll want to track and update task start and finish dates.

> **To enter actual start and finish dates for a task**

1 On the **View Bar**, click **Gantt Chart**.

2 In the **Task Name** field, select the task you want to update.

3 On the **Tools** menu, point to **Tracking**, and then click **Update Tasks**.

4 Under **Actual**, type the dates in the **Start** and **Finish** boxes.

   The dates you type will appear in the Actual Start and Actual Finish fields of the selected task.

You can view actual dates by inserting the Actual Start and Actual Finish columns into any task table or by applying the Tracking table to a task sheet view.

Enter actual start and finish dates here.

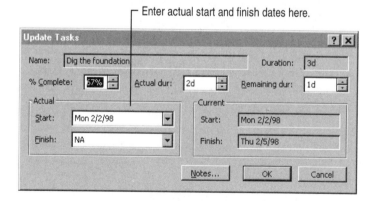

If several tasks started and finished on time—that is, their actual start and finish dates are the same as the planned dates that appear in the Start and Finish fields—you can set the actual start and actual finish information for all of those tasks at once. When you use the following procedure, Microsoft Project inserts the dates from the Start and Finish fields into the Actual Start and Actual Finish fields of the selected tasks.

> **To enter actual start and finish dates for several on-time tasks at once**

1   On the **View Bar**, click **Gantt Chart**.

Select nonadjacent tasks by holding down CTRL while you select.

2   In the **Task Name** field, select the tasks that started and finished on time.

3   On the **Tools** menu, point to **Tracking**, and then click **Update Project**.

4   Click **Selected tasks**.

Enter the Actual Duration of a Task

The actual duration of a task has important side-effects. If it's different than the baseline duration, it can change the project finish date. Also, when you enter the actual duration of a task, Microsoft Project updates the duration of the task remaining in the schedule, the actual start date, and the percentage of the task that is complete.

If you know how long a task has been worked on and it's progressing as planned, you can enter the actual duration for the task. For example, if a 5-day task has been worked on for 2 days (and it's likely to be completed in 3 more days), you can enter an actual duration of 2 days.

However, if effort-driven scheduling is turned on (which it is by default) and you've assigned resources to tasks, you should not change either the scheduled or the actual duration of tasks. Instead, adjust the amount of work for the resource or resource units to change the task duration.

By adjusting the amount of work, you can be sure that your schedule will reflect project reality. For example, when a task takes longer to complete than planned, then the actual duration of the task will be greater than the scheduled duration. In that case, when you enter the actual amount of work for the task, Microsoft Project changes the actual finish date to reflect the increased amount of work and also increases the task duration.

If you incrementally enter an actual duration for a task that is greater than the scheduled duration (and effort-driven scheduling is turned on), the actual work remains fixed. When the actual duration exceeds the scheduled duration, Microsoft Project assumes that the amount of work should stay fixed. It compensates by recalculating a lower number of resource units (that is, fewer hours worked per day on the task).

For example, a single resource is assigned at 100% resource units to a 2-day task (or 16 hours of work). The task ends up taking 3 days (24 hours or work). Incrementally, you enter an actual duration of 3 days (say, as the task progresses, an actual duration first of 1 day, then 2 days, and finally 3 days). After you make your final entry for the actual duration, Microsoft Project holds the work amount constant at the initial 16 hours, changes the scheduled duration to 3 days, and then recalculates the resource units to be 67%. That is, instead of showing the resource working on the task 8 hours on each of the 3 days it actually took to complete the task—which was really the case—Microsoft Project shows the resource working on the task each of the 3 days for 0.67 x 8 hours = 5.33 hours per day.

In short, change the actual work instead of the actual duration, to be on the safe side.

➤ **To enter the actual duration of a task**

1   On the **View Bar**, click **Gantt Chart**.

2   Select the task for which you want to enter the actual duration.

3   On the **Tools** menu, point to **Tracking**, and then click **Update Tasks**.

4   In the **Actual dur** box, enter the actual duration of the task.

If you think the task is going to be finished sooner or later than originally scheduled, you can enter a new value in the Remaining dur box.

Indicate Progress on a Task as a Percentage

When a task is in progress, you can indicate how much progress has been made by entering the percentage of the total task duration that has been completed. A task is zero percent complete when it has not yet begun, and it is 100 percent complete when it is finished. For example, if 2 days of work have been completed on a 5-day task, then you'd enter 40% complete. For a summary task, Microsoft Project calculates a percentage complete that's based on the progress of its subtasks.

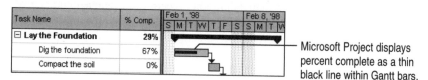

Microsoft Project displays percent complete as a thin black line within Gantt bars.

When you enter the percentage complete for a task that's between 0 and 100, Microsoft Project changes the actual start date to match the scheduled start date and calculates the actual duration and remaining duration. When you enter 100% complete for a task, Microsoft Project changes the actual finish date to match the scheduled finish date and changes the actual duration to match the scheduled duration. If the task was critical, Microsoft Project changes it to noncritical.

➤ **To indicate progress on a task as a percentage**

1   On the **View Bar**, click **Gantt Chart**.

2   In the **Task Name** field, select the task you want to update.

3   Click **Task Information** 🗒, and then click the **General** tab.

4   In the **Percent complete** box, type a whole number between 0 and 100.

To quickly enter 0%, 25%, 50%, 75%, or 100% complete for the selected tasks, use the percent complete buttons on the Tracking toolbar.

By default, Microsoft Project indicates the percentage of the task that is complete as a thin, black line drawn horizontally through the middle of each task bar in the Gantt Chart view.

Update the Work Completed on a Task

If the availability of resources is crucial to your project and you want to track the work that each resource is performing, you can track task progress by updating the work completed on the task by each. For example, say the scheduled work for a task assigned to 2 resources is 20 hours. At the end of a day, a total of 10 hours of work has been completed, 7 hours by one resource and 3 hours by the other. You can enter the amount of hours each resource has worked on the task on that day.

After you update the actual number of hours a resource has worked on a task, Microsoft Project automatically calculates the remaining work.

➤ **To update the work completed on a task**

1   On the **View Bar**, click **Task Usage**.

2   On the **View** menu, point to **Table,** and then click **Tracking**.

3   Drag the divider bar to the right to view the **Act. Work** field.

4   In the **Act. Work** field, type the updated work value and the duration abbreviation for the assigned resource under the task for which you want to update the actual work value.

Drag the divider bar to the right to see the Actual Work field. ⌐

Task Name	% Comp.	Act. Dur.	Rem. Dur.	Act. Cost	Act. Work	Details
⊟ **Lay the Foundation**	**41%**	**2.85 days**	**4.15 days**	**$0.00**	**0 hrs**	Work
Dig the foundation	67%	2 days	1 day	$0.00	0 hrs	Work
Compact the soil	25%	0.25 days	0.75 days	$0.00	0 hrs	Work

If you don't want to track the amount of work performed by each resource assigned to a task, then simply type a value for the combined work done on the task by all the resources in the Act. Work field for the task (not for the individual resources, which occupy the rows beneath the task). Microsoft Project divides the actual and remaining work among the resources.

Update Actual Work on a Daily Basis

If your schedule is tight and you need to use your resources as efficiently as possible, you can track the actual work done by each resource on a daily basis. You can do this by using the timephased fields in the Resource Usage view. Timephased fields break down the project duration into days, weeks, months, and so on.

➤ **To update actual work on a daily basis**

1 On the **View Bar**, click **Resource Usage**.
2 On the **View** menu, point to **Table,** and then click **Work**.
3 On the **Format** menu, point to **Details**, and then click **Actual Work**.
4 To enter actual values for a resource, select the column for the day you want to track and type a value into the **Act. Work** field of the resource.
5 To enter actual values for a task assignment, select the column for the day you want to track and type a value into the **Act. Work** field of the task.

Update the Remaining Work on a Task Yourself

Microsoft project calculates the remaining work on a task by subtracting the actual work from the scheduled work. But sometimes you find out that there's more work remaining than Microsoft Project has calculated. In those cases, you can update the remaining work on a task yourself.

➤ **To update the remaining work on a task**

1 On the **View Bar**, click **Gantt Chart**.
2 On the **View** menu, point to **Table,** and then click **Work**.
3 In the **Remaining** field of the task you want to update, enter the remaining work value you want.

You may need to scroll right to see the Remaining field.

Insert a Time Gap Between Actual Work and Remaining Work

A resource may not always work on a task continuously from beginning to end. For instance, a resource might complete part of a task, get interrupted to go work on a more urgent task, and then resume work on the first task. If the interruption is short and doesn't significantly affect the finish date of the interrupted task, you may not want or need to track the interruption. But if the length of the interruption is significant or you simply want to track as precisely as possible, you can display a gap between the actual work and the remaining work on a task. The gap, or split, spans the stop and resumption dates.

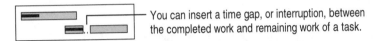 You can insert a time gap, or interruption, between the completed work and remaining work of a task.

➤ **To insert a split between actual work and remaining work**

1   On the **View Bar**, click **Gantt Chart**.

2   Click **Split Task** .

3   In the chart portion of the view, position the pointer over the incomplete part of the task you want to split.

4   Drag the task bar to the right to split the task and have a portion of it start later.

   Do not drag the finished portion of the task. If you drag the finished portion of the task, you'll move the entire task.

Reschedule Uncompleted Work to Start on the Current Date

If your project falls behind schedule and you and your team are scrambling to catch up, it can be all too easy to forget about tasks that should have been completed by the current date but weren't. Some of those tasks might have gotten "lost" somewhere near the beginning of the schedule, scrolled out of sight (unless you're in the habit of scrolling to the beginning of the schedule on a regular basis). You can account for all tasks that should have been completed by the current date by rescheduling uncompleted work to start on the current date.

You can reschedule uncompleted work for all tasks or for selected tasks. If a task has no work done on it, Microsoft Project calculates its new start date to be the current date or later, depending on any task dependencies. If a task is partially complete, Microsoft Project inserts a split between the completed work and the remaining work portions of the task. If a task has an inflexible constraint, such as Must Start On or Must Finish On, Microsoft Project may replace the inflexible constraint with a flexible constraint, such as Start No Earlier Than or As Soon As Possible. If you want to keep a constraint, you should reschedule the remaining work for a task manually.

➢ **To reschedule uncompleted work to start on the current date**

1 On the **View Bar**, click **Gantt Chart**.

2 In the **Task Name** field, select the tasks you want to reschedule.

If you want to reschedule all remaining work in the project, do not select any tasks.

3 On the **Tools** menu, point to **Tracking**, and then click **Update Project**.

4 Click **Reschedule uncompleted work to start**, and then type the date from which you want to reschedule all remaining work.

5 To reschedule the entire project, click **Entire project**.

To reschedule only the selected tasks, click **Selected tasks**.

Update Actual Costs for a Resource Assignment Manually

The cost of a resource assignment is the cost of one resource assigned to a particular task. The resource assignment cost can include items such as the standard rate paid to the resource, delivery fees, setup charges, and a per-use cost.

By default, Microsoft Project calculates the actual cost of a resource assignment as the task progresses, according to the accrual method you choose. If you want to enter the actual cost of a resource assignment yourself, you need to turn off automatic calculation and then enter your own cost after the remaining work on the task is zero.

➢ **To update actual costs for a resource assignment**

1 On the **Tools** menu, click **Options**, and then click the **Calculation** tab.

2 Clear the **Actual costs are always calculated by Microsoft Project** check box.

3 Click **OK**.

4 On the **View Bar**, click **Task Usage**.

5 On the **View** menu, point to **Table,** and then click **Tracking**.

6 Drag the divider bar to the right to view the **Act. Cost** field.

7 In the **Act. Cost** field, type the actual cost for the assignment for which you want to update costs.

Update Actual Costs on a Daily Basis

Just as you can track actual work on a daily basis, you can also track actual costs on a daily basis. You can track the actual costs of tasks as well as resource assignments. Typically, you'd track actual costs on a daily basis when costs are an important concern in your project. For example, you may be working with a limited budget.

By default, Microsoft Project calculates the actual cost of a task according to the accrual method you choose. If you want to enter the actual cost of a resource assignment yourself, you need to turn off automatic calculation and then enter your own cost after the remaining work on the task is zero.

> **To update actual costs on a daily basis**

1 On the **Tools** menu, click **Options**, and then click the **Calculation** tab.

2 Clear the **Actual costs are always calculated by Microsoft Project** check box.

3 Click **OK**.

4 On the **View Bar**, click **Task Usage**.

5 On the **View** menu, point to **Table,** and then click **Tracking**.

6 On the **Format** menu, point to **Details**, and then click **Actual Cost**.

7 To enter actual values for a task, select the column for the day you want to track and type a value into the **Act. Cost** field of the task.

8 To enter actual values for a resource assignment, select the column for the day you want to track and type a value into the **Act. Cost** field of the resource.

You can type in your own
values for the actual cost. ⌐

Dig the foundation	$160.00	Work	7h	8h
		Act. Cost	$140.00	$20.00
Diggers	*$160.00*	Work	7h	8h
		Act. Cost	$140.00	$20.00

Prevent Resource Information from Being Updated When Task Status is Updated

By default, when you update information for a task that has resources assigned to it, Microsoft Project automatically updates the tracking information for the assigned resources. When Microsoft Project updates the resource information, it treats each assigned resource equally. For example, if you indicate that a 4-day (32-hour) task with 2 assigned resources is 50% complete, then Microsoft Project calculates 8 hours of work performed by each resource.

But different assigned resources can work different amounts of hours in the same time period. Instead of working 8 hours each, one resource may have worked 10 hours and the other only 6 hours. You can specify the tracking information for each resource independent of the task information by turning off the automatic updating of resource tracking information.

> ➢ **To prevent resource information from being updated**
>
> 1 On the **Tools** menu, click **Options**, and then click the **Calculation** tab.
>
> 2 Clear the **Updating task status updates resource status** check box.

ANALYZING THE VARIANCE BETWEEN ACTUAL DATA AND BASELINE DATA

A variance is any difference between baseline data and actual data. For example, if the baseline start date for a task is February 12 and its actual start date is February 10, there's a variance of 2 days. Variances alert you to potential problems in your schedule that may need correcting. But variances can be good, as when a task starts 2 days earlier than planned, as well as bad. To determine the exact effect a variance has on your schedule, you can analyze the variance. Microsoft Project can display variances only when you've set a baseline.

Among the most important variances you should look for when comparing your updated schedule to the baseline plan are:

- Tasks that are starting or finishing late.

- Tasks that require more or less work than scheduled.

- Tasks that are progressing more slowly than planned.

- Tasks that are costing more than you planned for the actual work that's been completed.

- Resources that aren't working hours as scheduled.

After you find variances, you need to determine which corrective action, if any, you need to take. For example, some of the things you can do to speed up critical tasks are adjust task dependencies, assign overtime work, hire or assign additional resources, add shifts, and decrease the amount of work required to complete a task. To resolve resource allocations, you could reassign resources, delay tasks, and change working hours. To solve cost problems, you could adjust the budget, replace expensive resources with inexpensive ones, and delete tasks.

For more information about how to adjust your project plan, see the procedures in this chapter as well as in Chapter 8, "Reviewing and Fine-Tuning Your Project Plan."

Display Progress Lines to Determine Project Status

Looking at the variance for each task start and finish date may show that some tasks are early, some late, and others on time. You might not get a good impression of whether your project is, overall, ahead or behind schedule. One way to see quickly whether your project is ahead or behind schedule is to display progress lines on the Gantt Chart view.

A progress line is a vertical line that represents either the current date or a status date that you specify. Jutting out from a progress line are horizontal peaks connected to task bars representing tasks that are either in-progress or should have started prior to the current date or status date. A peak pointing leftward indicates a task that's either behind schedule or hasn't been completed. A peak pointing rightward indicates a task that's ahead of schedule. A progress line does not connect to completed tasks or tasks that start after the progress-line date.

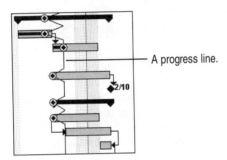

A progress line.

You can view more than one progress line at a time, either by inserting them manually or at set intervals automatically.

➢ **To display progress lines in your project**

1   On the **View Bar**, click **Gantt Chart**.

2   On the **Tools** menu, point to **Tracking**, and then click **Progress Lines**.

3   Click the **Dates and Intervals** tab.

4   Select the **Always display current progress line** check box.

5   To show progress for the project status date, click **At project status date**.

    To show progress for the current date, click **At current date**.

6   To show your progress relative to baseline data, under **Display progress lines in relation to**, click **Baseline plan**.

View Baseline Fields

The baseline you set consists of key information that you can use to track project progress. This information doesn't make up a separate plan, but rather is stored by Microsoft Project in baseline fields. When you want to compare actual data to baseline data, you can view baseline fields.

➤ **To view baseline fields**

1 On the **View Bar**, click **Tracking Gantt**.
2 On the **View** menu, point to **Table**, and then click **More Tables**.
3 In the **Tables** list, click **Baseline**, and then click **Apply**.

Microsoft Project displays the baseline dates in the Tracking Gantt view.

View Baseline Costs and Actual Costs on a Daily Basis

When costs matter, you probably want to track them closely and on a daily basis. You can do that by comparing baseline costs with actual costs in the Task Usage view, which breaks down costs (as well as work and other values) on a day-by-day timescale. In the Task Usage view, you can display both baseline costs and actual costs in detail.

➤ **To view baseline costs and actual costs on a daily basis**

1 On the **View Bar**, click **Task Usage**.
2 On the **View** menu, point to **Table**, and then click **Cost**.
3 On the **Format** menu, click **Detail Styles**, and then click the **Usage Details** tab.
4 In the **Available** fields list, hold down CTRL, click **Actual Cost**, **Baseline Cost**, and **Cost**.
5 Click **Show**.

Determine if Tasks Are Starting and Finishing on Time

Progress can only be measured against some reference point. In Microsoft Project, that reference point is the baseline start and finish data. To determine how your project is progressing, you need to compare the actual start and finish dates with the baseline start and finish dates. The Tracking Gantt view enables you to view both sets of dates at the same time. Based on your analysis of any variances you identify, you can adjust your schedule as necessary to keep your project on track.

Variance fields display the difference between baseline values and actual values. For example, if the baseline start date for a task is 2/2 and the actual start date is 2/5, the variance is 3 days.

> ➤ **To determine if tasks are starting and finishing on time**
>
> 1 On the **View Bar**, click **Tracking Gantt**.
>
> 2 On the **View** menu, point to **Table**, and then click **Variance**.
>
>   Microsoft Project displays the scheduled and baseline dates for each task.
>
> 3 Drag the divider bar to the right to view the **Variance** fields.

Determine if Tasks Are Using More or Less Work Than Planned

The amount of work required to complete a task affects the task duration as well as the workload of the resources assigned to a task. If your original work estimate for a task is off, the task could end up taking longer than planned or requiring additional resources to complete on time. If there's a difference between estimated and actual work, you may very well need to take corrective action.

> ➤ **To determine if tasks are using more or less work than planned**
>
> 1 On the **View Bar**, click **Gantt Chart**.
>
> 2 On the **View** menu, point to **Table**, and then click **Work**.
>
> 3 Drag the divider bar to the right to view the **Baseline** field.
>
> 4 Compare the values in the **Work** and **Baseline** fields.
>
>   To see the variance between the baseline work and actual work, look at the values in the **Variance** field.

Determine if Tasks Cost More or Less Than Planned

When you're working with a budget and tracking costs, you'll want to know if your tasks are running over budget before your project progresses too far. That way, you can either adjust your budget or reduce costs so that you don't go over budget before the project finish date.

In Microsoft Project, you can compare the total cost of a task—which consists of fixed costs plus resource costs—to the baseline cost and actual cost. Microsoft Project also calculates the remaining cost of a task that's in progress.

➤ **To determine if tasks cost more or less than budgeted**

1 On the **View Bar**, click **Gantt Chart**.

2 On the **View** menu, point to **Table**, and then click **Cost**.

3 Drag the divider bar to the right to view the **Total Cost** and **Baseline** fields.

4 Compare the values in the **Total Cost** and **Baseline** fields.

For the cost variance, look at the value in the **Variance** field.

Track Costs Over Time with the Earned Value Table

Are you spending more or less than you planned for the actual task work that's been completed? If you want to make sure that you complete all project tasks before you run out of money, you'll want to know the answer to this question. The answer lies in using the Earned Value table.

The Earned Value table displays, in terms of resource costs, the actual percentage of completion of each task. It enables you to estimate whether the task will finish under budget or over budget based on the cost incurred while the task is in progress. For example, if a task is 50 percent complete but has cost 75 percent of the budget allotted to it, the task will probably cost more than planned when it's completed. You can use the Earned Value table to analyze the cost of each task in this way.

➤ **To analyze costs over time with the Earned Value table**

1 On the **View Bar**, click **Gantt Chart**.

2 On the **View** menu, point to **Table**, and then click **More Tables**.

3 In the **Tables** list, click **Earned Value,** and then click **Apply**.

4 Drag the divider bar to the right to display all of the **Earned Value** table fields.

You can also view earned value data on a daily basis.

➤ **To view earned value data on a daily basis**

1 On the **View Bar**, click **Task Usage**.

2 On the **Format** menu, click **Detail Styles**, and then click the **Usage Details** tab.

3 In the **Available fields** list, hold down CTRL, click the fields you want to display, such as ACWP, BCWP, and BCWS, and then click **Show**.

10

Updating Task Information by Using E-Mail and the Web

Collecting up-to-date project information and incorporating it into your project plan is an essential activity if you want to track progress, but it can also be time-consuming. Periodically, you need to collect information from each resource assigned to a task that should have started by the current date. Then you need to enter this information into your plan, one task at a time. A faster and more convenient way to update your plan is to use the Microsoft Project workgroup feature.

A *workgroup* is a set of resources and their manager who work on the same project and are connected to an electronic communications system. Across this communications system, *workgroup members*, who are the resources who perform the tasks in your project, exchange project information with a *workgroup manager*, who is the person responsible for tracking the project.

The workgroup feature distributes responsibility for updating the project plan among the entire team; the workgroup manager doesn't have to do it all. After accepting a task assignment, each workgroup member periodically sends updated task information to the workgroup manager. The workgroup manager then incorporates this information into the project plan.

The workgroup manager exchanges task information with workgroup members by using the three types of Microsoft Project *workgroup messages*. The workgroup manager uses these messages to request task assignments, inform workgroup members of proposed schedule changes, and request actual task information. The workgroup members use these messages to accept or decline task assignments, provide feedback on proposed schedule changes, and send actual task information to the workgroup manager. The workgroup manager can insert all of the actual task information from a workgroup message directly into the project plan, without having to enter each piece of information separately and manually.

The kinds of communications systems you can use to exchange workgroup messages are e-mail, the World Wide Web, which is a part of the Internet, and a network used within an organization called an *intranet*, which looks and works like the World Wide Web. You can use any one of these systems or all three at the same time. Systems that use an intranet or the World Wide Web are called *web-based* systems.

You can use a workgroup for several reasons. You may decide to use a workgroup to request task assignments only. Or, you might only want to route project files for review (possible with e-mail systems only). But you get the full benefit from a workgroup when you use it to collect updated task information and incorporate that information into your project plan.

In this chapter, *workgroup member* will be used instead of *team member*, and *workgroup manager* instead of *project manager*. A topic that's for workgroup members only will have *workgroup members* in its title. A topic that's for workgroup managers only will have *workgroup manager* in its title.

HOW A WORKGROUP EXCHANGES TASK INFORMATION

Task information is exchanged between the workgroup manager and each workgroup member only, not between one workgroup member and another. This information is bundled into special electronic packets called workgroup messages. The three types of Microsoft Project workgroup messages are *TeamAssign*, *TeamUpdate*, and *TeamStatus* messages.

At the hub of the communications system, the workgroup manager can send workgroup messages to one workgroup member at a time, to several, or to all of them. Workgroup messages are received in an electronic inbox. In an e-mail system, both the workgroup member and the workgroup manager receive their workgroup messages in their respective e-mail inboxes. In a web-based system, each workgroup member receives workgroup messages in his or her *TeamInbox*, which is a web site that's specially set up to receive Microsoft Project workgroup messages. The workgroup manager receives web-based workgroup messages in the *WebInbox*, located within Microsoft Project.

The workgroup manager and workgroup members exchange task information by sending, receiving, and replying to workgroup messages. Whether you use e-mail, an intranet, or the World Wide Web, the cycle typically works like this:

1   The workgroup manager sends a TeamAssign request, which is a workgroup message requesting a task assignment, to a workgroup member.

2   The workgroup member sends the workgroup manager a reply to the TeamAssign request that indicates the workgroup member's acceptance or rejection of the task assignment.

    A TeamAssign message must be received by a workgroup member before the workgroup member can reply to a task assignment request (by using a workgroup message, that is).

3   If there's a change in a task's schedule, the workgroup manager can notify each workgroup member who's assigned to the task by sending those workgroup members a TeamUpdate message.

4   A workgroup member who receives a TeamUpdate message can send a TeamUpdate message to the workgroup manager to explain how the changes affect him or her.

    A workgroup member can send a TeamUpdate message to the workgroup manager at any time, without having to receive a TeamUpdate message from the workgroup manager first.

5   Periodically, to gather up-to-date progress information about each task, the workgroup manager sends each workgroup member a TeamStatus message, requesting actual information about tasks.

6   Each workgroup member responds to a TeamStatus message by sending a TeamStatus message with the requested task status information.

    A TeamStatus message must be received by a workgroup member before the workgroup member can send a TeamStatus message to the workgroup manager.

If you use a workgroup to route project files (which can only be done in an e-mail system), then one workgroup member can exchange project information with another workgroup member. But the specific task information that's required to keep a project plan up to date can only be exchanged between a workgroup member and a workgroup manager.

THE FIRST STEPS TO SETTING UP ANY WORKGROUP COMMUNICATIONS SYSTEM

Whether you want to use e-mail, an intranet, the World Wide Web, or any combination of these systems to exchange workgroup messages, you must do the following:

- Enter a resource list into your project plan. The resources on this list are the workgroup members for the project.
- Add each resource's workgroup identifier, such as an e-mail address or name, to your project plan, so that Microsoft Project can send a workgroup message to the correct workgroup member.
- Select a communications system for the workgroup.
- Set up each workgroup member with the system you select.

For information about entering a resource list into your project plan, see Chapter 6, "Assigning Resources to Tasks."

In addition to the four obligatory steps above, you can also perform one or more of the following optional steps when you set up a workgroup communications system:

- Change the workgroup messaging system for a particular workgroup member, for whom the default system may not be available.
- Customize workgroup messages to include the task information you want.

Add a Workgroup Member's Identifier to Your Project (Workgroup Manager)

Before a postal carrier can deliver mail to your home, he or she needs information that identifies your location uniquely, so that your mail doesn't end up at someone else's home. Likewise, Microsoft Project requires a unique identifier for each workgroup member. Microsoft Project uses this workgroup identifier to distinguish one workgroup member's inbox location from another, so that a workgroup message intended for a particular workgroup member reaches that workgroup member.

If you don't specify a workgroup identifier for a workgroup member, Microsoft Project uses the workgroup member's e-mail name as the workgroup identifier, by default. If an e-mail name isn't available, then Microsoft Project uses the name of the workgroup member that appears on your resource list, such as on the Resource Sheet view. Be aware that Microsoft Project allows you to use the same name for more than one resource on a resource list. To make sure that Microsoft Project can direct a workgroup message to the correct workgroup member, you should give each resource a unique name.

If a workgroup member's e-mail address is not the same as the workgroup member's name in Microsoft Project, you should add the member's e-mail address to the project

➢ **To add a resource's e-mail address to your project**

1   On the **View Bar**, click **Resource Sheet**.

2   On the **View** menu, point to **Table**, and then click **Entry**.

3   In the **Resource Name** field, select a resource whose e-mail address you want to add.

4   Click **Resource Information** 📋, and then click the **General** tab.

5   In the **Email** box, type the e-mail address for that resource, and then click **OK**.

   If the resource is located outside your organization, be sure to include the entire address. For example, if the resource's e-mail name is Jodie and that resource can be reached through an Internet service provider called Provider (whose web server is registered as provider.com), the following address would be correct:

   jodie@provider.com

6   Repeat steps 3 through 5 for all of the resources.

Select the Workgroup Messaging System (Workgroup Manager)

Before you can exchange workgroup messages, you have to select and set up a workgroup communications system (which isn't supplied by Microsoft Project). But which system should you select? You select the system whose requirements you can meet.

To use an e-mail–based communications system, you need access to a MAPI-compliant, 32-bit e-mail system.

To use a web-based communications system, you need access to a web server. You also need to notify workgroup members of the uniform resource locator (URL) address that points to the web server so that workgroup members can find their TeamInboxes by using a web browser. (URL is the standard for naming and locating a web site on the Internet. The person responsible for the web server can supply the URL.)

You can select an e-mail system only, an intranet only, the World Wide Web only, a combination of any two systems, or all three. By default, the choice you make will apply to each workgroup member. You can, however, change the communications system used by individual workgroup members.

In the following procedure, selecting a communications system doesn't make that system operational. You're simply enabling Microsoft Project to communicate with the system you select. You'll still need to set up each workgroup member's computer so that it can exchange workgroup messages across that communications system.

➢ **To select e-mail or a web as the system for workgroup communications**

1 On the **Tools** menu, click **Options**, and then click the **Workgroup** tab.

2 In the **Default workgroup messaging for resources** box, click the workgroup message option you want to use for most of your resources (you can change the message option for individual resources).

To send workgroup messages through a MAPI-compliant, 32-bit e-mail system, click **Email**.

To send workgroup messages through a web server (making use of an intranet or the World Wide Web), click **Web**.

To send workgroup messages through both a MAPI-compliant, 32-bit e-mail system and a web server (making use of an intranet or the World Wide Web), click **Email and Web**.

To prevent workgroup messages from being sent to resources, click **None**. (Select this option only if most of your resources don't have access to an e-mail system, an intranet, or the World Wide Web.)

3 If you chose a web server, enter the Internet address (URL) for the web server that is servicing the workgroup in the **Web Server URL (for resource)** box.

For example, the URL might point to a web server set up on the workgroup manager's computer. If the network identification for that computer has its name set to be "manager" and the web server files are in a folder named "project," then the URL for that computer would be as follows:

http://manager/project/

4 If you chose a web server, enter the path to where the web server software resides on the web server computer in the **Web Server root (for manager)** box.

The Microsoft Project workgroup feature will set up folders and files to manage the activity of the workgroup on this path. For example, if you install Microsoft Personal Web Server on your computer, and you want the folder for Microsoft Project information to be named "project," the path statement could be as follows:

\\manager\webshare\wwwroot\project

5 To apply your workgroup selections to all new projects, click **Set as Default**.

6 Click the **General** tab.

7 In the **User name** box, type the name by which you want to be identified in the workgroup messages you send.

8 If you selected **Web** or **Email and Web** on the **Workgroup** tab, Microsoft Project will notify you after you close the **Options** dialog box that it needs to copy files to the web server to set up the workgroup. To allow it to do so, click **Yes**.

Select the workgroup messaging option here.

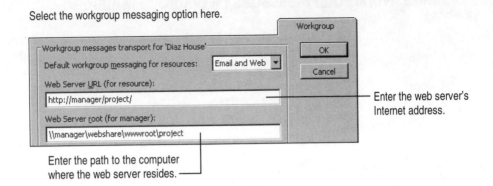

Enter the web server's
Internet address.

Enter the path to the computer
where the web server resides.

Change the Workgroup Messaging System for a Workgroup Member (Workgroup Manager)

When you select a workgroup messaging system on the Workgroup tab of the Options dialog box, that system becomes the default for all workgroup members. If a workgroup member doesn't have access to the default system, however, you can change the communications system used by that workgroup member.

➢ **To change the workgroup messaging system for a workgroup member**

1   On the **View Bar**, click **Resource Sheet**.

2   Select the resource or resources (CTRL + click) whose workgroup messaging option you want to change.

3   Click **Resource Information** 📖, and then click the **General** tab.

4   In the **Workgroup** box, click the method of workgroup messaging most appropriate for the workgroup member.

To follow the settings on the **Workgroup** tab of the **Options** dialog box, click **Default**.

If you choose an option other than Default, that option will be applied to the selected resource or resources.

Customize Workgroup Messages (Workgroup Manager)

Each type of Microsoft Project workgroup message conveys certain task information by default. This information is contained in fields. For example, the TeamStatus message contains the Task Name, Work, Start, and Finish fields. If you want to track different task information, you can customize the TeamStatus message or any of the other two workgroup message types.

You can customize a workgroup message type by adding fields, removing fields, changing the report period, and tracking overtime work.

➤ **To customize workgroup messages**

1 On the **Tools** menu, point to **Customize**, and then click **Workgroup**.

2 To add a field, click **Add**. In the **Field** box, click the field you want, and then click **OK**.

   To change the name of the field you select in the **Field** box, type its new name in the **Title** box, and then click **OK**.

3 To remove a field, click the field you want to remove, and then click **Remove**.

4 To change the time interval in which workgroup members report completed work, click the interval you want to use from the **Ask for completed work** box.

   To report the number of hours per day that a workgroup member has worked on a task, click **broken down by day**.

   To report the number of hours per week that a workgroup member has worked on a task, click **broken down by week**.

   To report the total number of hours a workgroup member has worked on a task during the entire reporting period, click **as a total for the entire period**.

5 To track overtime work, click **Track overtime work**.

6 To return workgroup messages to their default settings, click **Return to Default Settings**.

SETTING UP A WORKGROUP THAT USES E-MAIL

A workgroup that uses an e-mail system can exchange workgroup messages as well as route project files. The requirements for setting up a workgroup that uses e-mail are almost the same for the workgroup manager and the workgroup members. For instance, everyone in the workgroup must be connected to a network that can convey e-mail messages. But while the workgroup manager must have Microsoft Project installed on his or her computer, it's optional (but recommended) for workgroup members. With the addition of one setup step, a workgroup member who doesn't have Microsoft Project can still receive workgroup messages.

E-Mail Workgroup Requirements

The following table shows you the requirements that workgroup members and the workgroup manager must fulfill in order to exchange workgroup messages across an e-mail communications system.

Requirement	Workgroup member	Workgroup manager
Connected to a network, such as a LAN.	Required	Required
Use a MAPI-compliant, 32-bit e-mail system, such as Microsoft Outlook.	Required	Required
Microsoft Project installed on computer.	Optional	Required
Install WGsetup.exe on computer	Only if Microsoft Project isn't installed.	Not applicable to workgroup manager, who must have Microsoft Project installed.

A LAN, or local area network, is one kind of network that's capable of conveying e-mail messages.

The e-mail system (or e-mail program) you use must comply with the Messaging Application Programming Interface (MAPI). MAPI is the standard programming interface proposed and supported by Microsoft for accessing electronic messaging. Examples of MAPI-compliant e-mail programs are Microsoft Outlook, Microsoft Exchange, Microsoft Mail, LotusNotes 4.5, and cc:Mail 7.0. In addition, the e-mail program you use must be a 32-bit program.

Enable Workgroup Members without Microsoft Project to Exchange Workgroup Messages (Workgroup Manager)

Although the workgroup manager must have Microsoft Project installed on his or her computer in order to exchange workgroup messages across an e-mail system, workgroup members can exchange workgroup messages even if they don't have Microsoft Project. Those workgroup members can install WGsetup.exe, which is on the CD included with Microsoft Project. Once they've installed WGsetup.exe and met the other messaging requirements, workgroup members without Microsoft Project will be able to exchange workgroup messages on an e-mail system.

> ➢ **To enable workgroup members without Microsoft Project to exchange workgroup messages**

Workgroup members can also install WGsetup.exe from a network folder.

1 The workgroup manager copies WGsetup.exe from the Microsoft Project for Windows CD onto 2 disks.

On disk 2, copy Prj98-2.cab. On disk 1, copy all the other files.

2 The workgroup manager gives the 2 disks with WGsetup.exe to a workgroup member who doesn't have Microsoft Project.

3 The workgroup member inserts the first disk into his or her computer's disk drive.

4 After clicking the **Start** button and then **Run**, in the **Open** box, the workgroup member types:

a:**\WGsetup.exe**

5 Click **OK**, and then follow the instructions.

SETTING UP A WORKGROUP THAT USES A WEB-BASED SYSTEM

With so many organizations currently hooked up to an intranet or the World Wide Web, one of the advantages of setting up a web-based workgroup is that the web "network" may already be in place. The workgroup won't need a special network to convey workgroup messages, the way an e-mail-based system requires a LAN or something similar.

If an intranet or a connection to the World Wide Web already exists, then one of the few additional requirements is to install a web server for the workgroup. This requirement is easy to fulfill, because Microsoft Project comes with Personal Web Server, which can be installed on any one of the computers in the workgroup, but is usually installed on either the workgroup manager's computer or a dedicated server. Easier still: If one of your workgroup computers is running Windows NT Server 4.0 or later, there's no need to install a web server. By default, Windows NT Server 4.0 has an activated web server, the Internet Information Server (IIS).

After your web-based workgroup is set up, you can customize it by removing workgroup members and setting workgroup-message notification options.

Web-Based Workgroup Requirements

The following table summarizes the requirements that workgroup members and the workgroup manager must fulfill before they can exchange workgroup messages across a web-based system. Some requirements are different for an intranet-based system than they are for a system based on the World Wide Web.

Requirement	Workgroup members	Workgroup manager
Web server	Required	Required
Web browser	Required	Optional
Microsoft Project	Optional	Required
Internet connection (World Wide Web only)	Required	Required
Internet address (World Wide Web only)	Required	Required
Network access (intranet only)	Required	Required
Network identifier (intranet only)	Required	Required

The *web server* can be any computer that connects the workgroup to an intranet or the World Wide Web. If your organization has a dedicated web server, you can ask the person who administers it to set up a share volume for your workgroup. The administrator will also need to supply you with the web server's network address (URL) and network path (UNC), information that the workgroup manager needs to specify in Microsoft Project. Alternatively, you can make any computer in your workgroup a web server by installing Microsoft Personal Web Server. The computer has to have Windows 95 installed and access to your organization's intranet or the World Wide Web.

A *web browser*, such as Netscape Navigator or Microsoft Internet Explorer, enables workgroup members to display workgroup messages on their TeamInboxes, which are web sites dedicated to exchanging Microsoft Project workgroup messages.

For a workgroup to be able to exchange workgroup messages across the World Wide Web, it must be connected to the Internet. The workgroup can have a direct server connection to the Internet, or it can access the Internet through an Internet service provider.

If the workgroup is going to use an intranet to exchange workgroup messages, then each computer in the workgroup must have a unique network identifier, which enables Microsoft Project to identify and distinguish the participating computers on the intranet and communicate with them.

Install the Microsoft Personal Web Server (Workgroup Manager)

The central component of any web-based workgroup is the web server. It acts as an electronic traffic cop directing workgroup-message traffic to the right inbox. Having a web server is essential.

You might already have one. If one of the computers in the workgroup has Windows NT Server 4.0 or later installed on it, then you can use that computer as the web server. Included in Windows NT Server 4.0 is a web server, the Internet Information Server (IIS). Before it can work with the TeamInbox correctly, however, IIS has to be configured to both read and execute information. For more information about configuring IIS properly, contact your system administrator.

If no computer in the workgroup is currently functioning as a web server, you can install the Microsoft Personal Web Server, which is included on the Microsoft Project for Windows CD only, not on disk. The Microsoft Personal Web Server can reside on any computer in the workgroup and can be the web server for a messaging system based on either an intranet or the World Wide Web. The computer on which Microsoft Personal Web Server is installed must have Windows 95, be connected to the Internet or intranet, and be running any time a workgroup member needs to use the TeamInbox.

The web server's URL must include the network identification of the computer on which the web server is installed. For example, if the computer's network identification is WorkgroupManager, then the URL for the web server on that computer would be:

http://WorkgroupManager/

➤ **To install and adjust the settings for the Microsoft Personal Web Server**

1   Install the Microsoft Personal Web Server from the Microsoft Project CD.

Insert the Microsoft Project CD into your CD-ROM drive. In **Windows Explorer**, double-click the **CD drive icon**, double-click **Pws10a.exe** in the **ValuPack\PWServer** folder, and then follow the instructions.

2   When you've finished installing the web server, click the **Start** button, point to **Settings**, and then click **Control Panel.**

3   Double-click **Personal Web Server**.

4   Click the **Administration** tab, and then click **Administration**.

This action will launch your web browser and open to a settings file that has been newly installed to your computer.

5   Scroll down if necessary, and then click **WWW Administration**.

6   Click the **Directories** tab.

7   For the directory C:\WebShare\wwwroot, click **Edit** under the **Action** column.

8   Scroll down if necessary, and then select the **Execute** check box in the **Access** section.

9   Scroll down further, and then click **OK**.

After you install the Microsoft Personal Web Server, you'll need to share out the web server folder.

➤   **To share out the web server folder for workgroup members to access**

1   In Windows Explorer (not the Internet Explorer), click the **Webshare** folder.

2   On the **File** menu, click **Properties**, and then click the **Sharing** tab

3   Click **Shared As**, and then click **Add**.

4   In the **Name** list, hold down CTRL, and then click the name of each workgroup member who will be receiving workgroup messages.

5   Click **Full Access**, and then click **OK**.

6   Click **Web Sharing**, and then select the **Share folder for HTTP**, **Read Only**, and **Execute Scripts** check boxes.

Set Notification Options for Receiving New Workgroup Messages on the Web (Workgroup Manager)

Microsoft Project provides two options for alerting a workgroup participant that he or she has received a workgroup message on the web. One option applies to workgroup members, and the other option applies to the workgroup manager.

A TeamInbox by itself can't notify a workgroup member that a workgroup message has arrived. But when a web-based system is paired with an e-mail system, you can specify that Microsoft Project send notification messages to workgroup members' e-mail inboxes whenever a TeamInbox receives workgroup messages. Each notification message includes a hyperlink back to a member's TeamInbox. The workgroup member opens the notification message in the e-mail inbox, then clicks the hyperlink to "jump" to the TeamInbox. This option can work only if workgroup members use e-mail and an intranet as the messaging system or the World Wide Web, which includes an e-mail account for each workgroup member who's connected to it. If no e-mail system is available, workgroup members must check their TeamInboxes frequently for workgroup messages.

The workgroup manager receives web-based workgroup messages in the WebInbox, located within Microsoft Project. You can choose to have Microsoft Project display a dialog box when a workgroup message is received.

➤ **To set notification options for receiving a new workgroup message**

1   On the **Tools** menu, click **Options**, and then click the **Workgroup** tab.

2   Click the notification option that best suits your needs:

If you'd like Microsoft Project to notify you when workgroup members have replied to a web workgroup message you sent, select the **Notify when new web messages arrive** check box. If you're in Microsoft Project when a reply arrives, a tone will sound and a dialog box will appear asking if you want to open the WebInbox. If you're not in Microsoft Project when a reply arrives but Microsoft Project is running, a tone will sound and the Microsoft Project task box will blink on the Windows taskbar.

If workgroup members are using the TeamInbox and a MAPI-compliant, 32-bit e-mail system, select the **Send hyperlink in E-mail note** check box to send an e-mail notification with a hyperlink embedded in it when a web workgroup message is sent. When workgroup members open the notification and click the hyperlink, it opens their web browser so they can log on and respond to the workgroup message.

3   To have your workgroup selections apply to all new projects, click **Set as Default**.

Remove a Workgroup Member from a Web-Based Workgroup (Workgroup Manager)

If a workgroup member leaves the project, you can remove that member from the workgroup. Removing a workgroup member from a workgroup means that you remove the member from the WebInbox, which clears the workgroup member's assignments from the web-based tracking files that reside on the web server.

➤ **To remove a workgroup member from a workgroup**

1   In Microsoft Project, open the file that was tracking the resource's contribution in a task view.

2   On the **Tools** menu, point to **Workgroup**, and then click **WebInbox**.

If necessary, enter your password.

3   Click **Remove Resource**.

4   In the **Remove Resource** dialog box, select the resource that you would like to remove from your workgroup, and then click **Remove**.

5   Click **Yes**.

TRACKING AND UPDATING WORKGROUP ASSIGNMENTS

Whether you use an e-mail system, an intranet, or the World Wide Web, tracking and updating tasks assigned to workgroup members can be fast and efficient. The workgroup manager doesn't have to walk around to or phone workgroup members to collect up-to-date task information. From his or her computer, the workgroup manager can send workgroup messages to workgroup members and then quickly incorporate replies into the project plan.

The workgroup manager sends task assignment requests to workgroup members, and in turn receives confirmations and task status updates. To convey important task-tracking information, the workgroup participants exchange Microsoft Project TeamAssign, TeamUpdate, and TeamStatus messages.

If a workgroup uses an e-mail system only, then both the workgroup member and the workgroup manager receive workgroup messages in their respective e-mail inboxes only. If a workgroup uses a web-based system only, then the workgroup members receive workgroup messages in their TeamInboxes, and the workgroup manager in the WebInbox in Microsoft Project.

Open the E-Mail Inbox (Workgroup Members and Workgroup Manager)

If you use an e-mail system to exchange workgroup messages, then both the workgroup manager and the workgroup members will need to open their e-mail inboxes before they can view and act on the workgroup messages they receive. Opening an e-mail inbox and viewing a message require similar basic steps in most e-mail programs.

➢ **To open an e-mail inbox**

1   Start the e-mail program.

Only a 32-bit, MAPI-compatible e-mail program can receive workgroup messages.

2   Click or double-click on the inbox icon.

You'll probably see a list of messages.

3   Double-click the message you want to view.

Open the WebInbox (Workgroup Manager)

Any workgroup message sent from a TeamInbox is received by the workgroup manager's WebInbox, which is located within Microsoft Project. To open the WebInbox, Microsoft Project must be opened first. Typically, only the workgroup manager opens the WebInbox.

➤ **To open the WebInbox**

1 Open Microsoft Project.

2 On the **Tools** menu, point to **Workgroup**, and then click **WebInbox**.

3 If you've set up a password for the WebInbox, you'll be prompted for the password. Enter your password.

Open the TeamInbox (Workgroup Members)

When the workgroup uses a web-based system, any workgroup message sent from the workgroup manager is received in a workgroup member's TeamInbox. To view and reply to a workgroup message, the workgroup member will have to first open the TeamInbox.

➤ **To open the TeamInbox**

1 Start your web browser.

2 In the **Address** box, enter the URL of the web server that is servicing your workgroup, the file name of the workgroup program, **mspjhttp.exe**, and a question mark.

For example, if the web server name is "manager," then the URL for the web server (plus the workgroup program file name) is:

http:// manager/project/mspjhttp.exe?

Your workgroup manager can tell you the name of the URL.

3 In the **User Name** box, click your name.

If the workgroup manager has not yet assigned you to any tasks, you will not be able to log on to the TeamInbox and your name will not be listed.

4 In the **Password** box, enter your password.

If you haven't logged on to the TeamInbox before, leave the Password box empty. If you try to enter a password, you'll get an error message.

5 Click **Go**.

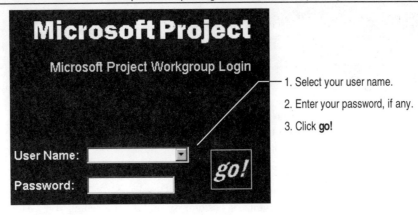

1. Select your user name.

2. Enter your password, if any.

3. Click **go!**

Send a TeamAssign Request (Workgroup Manager)

The process of using the Microsoft Project workgroup feature to track task progress and incorporate updated task information into the project plan can begin only after a workgroup member receives a TeamAssign message from the workgroup manager. The TeamAssign message requests that the workgroup member work on one or more specified tasks. The workgroup member can either accept or decline the task assignments.

➤ **To send a TeamAssign task request**

1   Select the tasks to which you want to assign a resource.

2   On the **Tools** menu, point to **Workgroup**, and then click **TeamAssign**.

3   To send a request about the selected task only, click **Selected task**, and then click **OK**.

   To send a request about all the tasks in your project, click **All tasks**, and then click **OK**.

4   In the **Subject** box, type the subject of the request.

   You can use the default subject, which is TeamAssign.

5   In the message area, type your message.

6 If a resource hasn't already been assigned to the task:

Select the **To** field for a task, and then click **Assign Resources** .

In the **Name** field, select the resources you want, and then click **Assign**.

As an alternative, in the **To** field for a task, type the e-mail name of the resource you want to assign to the task, and then press ENTER. Resources already assigned to the task that haven't confirmed their assignment are listed automatically in the **To** field. If a resource is new, it's added to the resource pool when you send the message.

7 Repeat step 6 for each task to which you're assigning a resource for the first time.

8 Click **Send**.

In the Indicators field of those tasks for which you've requested a resource, an envelope icon with a question mark appears, signifying that you've sent an assignment request but haven't yet received a response from the resource.

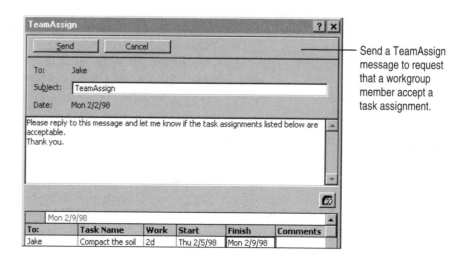

Send a TeamAssign message to request that a workgroup member accept a task assignment.

Accept or Decline a TeamAssign Request (Workgroup Members)

After receiving a TeamAssign request, a workgroup member can send a reply to the workgroup manager that accepts or declines the request. If the workgroup member accepts the request, the workgroup manager can begin to use the Microsoft Project workgroup feature to track the task and incorporate actual information about that task into the project plan. The workgroup feature can be used to track only those tasks that have a workgroup member assigned to them (because actual task information must be sent by a person working on the task). For example, TeamUpdate and TeamStatus messages can be sent only to a workgroup member assigned to a task.

If a workgroup member declines a task assignment request, the workgroup manager may need to send another, perhaps revised, request to the original workgroup member or to another member until the request is accepted. Some of the reasons for declining a request are that the workgroup member is unavailable during the time the task must be accomplished or the workgroup member wants to revise the assignment.

If you're a workgroup member and you receive a TeamAssign message that requests your acceptance of an assignment, you can check your schedule to determine your availability, and then accept or decline the assignment. If you use the TeamInbox or Microsoft Outlook, the tasks you accept are automatically added to your task list in that program.

> **To accept or decline a TeamAssign request**

1   In your e-mail program or TeamInbox, open the TeamAssign message.

To open a TeamAssign message in your TeamInbox, click the envelope icon .

To open a TeamAssign message in your e-mail program, click **Reply**.

2   In the message area, type a reply.

3   Do one of the following to accept or decline the task assignment request:

To accept the request, type **Yes** in the **Accept?** field (e-mail) or select the **Accept?** check box (TeamInbox).

To decline the request, type **No** in the **Accept?** field (e-mail) or clear the **Accept?** check box (TeamInbox).

4   Click **Send**.

If a workgroup member uses a TeamInbox, accepted task assignments are automatically added to the TeamInbox Task List.

Send a TeamAssign reply message to
accept or decline a task assignment.

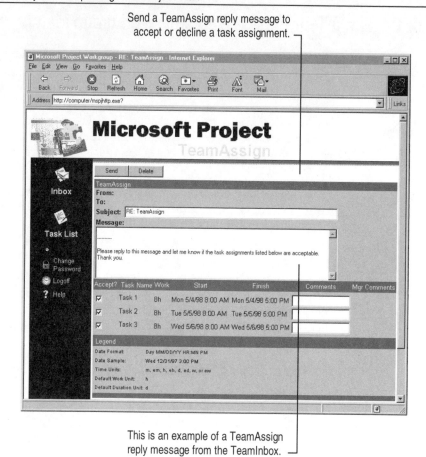

This is an example of a TeamAssign
reply message from the TeamInbox.

Send a TeamUpdate Message (Workgroup Manager)

Whenever there's a change in the schedule, the workgroup manager can send a TeamUpdate message to all those workgroup members whose tasks are affected by the change. For example, if the project deadline is shortened by 2 weeks, the workgroup manager may inform certain workgroup members that they need to complete their tasks sooner than planned.

Using a TeamUpdate message to notify workgroup members about a schedule change gives those workgroup members a chance to inform the workgroup manager about how the change affects their work. This feedback from workgroup members can be invaluable in helping the workgroup manager to avoid schedule problems.

> ## To send a TeamUpdate message

1   On the **Tools** menu, point to **Workgroup**, and then click **TeamUpdate**.

2   In the **Subject** box, type the subject of the update.

3   In the message area, type your message.

4   Click **Send**.

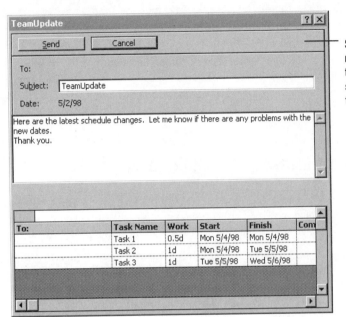

Send a TeamUpdate message to notify team members of schedule changes that affect them.

Reply to a TeamUpdate Message (Workgroup Members)

The workgroup manager sends a TeamUpdate message to inform a workgroup member that there's been a change in the schedule that may affect the tasks assigned to the workgroup member. The workgroup member can reply to a TeamUpdate message by sending a TeamUpdate message to the workgroup manager that describes how the schedule change affects his or her tasks.

➢ **To reply to a TeamUpdate message**

1 In your e-mail program or your TeamInbox, open the TeamUpdate message.

To open a TeamUpdate message in your TeamInbox, click the envelope icon ✉.

To open a TeamUpdate message in your e-mail program, click **Reply**.

2 Review the changed schedule dates, and then do one of the following:

Reply to the message. In your TeamInbox, type your reply in the **Message** box, and then click **Send**. In your e-mail program, type your reply in the **Message** box, and then click **Send**.

In your TeamInbox, change your record of the tasks to reflect the update, and then click **Update Task List**.

Close the message without replying. In your TeamInbox, click **Inbox**. In your e-mail program, click **Close**.

Send a TeamStatus Message (Workgroup Manager)

The TeamStatus message lies at the heart of the Microsoft Project workgroup feature. It replaces a lot of legwork and involves all workgroup members—not just the workgroup manager—in the process of collecting actual project data.

A workgroup manager sends a TeamStatus message to a workgroup member to get actual data on one or more of the workgroup member's tasks. The workgroup member responds by sending a TeamStatus message that contains the actuals requested by the workgroup manager. The workgroup manager can insert the actuals from this TeamStatus reply directly into the project plan.

➢ **To send a TeamStatus message**

1 Select the task for which you want status information.

To get status information on several tasks, select each of the tasks.

2 On the **Tools** menu, point to **Workgroup**, and then click **TeamStatus**.

3 To send a request about the selected task only, click **Selected task**, and then click **OK**.

To send a request about all the tasks in your project, click **All tasks**, and then click **OK**.

4 In the **Subject** box, type the subject of the status request.

5 In the message area, type your message.

6 Click **Send**.

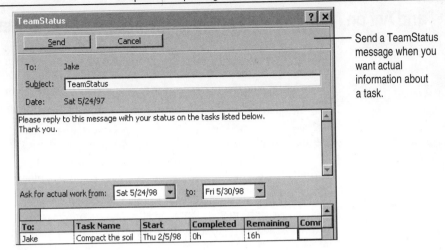

Send a TeamStatus message when you want actual information about a task.

Reply to a TeamStatus Message (Workgroup Members)

The TeamStatus message a workgroup member receives from the workgroup manager requests information about the progress of specified tasks. After receiving a TeamStatus message, the workgroup member checks on the progress of the tasks, enters actual information into a TeamStatus message, and then sends a TeamStatus message with the new information to the workgroup manager. The workgroup manager receives the TeamStatus message, and then can insert the information from the message into the project plan.

➢ **To respond to a TeamStatus message**

1   In your e-mail program or your TeamInbox, open the TeamStatus message.

To open a TeamStatus message in your TeamInbox, click the envelope icon .

To open a TeamStatus message in your e-mail program, click **Reply**.

2   In the appropriate fields, enter information about the task's actual status for each period.

For example, type the actual start date in the Start field and remaining work in the Remaining Work field.

3   In the **Message** box, type your message.

4   Click **Send**.

View and Act on New Workgroup Messages (Workgroup Manager)

The workgroup manager needs to respond only to TeamAssign and TeamStatus messages received from workgroup members, not to TeamUpdate messages. TeamAssign and TeamStatus messages contain data that can be automatically incorporated into the project plan. TeamUpdate messages do not.

A TeamAssign message received from a workgroup member contains the workgroup member's acceptance or rejection of a task assignment. To keep track of whether a task has been assigned to a workgroup member, the workgroup manager needs to add the information from a TeamAssign message to the project plan.

A TeamStatus message received from a workgroup member contains actual information about a task, information that indicates a task's progress. To track task progress and keep the schedule up to date, the workgroup manager needs to incorporate the information from a TeamStatus message into the project plan.

A TeamUpdate message received from a workgroup member, on the other hand, contains no data that can be automatically incorporated into the project plan, and so the workgroup manager doesn't need to respond to a TeamUpdate message. Typically, a TeamUpdate message received by the workgroup manager contains comments about how a schedule change affects a workgroup member's tasks. The workgroup manager may read these comments without replying to them. There's also no way to automatically update the project plan so that it includes comments from a TeamUpdate message.

The following procedures apply only to the workgroup manager's responses to TeamAssign and TeamStatus messages.

➤ **To view and act on new workgroup messages if you use a web-based system**

1   On the **Tools** menu, point to **Workgroup**, and then click **WebInbox**.

2   Enter your password, if you have one, and then click **OK**.

   The WebInbox displays any messages that haven't been deleted.

3   Select the message you want to view, and then click **View**.

4   To accept the workgroup member's reply and incorporate it into your project file, click **Update Project**.

   Microsoft Project updates the project file, returns you to the WebInbox, and marks the workgroup member's reply message as updated.

5   To update all messages all at once, click **Update All**.

6   To return to the WebInbox without acting on the message, click **Cancel**.

➢ **To view and act on new workgroup messages if you use an e-mail system**

1   In your e-mail inbox, double-click the reply message to view it.

2   To reply to the workgroup message, click **Reply**, type your response, and then click **Send**.

3   To update your project file, click **Update Project**.

4   To return to the inbox without acting on the message, click **Cancel**.

MANAGING TASKS IN THE TEAMINBOX

When a workgroup member accepts a TeamAssign request in a TeamInbox, the task assignments in the TeamAssign message are automatically inserted into the Task List of the TeamInbox. The workgroup member can use the Task List to track, indicate, and report on the status of each task. For example, the workgroup member can specify whether a task is completed, in progress, or not yet started. Also, the workgroup member can send up-to-date task information from the Task List to the workgroup manager.

Manage TeamInbox tasks in the Task List. ──

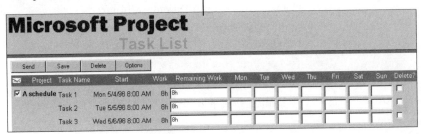

The workgroup member can use the Task List to:

- Update tasks by entering actuals for each task.
- Send updated task status to the workgroup manager.
- Change the report period and other options of the Task List.
- Delete tasks that are no longer active.
- Save task updates in the Task List.

All of the procedures in this section are to be done by workgroup members only.

Update Tasks in the Task List and Send Them (Workgroup Members)

For each task assignment that's been accepted by a workgroup member, the Task List displays important task status information in fields, such as the Start field, the Finish field, and so on. As a task progresses, the workgroup member can change the values in the Task List fields to indicate the task's current status. Periodically, the workgroup member sends task status information to the workgroup manager, who can then incorporate the information into the project plan.

Workgroup members should save after each time they update task status, even if they don't send the updated information to the workgroup manager.

➢ **To update a task in the Task List and send it to the workgroup manager**

1   Open your TeamInbox.

2   Click **Task List**.

3   If your Task List includes tasks from multiple projects, select the check box for the group of tasks for which you want to send updates.

4   In the fields provided for entering the work performed on a task, enter the actual amount of work performed for each period.

If you have overtime hours in a period, enter those hours in an overtime field for that task, if an overtime field is displayed.

In the **Remaining Work** field, type the amount of time you think it will take to complete the task.

5   To save your task updates without sending them to the workgroup manager, click **Save**.

6   To send your updates to the workgroup manager, click **Send**.

Change the Report Period and Other Options in the Task List (Workgroup Members)

Workgroup members can change the report period, the timescale, and the day on which the week starts in the Task List. They can also choose to display overtime work.

The report period can span any two dates and be displayed by day, week, or total for the entire period. For example, if the report period spans 14 days, the Task List could display one column for each day (14 columns) or week (2 columns) or for the entire period.

If the timescale is changed, then all the work values currently saved in the Task List will be erased.

➢ **To change the options for your Task List**

1   Open your TeamInbox.

2   Click **Task List**, and then click **Options**.

3   In the **Period From** and **to** boxes, enter the new dates for the report period. These two dates are included as part of the report period.

4   In the **Broken down by** box, click the timescale by which the Task List will display tasks.

5   To change the day on which the week starts, click the day you want in the **Week starts on** box.

6   To display overtime work in the Task List, click **Display Overtime Work**.

7   To save your changes, click **Set new period options**.

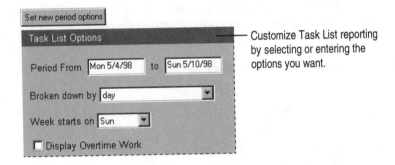

Customize Task List reporting by selecting or entering the options you want.

Delete Tasks in the Task List (Workgroup Members)

If a task is cut from a project or a workgroup member completes a task and reports its completed status to the workgroup manager, the task can be deleted from the Task List.

➢ **To delete a task**

1   Click **Task List**.

2   For each task that you want to delete, select the **Delete?** check box.

3   Click **Delete**.

ROUTING PROJECT FILES (E-MAIL ONLY)

One of the advantages of using an e-mail system is that the workgroup can route a project file. Routing a project file enables all workgroup members to review a project before it becomes final. You might also route a project file whenever there's been a major change to the schedule. To review the schedule, recipients must have Microsoft Project.

A project file is routed by attaching it to an e-mail message and then sending it to one or more persons at a time. A project file can be routed in a predetermined order.

Send a Project File (Workgroup Manager and Workgroup Members)

When you decide that other people in the group need to review a new or revised project schedule, you can attach the schedule to an e-mail message and route it. To start routing a project file, you first need to send it. You can send it to one or more persons at a time.

➢ **To send an entire project file**

1   Open the project file.
2   On the **File** menu, point to **Send To**, and then click **Mail Recipient**.
3   In the **To** box, type the e-mail names of the recipients.
4   In the message area, type your message.
5   Click **Send**.

Route a Project File (Workgroup Manager and Workgroup Members)

Routing a project file usually means that the file is sent by e-mail to one or more persons on a routing list and then eventually returned to the original sender. With Microsoft Project, a file can be routed so that one person at a time receives it, reviews it, and sends it to the next person, or it can be routed to each person on the routing list at the same time.

➢ **To route a project file**

1   On the **File** menu, point to **Send To**, and then click **Routing Recipient**.

2   Click **Address**, hold down CTRL, click the names of the recipients, click **To**, and then click **OK**.

3   To change the order of the recipients, click a name, and then click a **Move** button.

4   In the **Subject** box, type the purpose of the routing message.

5   In the **Message text** box, type instructions or other information.

6   Under **Route to recipients**, click the delivery option you want.

7   If you don't want the file returned to you after the last recipient on the routing list receives the project, clear the **Return when done** check box.

8   If you don't want to be notified each time the file is routed to the next recipient on the routing list, clear the **Track status** check box.

9   If you aren't ready to send the file, click **Add Slip** to save the routing slip with the project file.

10 To send the project file to the recipients, click **Route**.

View and Forward a Routed Project File (Workgroup Manager and Workgroup Members)

When you receive a routed project file, you can do one of two things. If you're the last person on the routing list, you can send the project file to the person who originated the routing message. If you're not the last person on the routing list, you can forward the project file to the next person on the list.

➢ **To forward a routed project file**

1   In your e-mail program, open the routed message.

2   To open the project, double-click the Microsoft Project icon in the e-mail message.

3   Review and modify the project, and then click **Save** 🖫.

4   On the **File** menu, point to **Send To**, and then click **Next Routing Recipient**.

5   To send the project to the next recipient on the routing list, click **OK**.

Part 4

Viewing, Formatting, and Printing Project Information

Though Microsoft Project can store thousands of pieces of information, you're probably only interested in viewing a small subset of that information at a time. Today, you might want to see how much certain tasks cost. Tomorrow, you might want to see which resources are overallocated. Any time you use Microsoft Project, you can view only the information you're interested in, and not a piece of data more or less.

When you're viewing project information, you may want that information to look a certain way. For example, you might want the names of critical tasks to stand out. Or, you may need to change the date format to conform with your organization's standards. Microsoft Project provides you with many ways to change the appearance of project information to suit your needs.

Occasionally, you'll want to share a set of particularly useful—and well-formatted—project information with team members, upper management, or clients. In some instances, you might send this information electronically. But in others, it might be more advantageous to share a hard copy of the information. Microsoft Project enables you to print views as well as a number of predefined reports that meet a wide variety of reporting needs.

Part 4, which consists of chapters 11, 12, and 13, explains how to view, format, and print project information.

11

Viewing the Information You Want: Using Views, Tables, Filters, and Details

Your project plan can contain hundreds if not thousands of separate pieces of information about tasks, resources, and assignments. It stores durations, start dates, finish dates, predecessor tasks, successor tasks, assigned resources, resource units, pay rates, working days and times, total costs, baseline costs, actual costs, per-use costs, notes, hyperlinks, and much more.

All of the information in your project plan couldn't fit on your computer screen at the same time. Nor, most likely, would you want it to. Typically, you're interested in seeing one specific set of information at a time. Perhaps now you want to see the costs of those tasks that begin after a certain date. Later you may want to see which resources have spare time to work on tasks that are taking longer than planned. You can see just the information you're interested in by using views, tables, filters, and details.

A *view* displays a specific set of task, resource, or assignment information. Although there are some views that can only display information, you can use most views to enter and edit information. Each view displays information in a particular format. For example, the Resource Sheet view displays resource information in a table format; the Resource Graph, in a graph format. You can change the view that's displayed on your computer screen, as well as the set of information displayed in each view, most commonly by changing the table, filter, or set of details applied to the view. By default, Microsoft Project displays the Gantt Chart view with the Entry table and the All Tasks filter.

A *table* is a set of fields arranged in columns and rows, like a spreadsheet. Each column displays a particular kind of information. For example, the Start column shows on which day a task begins. Each row displays information for a specific task, resource, or assignment. The columns that belong to a particular table display related information—information that you'd likely want to see all at once. For example, the Entry table for tasks consists of the Duration, Start, Finish, Predecessors, and Resource Names columns. You can, however, change the categories of information that appear in a table by adding and removing columns. Tables can be applied only to views that have a table portion, called sheet views.

A *filter* is a set of criteria for displaying a specific group of related tasks, resources, or assignments. For example, you can use one filter to display tasks that use a particular resource only, another to display overallocated resources only, and another to display in-progress assignments only. Although you can apply a filter to every view except the PERT Chart view, there's one type of filter, called an AutoFilter, that you can apply only to the table portion of sheet views.

Details are sets of related information that display detailed task, resource, or assignment information. They play much the same role as tables do, except that details can be applied to some views that have no table portion, such as form views, and to views that have a table portion as well as a details portion (only the Task Usage and the Resource Usage views have both). Details also differ from tables in that you can't change the information that appears within a particular set of details (as you can with a table by adding or removing columns). You can only replace one set of details with another (as in a form view) or add or remove a set of details (as in the Task Usage and Resource Usage views).

Though views, tables, filters, and details differ in how they affect the project information displayed, they are united by a common principle: In a broad sense, each acts as a "filter" of project information. Views are the largest filters; they "let through" a category of information: task, resource, or assignment. Tables and details narrow the information displayed to a specific set of task, resource, or assignment information. Filters narrow the information displayed still further, to a specific set of tasks, resources, or assignments.

Tables, filters, and details are the most common but not the only ways to change the information that appears in a view. For example, you can change the text that appears next to Gantt bars in the Gantt Chart view, the Tracking Gantt view, the Milestone Rollup view, and other views that have Gantt bars. You can also change the information that appears on the Resource Graph and in the PERT Chart view's PERT boxes. Because many people change the text that appears next to Gantt bars at the same time as they change the appearance of Gantt bars, information about changing Gantt bar text is in Chapter 12, "Making Your Project Look the Way You Want." However, information about changing the information that appears on the Resource Graph and PERT Chart views is in this chapter, in the section "Displaying Information in Views That Have Details and Non-Table Formats."

A QUICK GUIDE TO THE WAYS YOU CAN CHANGE THE INFORMATION DISPLAYED IN EACH VIEW

If you're familiar with how to use tables, filters, and details to display the information you want, you can use the following table to help you change the information that appears in each view. To get detailed information about specific views, tables, filters, and details, see the other sections in this chapter.

View or set of views		Tables?	Filters?	AutoFilters?	Details?	Other?
Gantt Chart Leveling Gantt Bar Rollup Milestone Date Rollup	Detail Gantt Tracking Gantt Milestone Rollup	Yes	Yes	Yes	No	Yes: You can change the text that appears next to the Gantt bars.
Resource Usage Task Usage		Yes	Yes	Yes	Yes	No
Resource Sheet Task Sheet PA_Expected Gantt PA_Pessimistic Gantt	PA_PERT Entry Sheet PA_Optimistic Gantt	Yes	Yes	Yes	No	No
PERT Chart		No	No	No	No	Yes: You can change the information in PERT boxes.
Calendar Task PERT		No	Yes	No	No	No
Resource Graph		No	Yes	No	No	Yes: You can change the information displayed for individual and selected resources.
Task Form Task Name Form Task Details Form	Resource Form Resource Name Form	No	Yes	No	Yes	No
Resource Allocation (top pane) Resource Allocation (bottom pane)		Yes Yes	Yes No	Yes No	Yes No	No No
Task Entry (top pane) Task Entry (bottom pane)		Yes No	Yes No	Yes No	No Yes	Yes: Change bar text. No

SELECTING VIEWS TO DISPLAY INFORMATION OF A PARTICULAR TYPE AND FORMAT

The large amount of information stored in a typical project plan wouldn't make any sense to you if it were all splattered randomly across your computer screen. That's why Microsoft Project uses views to display and organize subsets of project information. You can think of a view as the first step in a simple winnowing process to display only the information you want. For example, by default, each view shows only task, resource, or assignment information. When you choose a view, you display one of these types of information.

But views can help you display even more specific information than that. Consider two views that display task information, the Gantt Chart view and the PA_Optimistic Gantt view. By default, the Gantt Chart view displays task duration, start and finish dates, predecessor tasks, and resource names. The PA_Optimistic Gantt view, on the other hand, displays your optimistic estimates for task durations and start and finish dates. You can choose a view not only to display task, resource, or assignment information, but also to display a specific set of default information about tasks, resources, or assignments.

Quite often, though, two views can display the same information. For example, the Calendar view can display information that can also be displayed in the Gantt Chart view. Which one should you choose? The Calendar view displays task information in a monthly calendar format; the Gantt Chart view, in a table and graphical bar format. You can choose the view that enables you to display information in a format that you prefer to work with or suits a particular purpose at a particular time.

Microsoft Project comes with 26 predefined views that can be categorized into the following formats: sheets, charts, graphs, forms, and calendars. You can switch from one view to another, change the information that appears in a view, customize the appearance of most views to meet your needs, create your own views, and print views. By using the predefined view or custom view that best meets your needs, you can perform your project management tasks more efficiently at each stage of your project.

Determining the Right View for Your Purpose

Before you choose a view, you first need to decide whether you want to display task, resource, or assignment information. The available Microsoft Project views can be roughly categorized as task views, resource views, and assignment views (there's some overlap among them; for example, a task view may contain some resource or assignment information). Next, you need to decide which format you prefer to work with or that suits your particulacr purpose (such as printing project information). You can choose a view that displays the type of information you want, in a specific format.

Microsoft Project views come in the following five formats:

- *Sheet views* contain table portions that are arranged in columns and rows, like a spreadsheet. They provide the best way to enter or edit project information. Tasks or resources are listed vertically, usually on the left side of the view. Each column specifies a type of information, such as task duration or standard pay rate.

- *Chart views* display task information in a graphical way, so you can quickly see the relationships between tasks.

- *Graph views* display information on a set of axes as a curve, an area under a curve, a stepped line, or a set of bars. There's only one predefined graph-type view, the Resource Graph view, but you can create customized graph views.

- *Form views* look like forms you fill out at the doctor's office or at the motor vehicle bureau. They provide a way to enter and edit detailed task or resource information. Most often, they're used with another view in a combination view.

- *Calendar views* display task information in a calendar format, so that you can quickly see which tasks are scheduled for a particular a day, week, or month. There's only one predefined calendar-type view, the Calendar view, but you can create customized calendar views.

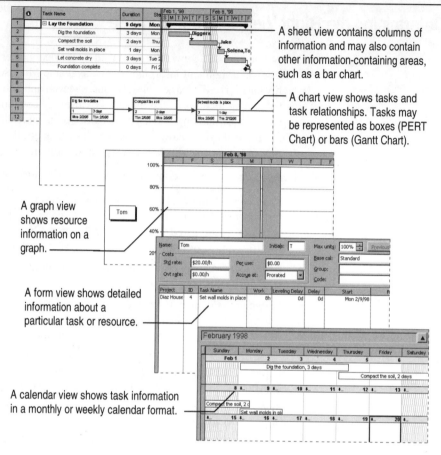

A sheet view contains columns of information and may also contain other information-containing areas, such as a bar chart.

A chart view shows tasks and task relationships. Tasks may be represented as boxes (PERT Chart) or bars (Gantt Chart).

A graph view shows resource information on a graph.

A form view shows detailed information about a particular task or resource.

A calendar view shows task information in a monthly or weekly calendar format.

The following three tables help you to choose the right view for each situation.

Task Views

To enter, change, or display task information, use the task view that meets your needs.

Task view	Type	Description
Bar Rollup	Sheet and chart	A Gantt Chart that displays each task as a task bar on a summary task bar. When used in conjunction with the Rollup_Formatting macro, you can hide subtask bars, while still seeing the individual tasks represented and named on a summary task bar.
Calendar	Calendar	A monthly calendar that displays each task as a task bar. The length of each task bar corresponds to the task's duration. Use this view to see tasks scheduled in a specific day, week, or month.
Detail Gantt	Sheet and chart	A Gantt Chart whose bar chart portion shows slack and slippage. Use this view to determine how much a task can slip without causing other tasks to slip.
Gantt Chart	Sheet and chart	A list of tasks and task information in the sheet portion of the view, and Gantt bars showing tasks and durations over time in the bar chart portion. Use this view to enter and edit task information and schedule tasks.
Leveling Gantt	Sheet and chart	A Gantt Chart that shows task-delay information in the sheet portion, and the delay added to tasks during leveling in the bar chart portion. Use this view to see the amount of delay added by resource leveling.
Milestone Date Rollup	Sheet and chart	A Gantt Chart that displays the start date for each task as a milestone symbol on a summary task bar. When used in conjunction with the Rollup_Formatting macro, you can hide subtask bars, while still seeing the individual tasks represented and named on a summary task bar.

Task view	Type	Description
Milestone Rollup	Sheet and chart	A Gantt Chart that displays each task as a milestone symbol on a summary task bar. When used in conjunction with the Rollup_Formatting macro, you can hide subtask bars, while still seeing the individual tasks represented and named on a summary task bar.
PA_ Expected Gantt	Sheet and chart	A Gantt Chart in which you enter your expected values for task durations, start dates, and finish dates. Use this view in conjunction with PERT analysis tools to evaluate a probable schedule based on an expected-case scenario.
PA_ Optimistic Gantt	Sheet and chart	A Gantt Chart in which you enter your optimistic values for task durations, start dates, and finish dates. Use this view in conjunction with PERT analysis tools to evaluate a probable schedule based on a best-case scenario.
PA_ PERT Entry Sheet	Sheet	A Gantt Chart in which you enter your expected, best-case, and worst-case durations for tasks, before you use PERT analysis tools to calculate the most likely durations. Use this view in conjunction with PERT analysis to compare the duration values among the various scenarios.
PA_ Pessimistic Gantt	Sheet and chart	A Gantt Chart in which you enter your pessimistic values for task durations, start dates, and finish dates. Use this view in conjunction with PERT analysis to evaluate a probable schedule based on a worst-case scenario.
PERT Chart	Chart	A flow chart that shows all tasks and the dependencies between them. Use this view to get an overview of task sequence or to add, change, or remove task dependencies. You can also use it to create a schedule or add tasks.

Task view	Type	Description
Task Details Form	Form	A form for entering, editing, and reviewing detailed information about a specific task. Use this view in the bottom pane of a combination view, with the Gantt Chart view in the top pane.
Task Entry	Sheet, chart, and form	A combination view that shows the Gantt Chart view in the top pane and the Task Form view in the bottom pane. Use this view to add, edit, and review information about the task you select in the Gantt Chart view.
Task Form	Form	A form for entering, editing, and reviewing information about a specific task. Use this view in the bottom pane of a combination view, with the Gantt Chart view in the top pane.
Task Name Form	Form	A simpler version of the Task Form, one in which only the task name appears at the top, but with the same details as appear in the Task Form at the bottom of the view. Use this view for entering and editing the task name and specific sets of task details.
Task PERT	Chart	A flow chart that shows the predecessors and successors of one task. Use this view to display all the tasks linked to a specific task. This view is most useful when displayed in the bottom pane of a combination view, with the Gantt Chart or the Task Sheet in the top pane.
Task Sheet	Sheet	A list of tasks and a table of task information. Basically, it's the Gantt Chart without Gantt bars. Use this view to enter and edit task information.
Tracking Gantt	Sheet and chart	A Gantt Chart view that shows baseline estimates and actual data for each task in the bar chart portion. After you save a baseline and have begun entering actual data, use this view to compare the planned schedule with the actual schedule.

Resource Views

To enter, change, or display resource information, use the resource view that meets your needs.

Resource view	Type	Description
Resource Allocation	Sheet and chart	A combination view with the Resource Usage view in the top pane and the Leveling Delay Gantt view in the bottom pane. Use this resource view to find and resolve resource overallocations.
Resource Form	Form	A form for entering, editing, and reviewing information about a specific resource.
Resource Graph	Graph	A graph showing resource allocations, costs, and work over time for an individual resource or group of resources. Use this view to see how much resources are overallocated, the percentage of total work time each resource is assigned to work, and resource costs.
Resource Name Form	Form	A simpler version of the Resource Form, one in which only the resource name appears at the top, but with the same details as appear in the Resource Form at the bottom of the view. Use this view for entering and editing the resource name and specific sets of resource details.
Resource Sheet	Sheet	A list of resources and a table of resource information. Use this view to enter and edit resource information.

Assignment Views

To enter, change, or display assignment information, use the assignment view that meets your needs.

Assignment view	Type	Description
Resource Usage	Sheet	A list of resources showing assigned tasks grouped under each resource, a table of resource information, and a set of details about resources and their assigned tasks. Use this view to see the tasks that are assigned to specific resources, set resource contours, and show cost or work allocation information for each resource.
Task Usage	Sheet	A list of tasks showing assigned resources grouped under each task, a table of task information, and a set of details about tasks and their assigned resources. Use this view to see the resources that are assigned to specific tasks and to set resource contours.

Display a View

Whenever you're working with Microsoft Project, you're looking at a view (assuming the view is not covered by a dialog box, that is). By default, the first time you start Microsoft Project, it displays the Gantt Chart view. However, each time you open an existing project file, it displays the view that appeared on your screen when you last saved the file. If you want to work with a different kind or set of information or with the same kind of information but in a different format, you can switch to a different view.

When you switch to another view, you don't add information to or remove information from your project. You only change the subset of project information that's displayed.

➢ **To display a view**

- On the **View Bar**, click the view you want.

  To select a view that doesn't appear on the **View Bar**, click **More Views**, click the view you want in the **Views** list, and then click **Apply**.

Display a Second View in the Bottom Pane (Combination Views)

Although you can change the information that appears in a view, each view can display only a limited amount of information at one time. And typically, a single view displays only one type of information: either task, resource, or assignment information.

To see a different set of information about a task, resource, or assignment, you can display a second view in the bottom half of the view area at the same time that you display a view in the top half. The result is a *combination view*.

The power of using a combination view is threefold:

- You can see more of the same type of information about a task, resource, or assignment in the top pane. For example, the Gantt Chart in the top pane might display a task's name, duration, and start and finish dates. The Task Sheet in the bottom pane might display fixed cost, total cost, baseline cost, actual cost, and remaining cost for a task.

- You can display a different type of information in each pane. For example, the Gantt Chart in the top pane displays task information. The Resource Graph in the bottom pane displays information about the resources assigned to the tasks in the top pane.

- The bottom view is automatically "slaved" to the top view. For example, when you select a task in the Gantt Chart view in the top pane, the Resource Graph in the bottom pane displays information about the resource assigned to the task (if you've assigned a resource to the task). When you select a different task in the Gantt Chart view, the Resource Graph displays information about that task's resource.

A combination view shows detailed information about a selected task or resource in the bottom pane.

The following restrictions apply to combination views:

- You can display at most two views at one time from the same project file. You can't split the view area into three or more view windows.

- In each view, you can choose the information you want to see, but you can't apply a filter or an AutoFilter to the bottom view, only to the top view (if filters can normally be applied to the top view). Among the ways you can change the information in the bottom view are by changing the table or changing the set of details.

- You can't display the PERT Chart and Calendar views in the bottom pane.

- You can replace the view in either pane one at a time. But if you choose to display a predefined combination view (such as the Resource Allocation view), the predefined combination view replaces both the top pane and the bottom pane of the currently displayed combination view.

> ### To display and close a second view in the bottom pane

Replace a view in a pane by selecting the view and then choosing another view.

1   On the **Window** menu, click **Split**.

By default, if the view in the top pane is a task view, the Task Form appears in the bottom pane. If the view in the top pane is a resource view, the Resource Form appears in the bottom pane.

2   Click the bottom pane to make the bottom view the active view.

3   On the **View Bar**, click the view you want to appear in the bottom pane.

To use a view that is not on the **View Bar**, click **More Views**, click the view you want to use in the **Views** list, and then click **Apply**.

4   To close the view, click **Remove Split** on the **Window** menu.

Regardless of which view is selected at the time you click Remove Split, Microsoft Project closes the bottom pane and fills the entire screen with the view in the top pane.

APPLYING TABLES TO DISPLAY DIFFERENT SETS OF INFORMATION IN A SHEET VIEW

Each sheet view includes a table portion that displays rows and columns of task, resource, or assignment information. Some sheet views, such as the Task Sheet and the Resource Sheet views, consist only of a table portion. Other sheet views, such as the Gantt Chart and the Resource Usage views, consist of both a table portion and another portion. The information in the table portion of a sheet view is, in fact, a table. A table can be either a predefined Microsoft Project table or a table you create.

A predefined Microsoft Project table consists of related columns of information. For instance, the Cost table for tasks (there's also a Cost table for resources) includes the Fixed Cost, Fixed Cost Accrual, Total Cost, Baseline Cost, Variance Cost, Actual Cost, and Remaining Cost fields. You can change the type of information displayed in a sheet view by changing the table displayed. By switching to the Work table, for instance, you can view information related to the work required to complete a task, such as the total work and the remaining work.

Determining the Right Table for Your Purpose

Microsoft Project displays each sheet view with a default table applied to it. For example, the Entry table is the default table for the Gantt Chart view, and the Usage table is the default table for the Resource Usage view. You can change the information displayed in the table portion of a sheet view by applying a different table to the view.

There are two kinds of tables. You can apply *task tables* to task sheet views (including the Task Usage view) and *resource tables* to resource sheet views (including the Resource Usage view). You can apply predefined tables or tables that you create. You apply the table that includes the columns of information you want to display.

Each table displays a set of columns of related information. ⌐

	Task Name	Duration	Start	Finish	Predecessors	Resource Nar
1	⊟ **Lay the Foundation**	**9 days**	**Mon 2/2/98**	**Fri 2/13/98**		
2	Dig the foundation	3 days	Mon 2/2/98	Thu 2/5/98		Diggers
3	Compact the soil	2 days	Thu 2/5/98	Mon 2/9/98	2	Jake

		Fixed Cost	Fixed Cost Accrual	Total Cost	Baseline	Variance	Actual	Remaining
4	Set wall molds in pla							
5	Let concrete dry	**$0.00**	Prorated	**$1,120.00**	**$0.00**	**$1,120.00**	**$0.00**	**$1,120.00**
6	Foundation complete	$0.00	Prorated	$480.00	$0.00	$480.00	$0.00	$480.00
7	⊟ **Put up the Frame**	$0.00	Prorated	$320.00	$0.00	$320.00	$0.00	$320.00
8	Construct outer wall	$0.00	Prorated	$320.00	$0.00	$320.00	$0.00	$320.00

		Act. Start	Act. Finish	% Comp.	Act. Dur.	Rem. Dur.	Act. Cost	Act. Work	
9	Con								$0.00
10	Con	**NA**	**NA**	**0%**	**0 days**	**9 days**	**$0.00**	**0 hrs**	$0.00
11	⊟ Add Plu	NA	NA	0%	0 days	3 days	$0.00	0 hrs	**$0.00**
12	Inlay	NA	NA	0%	0 days	2 days	$0.00	0 hrs	$0.00
		NA	NA	0%	0 days	1 day	$0.00	0 hrs	$0.00
		NA	NA	0%	0 days	3 days	$0.00	0 hrs	$0.00
		NA	NA	0%	0 days	0 days	$0.00	0 hrs	**$0.00**
		NA	**NA**	**0%**	**0 days**	**3 days**	**$0.00**	**0 hrs**	$0.00
		NA	NA	0%	0 days	1 day	$0.00	0 hrs	
		NA	NA	0%	0 days	1 day	$0.00	0 hrs	
		NA	NA	0%	0 days	1 day	$0.00	0 hrs	
		NA	**NA**	**0%**	**0 days**	**3 days**	**$0.00**	**0 hrs**	
		NA	NA	0%	0 days	1 day	$0.00	0 hrs	

Examples of task tables.

	Resource Name	Initials	Group	Max. Units	Std. Rate	Ovt. Rate	Cost/Use	Accrue At	Bas
1	Tom	T		100%	$20.00/hr	$0.00/hr	$0.00	Prorated	Star
2	Diggers	D		300%	$20.00/hr	$0.00/hr	$0.00	Prorated	Star
3	Selena	S		100%	$20.00/hr	$0.00/hr	$0.00	Prorated	Star
4	Jake	J							
5	Penelope	F							

	Cost	Baseline Cost	Variance	Actual Cost	Remaining
	$160.00	$0.00	$160.00	$0.00	$160.00
	$480.00	$0.00	$480.00	$0.00	$480.00
	$160.00	$0.00	$160.00	$0.00	$160.00
					$320.00
					$0.00

% Comp.	Work	Overtime	Baseline	Variance	Actual	Remaining
0%	8 hrs	0 hrs	0 hrs	8 hrs	0 hrs	8 hrs
0%	24 hrs	0 hrs	0 hrs	24 hrs	0 hrs	24 hrs
0%	8 hrs	0 hrs	0 hrs	8 hrs	0 hrs	8 hrs
0%	16 hrs	0 hrs	0 hrs	16 hrs	0 hrs	16 hrs
0%	0 hrs	0 hrs	0 hrs	0 hrs	0 hrs	0 hrs

Examples of resource tables.

To help you choose the right table for your purpose, the following lists show the predefined task and resource tables that come with Microsoft Project.

Task Tables

Task tables can be applied to the following views:

- Bar Rollup
- Detail Gantt
- Gantt Chart
- Leveling Gantt
- Milestone Date Rollup
- Milestone Rollup
- PA Expected Gantt
- PA Optimistic Gantt

- PA PERT Entry Sheet
- PA Pessimistic Gantt
- Task Entry (in the top pane only of this combination view)
- Task Sheet
- Task Usage
- Tracking Gantt

Task table	Description
Baseline	Displays baseline durations, start and finish dates, work, and costs.
Constraint Dates	Displays the type of constraint applied to each task (such as As Soon As Possible or Must Start On) and the constraint date.
Cost	Displays cost information, such as fixed cost, total cost, baseline cost, cost variance, actual cost, and remaining cost.
Delay	Displays resource-leveling information, including leveling delay (in terms of elapsed duration, or *edays*), duration, scheduled start and finish dates, successors, and resource names.
Earned Value	For tasks that have resources assigned, compares expected progress with the actual progress to date. Shows, in terms of resource costs, the actual percentage of completion of each task, so it can be used to forecast whether a task will finish under budget or over budget. Includes fields such as BCWS (budgeted cost of work scheduled) and SV (schedule variance).
Entry	So called because you can use it to enter task information as you start to create your project plan. Displays task names, durations, start and finish dates, predecessors, and resources. The default table for the Gantt Chart and Task Sheet views.
Export	Displays the 40 task fields that Microsoft Project can export in the .mpx file format. Use this table to export a file in the .mpx file format.
Hyperlink	Displays the web addresses and subaddresses of hyperlinks connecting tasks to web sites and intranet files.

Task table	Description
PA_Expected Case	Displays estimates for expected durations, start dates, and finish dates. Use with Microsoft Project's PERT analysis features to determine probable task durations and start and finish dates.
PA_Optimistic Case	Displays estimates for optimistic durations, start dates, and finish dates. Use with Microsoft Project's PERT analysis features to determine probable task durations and start and finish dates.
PA_PERT Entry	Compares optimistic, expected, and pessimistic task durations. Use with Microsoft Project's PERT analysis features to determine probable task durations and start and finish dates.
PA_Pessimistic Case	Displays estimates for pessimistic durations, start dates, and finish dates. Use with Microsoft Project's PERT analysis features to determine probable task durations and start and finish dates.
Rollup	Applied after you have run the Rollup_Formatting macro (Tools menu, Macro, Macros, Run), enables you to optimize the display of Gantt bars rolled up and overlaid on top of their respective summary task bars. It's the default table for the Bar Rollup, Milestone Date Rollup, and Milestone Rollup views.
Schedule	Displays scheduling information, including start and finish dates, late start and finish dates, free slack, and total slack. Enables you to see how late a task can start or finish without affecting the dates of successor tasks or the project's finish date.
Summary	Displays a summary of the most important task information, including task duration, start and finish dates, percent complete, cost, and work.
Tracking	Displays actual task information (as opposed to scheduled information), including actual start dates, actual finish dates, percent complete, actual duration, remaining duration, actual cost, and actual work.
Usage	Displays work, duration, and start and finish dates. It's the default table of the Task Usage view.
Variance	Displays scheduled start and finish dates, baseline start and finish dates, and the differences, or variances, between the two sets of dates.
Work	Displays work information, including baseline work, work variance, actual work, and remaining work. Enables you to compare scheduled work against baseline work, actual work, or remaining work.

Resource Tables

Resource tables can be applied to the following views:

- Resource Allocation (in the top pane only of this combination view)
- Resource Sheet
- Resource Usage

Resource table	Description
Cost	Displays cost information, such as total cost, baseline cost, cost variance, actual cost, and remaining cost.
Earned Value	Compares expected resource costs with the actual resource costs to date. Can be used to forecast whether resource costs for tasks will finish under budget or over budget. Includes fields such as BCWS (budgeted cost of work scheduled) and SV (schedule variance).
Entry	So called because you can use it to enter resource information as you create a resource list for your project plan. Displays resource groups, resource units, standard rates, overtime rates, cost per use, accrual method, and resource code. The default table for the Resource Sheet view.
Export	Displays the 18 resource fields that Microsoft Project can export in the .mpx file format. Use this table to export a file in the .mpx file format.
Hyperlink	Displays the web addresses and subaddresses of hyperlinks connecting resources to web sites and intranet files.
Summary	Displays a summary of the most important resource information, including resource groups, maximum units, peak resource usage, standard rates, overtime rates, cost, and work.
Usage	Displays the amount of work assigned to each resource. It's the default table of the Resource Usage view.
Work	Displays work information, including baseline work, work variance, actual work, overtime work, and remaining work.

Apply a Table

The first time you display a Microsoft Project sheet view, a default table will be attached to it. For example, the Entry table will be attached to the Gantt Chart view. However, each time you open an existing project file, each sheet view is displayed with the table that was attached to it when you last saved the file. To see other columns of information, you can apply a different table to the view. When you apply a different table to a sheet view, the new table replaces the old table. You can apply a task table only to a task view and a resource table only to a resource view.

When you replace one table with another, you do not add information to or remove information from your project. You only change the project information displayed at the moment. Also, the list of tasks or resources on the view remains the same. Only the other columns of information change.

➢ **To apply a table**

1   On the **View Bar**, click the view to which you want to apply a table.

   To select a view that doesn't appear on the **View Bar**, click **More Views**, click the view you want in the **Views** list, and then click **Apply**.

2   On the **View** menu, point to **Table**, and then click the table you want.

   To apply a table that isn't on the **Table** submenu, click **More Tables**, click the task or resource table you want, and then click **Apply**.

FILTERING TO DISPLAY ONLY CERTAIN TASKS OR RESOURCES

You choose the type of information you want to display—task, resource, or assignment—by choosing a task, resource, or assignment view. You choose the particular set of information that appears in a view by choosing a table or set of details. To display only certain tasks or resources (even in an assignment view), you choose a filter.

By default, each view displays all the tasks or resources in your project (though you may need to scroll to see them all). Often, however, you may want to focus on just those tasks or resources that share certain characteristics. For example, you might want to see only in-progress tasks or only overallocated resources.

For each view (except the PERT Chart view), you can determine which tasks or resources Microsoft Project displays or highlights by applying a *filter*. A filter contains instructions, called criteria, that specify the characteristics a task or resource must have in order to appear in a view. You change the filter applied to a view when you want to see information about different tasks or resources in the current format.

If none of the filters provided with Microsoft Project contains the task or resource criteria that you want, you can create a new filter or modify an existing one.

Determining the Right Filter for Your Purpose

Microsoft Project displays each view (except the PERT Chart view) with a default filter applied to it: The All Tasks filter is applied to each task view and the All Resources filter is applied to each resource view. You can display a subset of the tasks or resources that appear in a view by applying a different filter to the view.

There are two major groups of filters: *task filters*, which you apply to task views, and *resource filters*, which you apply to resource views. Each of these groups contains three types of filters: standard, interactive, and AutoFilters. You can apply predefined filters or filters that you create. You apply the filter that contains the criteria for the task or resource information you want to display in a view.

- A *standard* filter identifies tasks and resources based on one or two commonly used criteria. For example, when you apply the Completed Tasks filter, Microsoft Project displays only completed tasks. Most Microsoft Project filters are of this type.

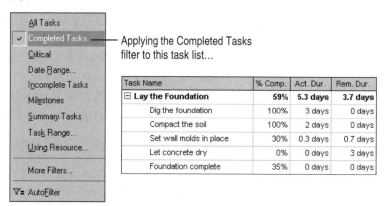

Applying the Completed Tasks filter to this task list...

...results in only 100% completed tasks being displayed.

- An *interactive* filter prompts you to enter filtering criteria. You enter either a single value or a range of values. For example, when you apply the Date Range filter for tasks, you specify two dates that bracket a time period. Microsoft Project then displays only those tasks that start or finish within that time period.

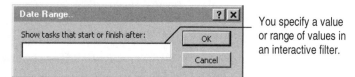

You specify a value or range of values in an interactive filter.

- An *AutoFilter*, available only in sheet views, displays tasks or resources that share a piece of information contained in a specific column. (A Microsoft Project AutoFilter works just like a Microsoft Excel AutoFilter.) Each column has one AutoFilter. The criteria in each AutoFilter consist of all the different pieces of information listed in the column, plus some predefined criteria.

For example, if one or more tasks listed in the Gantt Chart view starts on 2/5/98, the AutoFilter for the Start field lists 2/5/98 among its filtering criteria. If you select 2/5/98 from the AutoFilter criteria list, Microsoft Project displays only those tasks that start on 2/5/98. The Start field AutoFilter also lists predefined criteria such as All, Tomorrow, This Week, and Next Month.

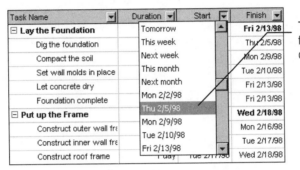

This AutoFilter for the Start field contains the criteria date 2/5/98, among others.

Down arrows next to column names indicate that the AutoFilter feature is on.

You can use a filter by itself or in combination with other filters. For example, you can use a Start field AutoFilter to display only tasks that start after 2/5/98. Then you can narrow your focus by applying the Critical filter to display only critical tasks that start after 2/5/98. Or, instead of or in addition to the Critical filter, you can select the > 1 day criterion in the Duration field AutoFilter to display only those critical tasks that start after 2/5/98 and have durations greater than 1 day. By using various combinations of filters, you can focus on exactly the tasks or resources you want.

To help you choose the right filter for your purpose, the following lists show the predefined task and resource filters that come with Microsoft Project.

Task Filters

Each task filter can be applied to any task view except the PERT Chart view.

Task filter	Type	Description
All Tasks	Standard	Displays all the tasks in your project plan.
Completed Tasks	Standard	Displays all tasks that have been marked as 100% completed.
Confirmed	Standard	Displays each task whose resources have agreed to perform the task. (A task is confirmed when each resource requested for the task accepts the task in a workgroup TeamAssign message and a Yes appears in the Confirmed field for the task.)
Cost Greater Than	Interactive	Displays the tasks that have a total cost that's greater than the amount that you specify.
Cost Over budget	Standard	Displays all tasks that have a total cost that's greater than the baseline cost.
Created After	Interactive	Displays all the tasks that you added to your project plan on or after the date you specify.
Critical	Standard	Displays all the tasks that are on the critical path.
Date Range	Interactive	Displays all tasks that start or finish within the date range you specify.
In Progress Tasks	Standard	Displays all tasks that have started but haven't been completed.
Incomplete Tasks	Standard	Displays all tasks that haven't been completed.
Late/Overbudget Tasks Assigned To	Interactive	Displays the tasks assigned to the resource you specify that are costing more than budgeted or haven't yet been completed and will likely finish after the baseline finish date.
Linked Fields	Standard	Displays tasks to which information from other programs has been linked.
Milestones	Standard	Displays only milestone tasks.
Resource Group	Interactive	Displays the tasks assigned to the resources who belong to the resource group you specify.
Should Start By	Interactive	Displays all tasks that should have started by the date you specify but haven't.
Should Start/Finish By	Interactive	Displays those tasks that haven't started and finished within the date range you specify.

Task filter	Type	Description
Slipped/Late Progress	Standard	Displays tasks that either haven't finished by their baseline finish date or that haven't been progressing on schedule (by comparing the amount of work scheduled for the task, BCWS, against the amount of work that has been completed, BCWP, in the Earned Value table).
Slipping Tasks	Standard	Displays all tasks that are behind schedule (their actual start or finish dates are later than their baseline start or finish dates).
Summary Tasks	Standard	Displays all tasks that have subtasks indented underneath them.
Task Range	Interactive	Displays all tasks within the ID range you specify.
Tasks With Attachments	Standard	Displays tasks that have OLE objects attached or a note in the Notes box of the Task Information dialog box.
Tasks With Fixed Dates	Standard	Displays all tasks that don't have the constraints As Soon As Possible or As Late As Possible or that have an actual start date.
Tasks/Assignments With Overtime	Standard	Displays the tasks or assignments whose assigned resources are working overtime.
Top Level Tasks	Standard	Displays the highest-level summary tasks only.
Unconfirmed	Standard	Displays each task whose resources have not yet agreed to perform the task.
Unstarted Tasks	Standard	Displays all tasks that haven't started.
Update Needed	Standard	Displays tasks whose scheduling information, such as durations, start and finish dates, or resource reassignments, you've changed, and for which you need to send a TeamUpdate message to the affected resources (if you're using the workgroup messaging feature).
Using Resource	Interactive	Displays the tasks that are assigned to the resource you specify.
Using Resource In Date Range	Interactive	Displays the tasks that are assigned to the resource you specify and that start or finish between two dates that you specify.
Work Overbudget	Standard	Displays all tasks whose actual work is greater than their baseline work.

Resource Filters

Each resource filter can be applied to any resource view.

Resource filter	Type	Description
All Resources	Standard	Displays all the resources in your project plan.
Confirmed Assignments	Standard	Displays each resource who has agreed to perform all the tasks he or she has been asked to perform. (A resource's assignments are confirmed when the resource accepts each task assignment on a workgroup TeamAssign message and a Yes appears in the Confirmed field for the resource.)
Cost Greater Than	Interactive	Displays those resources whose scheduled cost is greater than the amount you specify.
Cost Overbudget	Standard	Displays all resources whose scheduled cost is greater than the baseline cost.
Date Range	Interactive	Displays all resources that have assignments that start or finish within the date range you specify.
Group	Interactive	Displays all resources belonging to the resource group you specify.
In Progress Assignments	Standard	Displays all resources that have started assignments that haven't been completed yet.
Linked Fields	Standard	Displays resources to which text from other programs has been linked.
Overallocated Resources	Standard	Displays all resources that are scheduled to do more hours of work than they are allocated to do in a given time period. Examples of overallocated resources are a resource scheduled to do 10 hours of work in one day but is allocated only 8 hours of work per day, and a resource scheduled to do 46 hours of work in one week but is allocated only 40 hours of work per week.
Resource Range	Interactive	Displays all resources within the ID range you specify.
Resources With Attachments	Standard	Displays resources that have OLE objects attached or a note in the Notes box of the Resource Information dialog box.
Resources/ Assignments With Overtime	Standard	Displays those resources that are working overtime, or those assignments on which resources are working overtime.
Should Start By	Interactive	Displays all resources with assignments that should have started by the date you specify but haven't.

Resource filter	Type	Description
Should Start/Finish By	Interactive	Displays those resources with task assignments that should have started or finished within the date range you specify.
Slipped/Late Progress	Standard	Displays resources assigned to tasks that either haven't finished by their baseline finish date or that haven't been progressing on schedule (by comparing the amount of work scheduled for the task, BCWS, against the amount of work that has been completed, BCWP, in the Earned Value table).
Slipping Assignments	Standard	Displays resources whose task assignments are behind schedule (their actual start or finish dates are later than their baseline start or finish dates).
Unconfirmed Assignments	Standard	Displays resources who haven't yet agreed to perform all the tasks they've been requested to perform (via a workgroup TeamAssign message).
Unstarted Assignments	Standard	Displays resources who have accepted but haven't yet started their assignments.
Work Complete	Standard	Displays resources that have completed all of their assigned tasks.
Work Incomplete	Standard	Displays all resources assigned to tasks that are marked as less then 100% complete.
Work Overbudget	Standard	Displays all resources that have scheduled work that's greater than baseline work.

Apply a Filter

There's always a filter attached to a view. The default filter for each task view (except the PERT Chart view) is the All Tasks filter. The default filter for each resource view is the All Resources filter. If you want all the tasks or resources in your project plan to appear in the current view, then you don't need to apply a different filter. If you want to focus on a subset of the tasks or resources in your project, however, then you do need to apply a different filter.

You can apply the filter that displays only those tasks or resources that share certain characteristics. For each filter, you can specify whether the filter displays only those tasks or resources that meet the filter criteria (and hides the tasks or resources that don't) or highlights the tasks or resources of interest in blue (while still displaying the other tasks or resources).

After you apply a filter, you can make all tasks or resources reappear by reapplying the All Tasks or All Resources filter, which removes the filtering effect from the view but leaves the filter itself in your project file.

➢ **To apply a filter**

1   On the **View Bar**, click a view.

   To select a view that doesn't appear on the **View Bar**, click **More Views**, click the view you want in the **Views** list, and then click **Apply**.

2   On the **Project** menu, point to **Filtered for**, and then click the filter you want to apply.

   To apply a filter that isn't on the **Filtered for** submenu or to apply a highlighting filter, click **More Filters.**

3   In the **Filters** list, click the filter you want.

4   Click **Apply** to apply the filter or click **Highlight** to apply a highlighting filter.

5   If you apply an interactive filter, type the requested values, and then click **OK**.

When you no longer need to see a subset of tasks or resources, you can display all of them again.

➢ **To display all tasks or resources**

•   On the **Project** menu, point to **Filtered for**, and then click **All Tasks** if a task filter is applied or **All Resources** if a resource filter is applied.

Filter Your View Quickly by Using AutoFilters

Standard and interactive filters typically contain fairly broad sets of criteria that distinguish one category of tasks or resources from another. For example, the Critical filter distinguishes the broad category "critical tasks" from the broad category "noncritical tasks." The Overallocated Resources filter distinguishes the broad category "overallocated resources" from the broad category "not overallocated resources."

Unlike standard and interactive filters, AutoFilters distinguish tasks or resources based on specific criteria; in fact, you typically use an AutoFilter to distinguish a subset of tasks or resources based on one very specific criterion. The reason you can do this is that an AutoFilter takes as its set of criteria the data that currently appears in one column in a sheet view. Change the data and the set of AutoFilter criteria changes also.

For example, suppose 5 tasks listed in the Gantt Chart view have durations of 3 days, 2 days, 4 days, 2 days, and 2 days. Each of these durations appears as a criterion in the AutoFilter for the Duration column. If you select the "2 days" criterion that appears in the AutoFilter's criteria list, then only those 3 tasks with durations of 2 days will be displayed.

AutoFilters not only enable you to distinguish tasks or resources by applying very specific criteria, but they also allow you to filter information quickly and easily. After you activate the AutoFilters feature, an AutoFilter button appears in the heading of each column. The high visibility of AutoFilters and the ease with which you can select a particular AutoFilter criterion enable you to filter tasks or resources rapidly.

You can narrow the information displayed by applying more than one AutoFilter at one time. You can also use AutoFilters in conjunction with standard and interactive filters.

The AutoFilter of each field includes the predefined criteria All and Custom in its criteria list. By clicking All, which is the default criterion for all fields, you remove the filter criterion from that field. By clicking Custom, you can create your own filter for that field. In addition to All and Custom, each AutoFilter also includes unique predefined criteria. For example, the AutoFilter for the Duration field includes the predefined criteria <= 1 day, > 1 day, <= 1 week, and > 1 week.

➢ **To apply an AutoFilter**

1   If AutoFilters are not turned on, click **AutoFilter** ⊽≡ .

    After you turn on the AutoFilter feature, AutoFilters appear in each sheet view, not just the current sheet view.

2   In the field to which you want to apply an AutoFilter, click the arrow in the column heading, and then click the value for which you want to filter the table.

    The arrow and field name for that column become blue.

3   To filter for an additional condition based on a value in another field, repeat step 2 in the other field.

4   To filter one field for two values or to apply comparison operators other than **Equals**, click the arrow in the column, and then click **Custom**.

5   If information changes, you can refresh your AutoFilter settings by clicking the arrow again, and then reselecting the filtering value.

6   To remove the filtering on a specific row, click **All** in the AutoFilter list for that column.

7   To turn off all AutoFilters, click **AutoFilter** ⊽≡ again.

If you apply a particularly useful custom AutoFilter frequently, it may be faster to save it and then apply it as a normal filter.

➢ **To save a custom AutoFilter as a normal filter**

1   If AutoFilters are not turned on, click **AutoFilter** $\boxed{\triangledown\text{=}}$.

2   Click the arrow in the column heading, click **Custom**, and then click **Save**.

3   Make any changes to the filter in the **Filter Definition** dialog box.

4   To display the custom filter on the **Filtered for** submenu (under the **Project** menu), select the **Show in menu** check box, and then click **OK**. Click **OK** again in the **Custom AutoFilter** dialog box.

CREATING OR MODIFYING A VIEW, TABLE, OR FILTER

The many predefined Microsoft Project views, tables, and filters can be used to display the information you want in most situations. Occasionally, however, none of the predefined views, tables, or filters may meet your needs. In that case, you can create a view, table, or filter from scratch, create one based on an existing one, or modify an existing one.

Your new or modified view, table, or filter is saved only with the project file in which you created or modified it, and you can use it only with that project file. You can, however, make it available to other project files by using the Organizer.

Create or Modify a View

The predefined views that come with Microsoft Project are designed to display the information you're most likely to want, in useful formats. However, if none of the predefined views meet your information or formatting needs, you can create a new view or modify an existing one.

If the view you want differs significantly from existing views, create a new view. When you create a new view, though, you're constrained to making the new view look like a predefined view; you can't make a new view look any way you want it to.

If the view you want is similar to a predefined view, you can modify a copy of the existing view and save the modified version under a different name. The original, predefined view remains unchanged.

If the view you want requires only minor changes to a predefined view, you can edit the view. When you edit a view, you change the original view and not a copy of it. After you save the changes you've made to an existing view, you can't automatically reset the view back to its original form. If you're not sure you need to edit a view, copy it, and then modify the renamed copy instead.

➤ **To create or modify a view**

1   On the **View Bar**, click **More Views**.

2   To create a view from scratch, click **New**, click **Single view** or **Combination view**, and then click **OK**.

   To create a view based on an existing view, click that view in the **Views** list, and then click **Copy**.

   To edit an existing view, click that view in the **Views** list, and then click **Edit**.

3   In the **Name** box, type a name for the view, select a screen type for a view created from scratch, select a table and a filter, and specify whether the filter should be a highlighting filter.

   To create a new combination view, click a view name in the **Top** box for the top pane and click a view name in the **Bottom** box for the bottom pane.

4   To display the new view on the **View Bar** and **View** menu, select the **Show in menu** check box.

5   Click **OK**.

6   To display the view, click **Apply**.

Create or Modify a Table

The predefined tables that come with Microsoft Project display many useful sets of task or resource information, most of which should satisfy your information needs most of the time. However, if none of the tables provided with Microsoft Project displays the combination of information you need, you can create a table from scratch, create a table based on an existing table, or edit an existing table.

When you create a table, you start with a blank table to which you add each column and specify details such as the column title, column width, and data alignment within a column. When you create a table based on an existing table, you modify a copy of the existing table to suit your needs, without changing the original table. When you edit an existing table, you change the original table, so you should edit a table only if you're sure you want it changed.

➢ **To create or modify a table**

1 On the **View** menu, point to **Table**, and then click **More Tables**.

2 To create or modify a task table, click **Task**, and then click a table in the **Tables** list.

To create or modify a resource table, click **Resource**, and then click a table in the **Tables** list.

3 To create a table from scratch, click **New**.

To create a table based on an existing table, click that table in the **Tables** list, and then click **Copy**.

To edit an existing table, click that table in the **Tables** list, and then click **Edit**.

4 In the **Name** box, type a name for the table.

5 In the **Field Name** column:

If you're creating a table from scratch, then for each field you want to include, click the field name, data alignment value, and column width value you want.

If you're copying or modifying an existing table, then for each field listed, click the field name, data alignment value, and column width value you want.

6 To add a column title other than the field name, type a title in the **Title** field, and then click a title alignment in the **Align Title** field.

7 In the **Date** format box, click a date format for date fields.

8 To display the table in the **More Tables** submenu, select the **Show in menu** check box.

9 To prevent the first column from scrolling, select the **Lock first column** check box.

10 Click **OK**.

11 To display the table, click **Apply**.

If the table you've created or modified can't be applied to the current view, the Apply button is unavailable. For example, if you've created a table based on Tracking, a task table, and the Resource Sheet is displayed, the Apply button will appear gray.

If an existing Microsoft Project table displays nearly all the information you need, you can modify it quickly by adding a column to it to display the "missing" information.

> **To modify a table quickly by adding a column**

1   In a sheet view, apply the table to which you want to add a column, and then select the column to the left of which you want to insert the new column.

2   On the **Insert** menu, click **Column**.

3   In the **Column Definition** dialog box, specify the field name, title, title alignment, data alignment and width of the column.

4   To set the column width to the longest item in the column, click **Best Fit**.

If you don't need the field information displayed in a column, you can remove (or hide) that column. When you hide a column, the information that's in the column isn't removed from your project file; it's simply hidden.

> **To remove a column from a table**

1   In a sheet view, select the column you want to remove.

2   On the **Edit** menu, click **Hide Column**.

Create or Modify a Filter

The predefined filters that come with Microsoft Project enable you to display many useful subsets of tasks or resources, each subset based on a different set of criteria. However, if none of the filters provided with Microsoft Project displays exactly the subset of tasks or resources you want, you can create a filter from scratch, create a filter based on an existing filter, or edit an existing filter.

When you create a filter, you start with a blank filter to which you add each criterion. When you create a filter based on an existing filter, you modify a copy of the existing filter without changing the original. When you edit an existing filter, you change the original filter.

➢ **To create or modify a filter**

1   On the **View Bar**, click any view except the PERT Chart.

    To select a view that doesn't appear on the **View Bar**, click **More Views**, click the view you want in the **Views** list, and then click **Apply**.

2   On the **Project** menu, point to **Filtered for**, and then click **More Filters**.

3   To create or modify a task filter, click **Task**, and then click a filter in the **Filters** list.

    To create or modify a resource filter, click **Resource**, and then click a filter in the **Filters** list.

4   To create a filter from scratch, click **New**.

    To create a filter based on an existing filter, click that filter in the **Filters** list, and then click **Copy**.

    To edit an existing filter, click that filter in the **Filters** list, and then click **Edit**.

5   In the **Name** box, type a new name for the filter.

6   Under **Filter**, click a field name and a test.

7   In the **Value(s)** field, click a value to test for or click a range of values separated by a comma (,).

    For example, if you clicked **is within** or **is not within** in the **Test** field, type "**From**"?,"**To**"? to create an interactive filter that requests a range of dates to test for.

8   If the filter will contain more than one criterion row, select additional conditions on the row immediately underneath the first row, and then click an operator in the **And/Or** field of the same row. You may need to use the left arrow key to see the **And/Or** field.

9   Click **OK**.

10 To apply the filter immediately, click **Apply**.

Delete a View, Table, or Filter from Your Project Plan

If you don't need particular views, tables, or filters or you don't want team members to use them, you can delete them. When you delete a view, table, or filter, you delete it from the project file only. A copy of it continues to be stored in the Microsoft Project global file, Global.mpt. Deleting a view, table, or filter does not delete information from your project file.

➤ **To delete a view, table, or filter from a project plan**

1   On the **Tools** menu, click **Organizer**, and then click the **Views** tab, the **Tables** tab, or the **Filters** tab.

2   If you clicked the **Tables** tab or the **Filters** tab, click **Task** or **Resource** (above the GLOBAL.MPT box on the left).

3   In the **Views** box, the **Tables** box, or the **Filters** box on the right, click the view, table, or filter you want to delete.

4   Click **Delete**.

A message appears, asking you if you really want to delete the selected item.

5   Click **Yes**.

6   Click **Close**.

DISPLAYING INFORMATION IN VIEWS THAT HAVE DETAILS AND NON-TABLE FORMATS

The majority of Microsoft Project views are sheet views, such as the Gantt Chart, Resource Usage, and PA_Optimistic Gantt views. To display the information you want in sheet views, you can apply tables and filters.

But some views display information in a non-sheet format. This category includes all views that contain no table portion—such as the Resource Graph, the PERT Chart, and the Task Form—as well as some sheet views that consist of both a non-table portion as well as a table portion, such as the Task Usage and Resource Usage views.

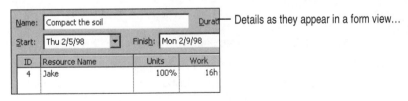

Details as they appear in a form view...

...and in a usage view.

Displaying the information you want in views that don't include table portions or include both table and non-table portions requires that you use one of several methods, the method you use depending upon the view. One of the most common methods is to change the set of details that appear in a view. You can change the set of details in the Task Usage view, the Resource Usage view, and in all the form views. But both the PERT Chart view and the Resource Graph view have unique methods for changing the information that appears on them.

Display the Details You Want in the Task Usage or Resource Usage View

If you don't see the usage information you want in the timescale, or details, portion of the Task Usage or Resource Usage view, you can display different information. For example, you can display actual costs, cumulative work, or the cost per resource for a given time period instead of the number of hours each resource is scheduled to work.

➢ **To change the details displayed**

1 On the **View Bar**, click **Task Usage** or **Resource Usage**.

2 On the **Format** menu, point to **Details**, and then click the type of information you want to display.

Display the Information You Want in the PERT Chart View

If the default information that appears in the PERT Chart view doesn't meet your information needs, you can display different task information in the PERT boxes. For example, instead of displaying the scheduled start and finish dates, you can display the constraint type and the task type.

➢ **To display the information you want in the PERT Chart view**

1 On the **View Bar**, click **PERT Chart**.

2 On the **Format** menu, click **Box Styles**, and then click the **Boxes** tab.

3 In the **1**, **2**, **3**, **4**, and **5** boxes, select the fields whose information you want to display in each part of the PERT box.

4 In the **Date format** box, click a date format.

Display Information for Both Individual and Selected Resources in the Resource Graph View

The Resource Graph view enables you to display information for both an individual resource and a selected group of resources at the same time. For example, you can compare the overallocation of a resource to that of the group to see if overallocated work can be assigned to another resource in the group. When you display information for both individual and selected resources, you see one graph for the individual resource and one graph for the selected resources. You can view these graphs side by side or overlap them.

➢ **To display information for individual or selected resources**

1   On the **View Bar**, click a task or resource view, other than the Resource Graph view.

2   On the **Window** menu, click **Split**.

3   Click the bottom pane.

4   On the **View Bar**, click **Resource Graph**.

5   On the **Format** menu, click **Bar Styles**.

6   In the **Show as** boxes, click the styles you want to use to represent the graph.

7   In the **Color** boxes, click the colors you want to use for the graph style.

8   In the **Pattern** boxes, click the patterns you want to use for the graph style.

9   If you want to show the numerical value for each graph at the bottom of the graphs, select the **Show values** check box.

10 If you want to show a line to indicate the availability of individual resources, select the **Show availability line** check box.

11 Click **OK**.

12 In the top pane, select all the tasks or resources for which you want to display information on the **Resource Graph** in the bottom pane.

Display the Information You Want in a Form View

The bottom portion of each form view displays information as a set of details. If the set of details that appears on a form view doesn't meet your information needs, you can display different information by selecting a different set of details. For example, you can display the resource cost or resource work for a task instead of assigned resources and predecessor tasks on the Task Form.

➢ **To display different information in a form view**

1 On the **View Bar**, click **More Views**, click the form view you want to use in the **Views** list, and then click **Apply**.

2 On the **Format** menu, point to **Details**, and then click the type of information you want to display.

12

Making Your Project Look the Way You Want

After you display the project information you want, you can make that information look the way you want. For example, you might decide that key information should stand out. Or, you might want to display the information graphically on the Gantt Chart view. To get a project overview, you may want to see more of your schedule at one time. To focus on a few tasks, you may want to see less of your schedule.

If the default appearance of a view doesn't meet your needs, you can change that appearance in a number of ways. For instance, you can:

- Change the appearance of information. For example, to make key information stand out, you can darken it by applying bold formatting.

- Display up to four sets of Gantt bars for each task. For example, you might display both a normal Gantt bar and one that shows the percent that a task is complete.

- Change the color, pattern, and shape of individual Gantt bars as well as of Gantt bars for specific task categories (such as the Gantt bars for critical tasks).

- Display a longer time period on a timescale to see more tasks at a time (but in less detail), or a shorter time period to see fewer tasks at a time (but in more detail).

These are just a few of the ways you can change the appearance of information in views. Microsoft Project also enables you to view all the text that's in a field, add information to Gantt bars, change the appearance of PERT boxes, show or hide specific task bars on the Calendar view, change the type of graph displayed on the Resource Graph view, and much more.

You can also import graphics from other programs. For information about importing, see Chapter 15, "Sharing Project Information with Other Programs and Projects."

A QUICK GUIDE TO THE FORMATTING YOU CAN APPLY TO EACH VIEW

Use the following table to find out the ways in which you can format each view.

To format this view or set of views		Perform the procedures contained in these sections
Gantt Chart	Bar Rollup	"Formatting Items Common to Many Views"
Detail Gantt	Milestone Date Rollup	"Formatting Items Common to Sheet Views"
Leveling Gantt	Milestone Rollup	"Formatting the Gantt Chart View"
Tracking Gantt		
PA_ Expected Gantt	PA_ Pessimistic Gantt	"Formatting Items Common to Many Views"
PA_ Optimistic Gantt		"Formatting Items Common to Sheet Views"
Resource Sheet	PA_ PERT Entry Sheet	"Formatting Items Common to Many Views" (All topics except for "Format the Timescale to See a Different Level of Detail")
Task Sheet		"Formatting Items Common to Sheet Views"
Resource Usage		"Formatting Items Common to Many Views"
Task Usage		"Formatting Items Common to Sheet Views"
		"Formatting the Task Usage and the Resource Usage Views"
PERT Chart		"Formatting Items Common to Sheet Views" (Only the topic "Format Individual Text")
		"Formatting the PERT Chart View"
Calendar		"Formatting Items Common to Many Views" (All topics except for "Format the Timescale to See a Different Level of Detail")
		"Formatting the Calendar View"
Resource Graph		"Formatting Items Common to Many Views"
		"Formatting the Resource Graph View"
Resource Allocation, a combination view		See the formatting procedures available for the Resource Usage view (top pane) and the Leveling Gantt (bottom pane).
Task Entry Form, a combination view		See the formatting procedures available for the Gantt Chart view (top pane) and the Task Form (bottom pane).
Resource Form	Task Form	No formatting is available for these views.
Resource Name Form	Task Details Form	
Task PERT	Task Name Form	

FORMATTING ITEMS COMMON TO MANY VIEWS

This section contains formatting procedures that can be applied to a wide variety of views, but not to all views. The following table shows you the views to which you can apply each formatting procedure in this section.

Formatting procedure	Views to which you can apply the procedure
Change the appearance of a category of tasks or resources	All views except the Task PERT view and form views.
Change the timescale to see a different level of detail	All views except the PERT Chart view, the Task PERT view, the Calendar view, the PA_PERT Entry Sheet view, and form views.
Change gridlines	All views except the PERT Chart view, the Task PERT view, the PA_PERT Entry Sheet view, and form views.

Change the Appearance of a Category of Tasks or Resources

On one day you may need to focus on critical tasks. On another day, you may want to point out overallocated resources to your supervisor. To visually distinguish a class of tasks or resources—or simply to change its appearance to suit your needs—you can change the appearance of predefined task and resource categories.

When you change the appearance of a category of tasks or resources, you change the appearance of all the information for each task or resource in that category, all at once. For example, if you make a category of tasks on the Gantt Chart view bold, the entire row of text for each task in the category appears bold. If you apply a different table, the appropriate rows in the new table will also appear bold. However, if you switch to the Task Sheet view, the task category that appears bold in the Gantt Chart view will appear as normal, unbolded text in the Task Sheet view. The formatting you apply to text in one view does not transfer to another view.

You change the appearance of task and resource information by changing the font, font style, font size, and color. A *font* is a family of characters—letters, numbers, and symbols—that share a particular look. For example, characters in the Arial font look like this:

Arial characters

Characters in the Rockwell font look like this:

Rockwell characters

There are thousands of fonts, a small portion of which you'll be able to display and print.

A *font style* is the "coating" you add to text, which in Microsoft Project can be regular (that is, no coating), bold, italic, or bold italic. You can apply a font style in addition to changing the font in which text appears. *Size* refers to the size of the text.

Here are some examples combining fonts, font styles, and font sizes (the number in each example refers to the font size):

Arial bold 10   ***Arial bold italic 12***   *Rockwell italic 10*

The capabilities of your computer and printer determine which fonts, font styles, and font sizes you can display and print.

You can change the appearance of categories of tasks and resources in all views except the Task PERT view and form views. The available categories that you can format vary from view to view.

➤ **To format a category of tasks or resources**

1. On the **View Bar**, click the view you want to reformat.

    To select a view that doesn't appear on the **View Bar**, click **More Views**, click the view you want in the **Views** list, and then click **Apply**.

2. On the **Format** menu, click **Text Styles**.

3. In the **Item to Change** box, click the task or resource category whose appearance you want to change, and then select formatting options for that category.

4. Repeat step 3 to change the formatting of other categories of information.

Change the Timescale to See a Different Level of Detail

Some of the most important information to keep on top of in any project is time-related information, such as task schedules or the day-by-day breakdown of the hours worked by resources. In Microsoft Project, there are a number of views that display time-related information on a timescale. Examples are the Gantt Chart view (the bar chart portion), the Resource Graph view, the Calendar view, and the Task Usage and Resource Usage views (the details area).

The way you want to display time-related information may vary. Sometimes you may want to see as much information as possible within a long time period. Other times you may want to focus on just a few events within a short time period. You can display time-related information within the time period you want by changing the timescale. When you display a longer time period on a timescale, you can see more events at one time, but in less detail. When you display a shorter time period, you can see fewer events, but in more detail. On views that have both major and minor timescales, such as the Gantt Chart view, you can adjust the scales independently.

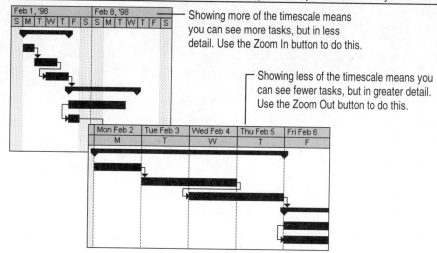

Showing more of the timescale means you can see more tasks, but in less detail. Use the Zoom In button to do this.

Showing less of the timescale means you can see fewer tasks, but in greater detail. Use the Zoom Out button to do this.

➢ **To change the timescale to see a different level of detail**

You can quickly zoom in and out of a view by clicking or .

1 On the **View Bar**, click **Gantt Chart** or another time-related view.

To select a view that doesn't appear on the **View Bar**, click **More Views**, click the view you want in the **Views** list, and then click **Apply**.

2 On the **Format** menu, click **Timescale**, and then click the **Timescale** tab.

3 In the **Units** boxes under **Major scale** and **Minor scale**, click the units of time you want to use.

4 To display only the major scale time unit, click **None** in the **Units** box under **Minor scale**.

5 In the **Label** boxes under **Major scale** and **Minor scale**, click the labels you want to use.

6 In the **Align** boxes under **Major scale** and **Minor scale**, click the alignment you want.

7 In the **Count** boxes under **Major scale** and **Minor scale**, type the numbers of intervals you want between the unit labels on the major scale and on the minor scale.

For example, if the major scale unit is months, and you type 1, the scale will be separated into 1-month segments.

8 To display a horizontal line between the major and minor scales, select the **Scale separator** check box.

9 To display vertical lines between unit labels, select the **Tick lines** check boxes.

10 To reduce or enlarge the timescale so that you can see more or less time in the same space, type a percentage in the **Enlarge** box.

Microsoft Project adjusts major and minor scales by the same amount.

Format Gridlines

Gridlines play a number of roles. They indicate time intervals, such as on the bar chart portion of the Gantt Chart view. They separate columns and rows of information, such as on any sheet or form view. And they separate titles both vertically, as in the columns on a sheet view, and horizontally, as on a timescale. Gridlines make it easier to read and interpret the information in a view.

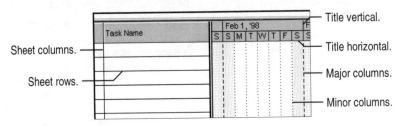

Examples of gridlines you can format on the Gantt Chart view.

You can enhance the effect that gridlines have by specifying the gridline patterns and colors that meet your needs, for each type of gridline that appears in a view. You can change the appearance of gridlines in all views except the PERT Chart view, the Task PERT view, and form views.

➤ **To format gridlines**

1   On the **View Bar**, click any view except the PERT Chart, the Task PERT, or a form view.

To select a view that doesn't appear on the **View Bar**, click **More Views**, click the view you want in the **Views** list, and then click **Apply**.

2   On the **Format** menu, click **Gridlines**.

3   In the **Line to change** list, click the type of gridline you want to change.

4   In the **Type** box under **Normal**, click the line pattern you want.

5   If you want to hide the selected line type, click the blank option in the **Type** box.

Later on, you can choose to display the selected gridline again.

6   In the **Color** box under **Normal**, click the line color you want.

7   If the gridline appears repeatedly and you want contrasting gridlines at specified intervals, click an interval, line type, and line color under **At interval**.

8   To skip a gridline at certain intervals, click the blank option in the **Type** box under **At interval**.

FORMATTING ITEMS COMMON TO SHEET VIEWS

Microsoft Project does some sheet-view formatting for you automatically; for example, it makes summary tasks bold. But if this automatic formatting doesn't highlight the information you want in just the way you want it, you can format these elements yourself. Column headings, individual pieces of information, and even entire categories of information can easily be rewritten, realigned, and reformatted.

You can format all sheet views in the following ways:

- Change the appearance of individual text.
- Change a column's name, width, and alignment.
- Format a category of tasks or resources.
- Change a column title.
- View all text in a field.
- Change the date format in date fields.

You can apply the formatting procedures in this section to these sheet-only views:

- Task Sheet
- Resource Sheet
- PA_PERT Entry Sheet

You can also apply the formatting procedures in this section to the sheet (or table) portions of the following views:

• Gantt Chart	• Task Usage	• Bar Rollup
• Detail Gantt	• Resource Usage	• Milestone Rollup
• Leveling Gantt	• PA_Expected Gantt	• Milestone Date Rollup
• Tracking Gantt	• PA_Optimistic Gantt	• Resource Allocation
	• PA_Pessimistic Gantt	• Task Entry

Change the Appearance of Individual Text

Looking at your project plan, maybe you noticed a task that's taking longer than planned, a resource that's available to work more hours, or a cost that's much less than you expected. To remain aware of the particular piece of text information, to call someone else's attention to it, or simply to distinguish the text from other text, you can change the appearance of that text.

You can change the appearance of text by changing its font, font style, font size, and color. For examples of how you can change these aspects of text, see "Change the Appearance of a Category of Tasks or Resources."

The capabilities of your computer and printer determine which fonts, font styles, and font sizes you can display and print.

You can change the appearance of individual pieces of text in the table fields of sheet views only.

➢ **To apply formatting to individual text**

  1 On the **View Bar**, click a sheet view, such as the Gantt Chart, Resource Sheet, or Task Usage view.

     To select a view that doesn't appear on the **View Bar**, click **More Views**, click the view you want in the **Views** list, and then click **Apply**.

  2 Select the text whose appearance you want to change.

  3 On the **Format** menu, click **Font**.

  4 Select the formatting options you want.

Change a Column's Name, Width, and Alignment

Microsoft Project provides default names for the column headings that appear in tables (which are displayed in sheet views only). For example, on the Entry table in the Gantt Chart view, the default name of the column that contains task start dates is Start. If a default column name doesn't tell you what kind of information is contained in the column or the name doesn't conform with your organization's standards, you can change the name that appears in the column heading. For example, you might change Start to Start Date.

You can also change the default column width to accommodate longer (or shorter) column names and data. In addition, you can specify whether column names and data are centered within the column or aligned left or right.

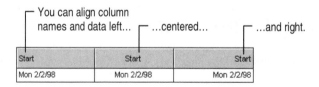

You can align column names and data left... ...centered... ...and right.

Start	Start	Start
Mon 2/2/98	Mon 2/2/98	Mon 2/2/98

The changes you make to a column's name, width, or alignment appear only in the table in which you make the changes. For example, if you change the name of the Start column to Start Date in the Entry table, the Start column in the Schedule table still appears with the name Start.

➢ **To change a column's name, width, or alignment**

1 On the **View Bar**, click the view you want to modify.

   To select a view that doesn't appear on the **View Bar**, click **More Views**, click the view you want in the **Views** list, and then click **Apply**.

2 Double-click the column heading whose name, width, or alignment you want to change.

3 To change the name of the column heading, type a new column heading for the field in the **Title** box.

4 To change the alignment of the column heading, select the alignment you want in the **Align title** box.

5 To change the column width, enter the width you want in the **Width** box.

6 To change the alignment of the column information, select the alignment you want in the **Align data** box.

View All the Data in a Field

A long piece of data in the field of a column sometimes gets cut off by the right edge of the column. The column isn't wide enough to display the entire piece of data. You can solve that problem by quickly adjusting the width of the column to match the length of the longest piece of data contained in that column.

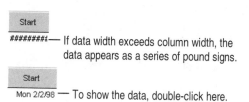

Start
######## — If data width exceeds column width, the
          data appears as a series of pound signs.

Start
Mon 2/2/98 — To show the data, double-click here.

- In a sheet view, double-click the border to the right of the column name.

  Microsoft Project automatically resizes the column width to the widest data in the column.

Change the Date Format for Date Fields

Dates appear in several fields, such as the Start and Finish fields that can be displayed in sheet views. By default, dates in date fields appear in the following format: Fri 2/6/98. If this format doesn't suit your needs, you can change it to any one of a number of date formats available in Microsoft Project. Examples of available date formats are 2/6/98, Fri 2/6/98 4:45 PM, 2/6, Feb 6, Feb 6 '98, and February 6, 1998.

You can change the date format no matter which view is displayed on your screen. However, you can only see the change in the date format on those views that have date fields. For instance, if you change the data format while the Resource Graph view is displayed, you won't see the new date format because the Resource Graph view doesn't have a date field.

> ## To change the date format for date fields

1 On the **Tools** menu, click **Options**, and then click the **View** tab.

2 In the **Date format** box, click the format you want to use.

You can also specify which date format you want to display in an individual table without affecting the date format that appears in all other tables.

> ## To change the date format in an individual table

1 On the **View** menu, point to **Table**, and then click **More Tables**.

2 In the **Tables** list, click the table for which you want to format the date, and then click **Edit**.

3 In the **Date format** box, click the date format you want to display.

FORMATTING THE GANTT CHART VIEW

The most frequently used of all Microsoft Project views, the Gantt Chart view can be formatted in more ways than any other view. This section provides procedures on how to format the graphical portion of the Gantt Chart view, with a focus on formatting Gantt bars. Although Microsoft Project applies default formatting to Gantt bars, you can change their look to include or highlight certain information, or to conform with organization standards. You can format Gantt bars manually or use the GanttChartWizard.

The procedures in this section explain how to format the graphical portion of the Gantt Chart view in the following ways:

- Change the color, shape, and pattern of a category of Gantt bars.
- Change the height of Gantt bars.
- Add the date or other information to Gantt bars.
- Create a custom Gantt Bar for a task category.
- Roll up a Gantt bar to a summary task bar.
- Display multiple Gantt bars for each task.
- Change the appearance of the link lines that connect Gantt bars.
- Change the appearance of nonworking time.

The procedures in this section apply to the following views: the Gantt Chart, the Detail Gantt, the Leveling Gantt, the Tracking Gantt, the Bar Rollup, the Milestone Rollup, the Milestone Date Rollup, and the Gantt Chart portions of the Resource Allocation and Task Entry views.

For information on formatting other parts of the Gantt Chart view, such as text, date formats, and gridlines, see the procedures in the "Formatting Items Common to Many Views" and "Formatting Items Common to Sheet Views" sections.

Change the Color, Shape, and Pattern of Gantt Bars

To help you focus on a particular set of tasks, you can change the appearance of the Gantt bars for all the tasks that belong to a predefined task category. For example, you can change the color, shape, or pattern of all milestone tasks or all summary tasks.

When you change the appearance of Gantt bars for a category of tasks, you change the appearance of all the Gantt bars for all the tasks in that category, all at once.

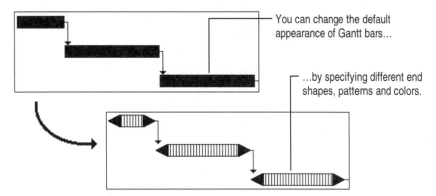

You can change the default appearance of Gantt bars...

...by specifying different end shapes, patterns and colors.

➢ **To change the color, shape, or pattern of a Gantt bar category**

1 On the **View Bar**, click **Gantt Chart**.

2 On the **Format** menu, click **Bar Styles**.

3 In the table, under **Name**, select the category (such as Task, Progress, or Summary) you want to change, and then click the **Bars** tab.

4 In the **Shape** boxes under **Start shape**, **Middle bar**, and **End shape**, click the Gantt bar shapes you want.

5 In the **Pattern** box under **Middle bar**, click a Gantt bar pattern.

6 In the **Color** boxes under **Start shape**, **Middle bar**, and **End shape**, click the Gantt bar colors you want.

   Some categories, such as Milestone and Task, have only a start shape. Others, such as Summary (for summary tasks), have shapes for the start and end components as well as for the middle bars.

You can also draw attention to an individual task by formatting its Gantt bar differently from other bars in that category. When you use the following procedure, you change the appearance of an individual Gantt bar without affecting any other Gantt bars.

➢ **To change the color, shape, or pattern of an individual Gantt bar**

1 On the **View Bar**, click **Gantt Chart**.

2 In the **Task Name** field, select the tasks whose Gantt bars you want to reformat.

3 On the **Format** menu, click **Bar**, and then click the **Bar shape** tab.

4 In the **Shape** boxes under **Start shape**, **Middle bar**, and **End shape**, click the Gantt bar shapes you want.

5 In the **Pattern** box under **Middle bar**, click a Gantt bar pattern.

6 In the **Color** boxes under **Start shape**, **Middle bar**, and **End shape**, click the Gantt bar colors you want.

Change the Height of Gantt Bars

Microsoft Project displays Gantt bars with a certain predefined, standard height that shows up clearly on your screen and in printed Gantt Chart views. However, if the bar chart portion of the Gantt Chart is cluttered with information, you might want to make room by reducing the bar height. Conversely, if you want to draw attention to the bars, you can increase bar height. When you adjust the bar height, you change the height of all Gantt bars.

➢   **To change the height of Gantt bars**

1   On the **View Bar**, click **Gantt Chart**.

2   On the **Format** menu, click **Layout**.

3   In the **Bar height** box, click the height of the Gantt bars in points.

Add Information to a Category of Gantt Bars

The Gantt Chart view is composed of two halves. On the left side is a table with columns of information. On the right side is a bar chart showing linked Gantt bars. Switching your focus from one side to the other can be time-consuming and annoying: First to the left side to see information about a task, and then to the right side to see a graphical representation of that task's dependencies.

If you prefer to work with the bar chart portion of the Gantt Chart view, you can display key information on or near each Gantt bar. That way, you won't have to continually refer to the information in the table. You might also add information to Gantt bars if you want to print the bar chart with key information.

By default, the names of assigned resources appear to the right of Gantt bars. You can also choose to display task names, cost, slack, remaining duration, and many other pieces of information. You can specify that the information appear at the top, bottom, left, and/or right of the Gantt bars, as well as inside them.

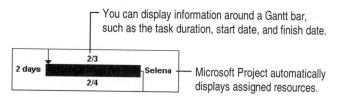

You can display information around a Gantt bar, such as the task duration, start date, and finish date.

Microsoft Project automatically displays assigned resources.

➢   **To add dates or other information to a Gantt bar category**

1   On the **View Bar**, click **Gantt Chart**.

2   On the **Format** menu, click **Bar Styles**.

3   In the table, select the type of Gantt bars (such as Task or Milestone) to which you want to add text, and then click the **Text** tab.

4   In the **Left**, **Right**, **Top**, **Bottom**, and **Inside** boxes, click the fields whose data you want to display on the Gantt bar.

If you display dates for a Gantt bar category, such as task start and finish dates, you can change the format for those dates. For example, you can change the date format from 2/6 to Feb 6 '98.

> ➤ **To change the format of dates on Gantt bars**
> 1   On the **Format** menu, click **Layout**.
> 2   In the **Date format for bars** box, click the date format you want.

Add Information to an Individual Gantt Bar

A particular task may have a very important role. For instance, perhaps it's more urgent to meet the date of one milestone than it is to meet the dates of other milestones. If you want to call attention to a specific Gantt bar, you can distinguish that Gantt bar from others in the same category by adding information to that Gantt bar only. You can add information to the left, right, top, bottom, and inside of an individual Gantt bar.

> ➤ **To add information to an individual Gantt Bar**
> 1   On the **View Bar**, click **Gantt Chart**.

You can also double-click a bar to format it or add information.

> 2   In the **Task Name** field, select the task whose Gantt bar you want to add information to.
> 3   On the **Format** menu, click **Bar**, and then click the **Bar Text** tab.
> 4   In the **Left**, **Right**, **Top**, **Bottom**, and **Inside** boxes, click the fields whose data you want to display on the Gantt bar.

Create a Custom Gantt Bar for a Task Category

Microsoft Project provides a default Gantt bar for each of several predefined task categories. For example, it provides a rectangular bar for normal tasks and a diamond shape for milestone tasks. If you want a Gantt bar for a task category that doesn't have its own bar, you can create a custom Gantt bar for that category. For instance, you can create a custom Gantt bar for critical tasks and in-progress tasks.

> ➤ **To create a custom Gantt bar for a task category**
> 1   On the **View Bar**, click **Gantt Chart**.
> 2   On the **Format** menu, click **Bar Styles**.
> 3   Select the row above which you want to insert a new Gantt bar, and then click **Insert Row**.

4   In the **Name** field of the new row, type a name for the new bar, and then press ENTER.

5   In the **Show For Tasks** field of the new row, click the category that the bar is to represent.

6   In the **From** and **To** fields, click the fields you want to use to position the start and finish points of the new Gantt bar. (In most cases, these will be the Start and Finish fields.)

   To create a symbol that represents a single date, such as for a milestone task, click the same field in both the **From** and **To** fields.

7   Click the **Bars** tab.

8   In the **Shape** boxes under **Start shape**, **Middle bar**, and **End shape**, click the Gantt bar shapes you want.

9   In the **Pattern** box under **Middle bar** and in the **Type** boxes under **Start shape** and **End shape**, click a Gantt bar pattern.

10 In the **Color** boxes under **Start shape**, **Middle bar**, and **End shape**, click the Gantt bar colors you want.

Roll Up a Gantt Bar to a Summary Task Bar

The bar chart portion of the Gantt Chart can become crowded, especially if your project contains many tasks. To make space, while still displaying important task information, you can *roll up* selected subtask bars into summary task bars.

When you roll up a subtask bar, it's displayed both on the summary task bar and as a separate bar, in its original location. To create space on the Gantt Chart, you can choose to hide the original bar after you've rolled it up. The summary task bar will show you at a glance the start and finish dates of the task bars you've rolled up.

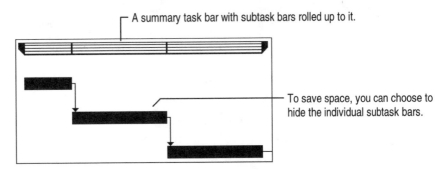

A summary task bar with subtask bars rolled up to it.

To save space, you can choose to hide the individual subtask bars.

> ➤ **To roll up a Gantt bar to a summary task bar**

1 On the **View Bar**, click **Gantt Chart**.

2 In the **Task Name** field, click the subtask you want to roll up.

3 Click **Task Information** 📋 , and then click the **General** tab.

4 Select the **Roll up Gantt bar to summary** check box.

The task bar is displayed as part of the summary task bar.

5 To hide the original subtask bar, select the **Hide task bar** check box.

Display Multiple Gantt Bars for Each Task

Typically, the one Gantt bar you display for each task contains all the information you apply to that Gantt bar. For instance, if you mark percent complete, the percent complete line appears inside the Gantt bar. If you apply a different color to Gantt bars for critical tasks—red, for example—then the entire bar will appear red.

Instead of showing each type of information on one Gantt bar, you can show each type of information on its own Gantt bar by displaying several Gantt bars for each task. Then each type of information can stand out more clearly. You can display up to four Gantt bars per task.

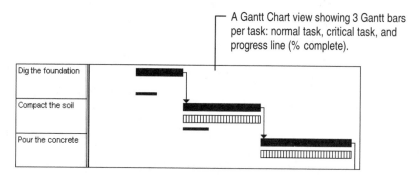

A Gantt Chart view showing 3 Gantt bars per task: normal task, critical task, and progress line (% complete).

> ➤ **To display multiple Gantt bars for each task**

1 On the **View Bar**, click **Gantt Chart**.

2 On the **Format** menu, click **Bar Styles**.

3 In one of the **Row** fields, type 1 for the information you want to appear first for each task.

4 In another **Row** field, type 2 for the information you want to appear second for each task.

5 If you want to display a third or fourth row of task information, type 3 or 4 in the **Row** field for the information you want to appear.

The Gantt bar (or Gantt bars) that have a 1 in the Row field will appear in the highest position for each task, and the Gantt bars that have a 4 in the Row field will appear in the lowest position.

Change the Appearance of Link Lines

After you link tasks, Microsoft Project displays link lines between the tasks. By default, an arrow points toward the successor task. If the default look doesn't suit you, you can change the appearance of link lines. You can even hide link lines completely.

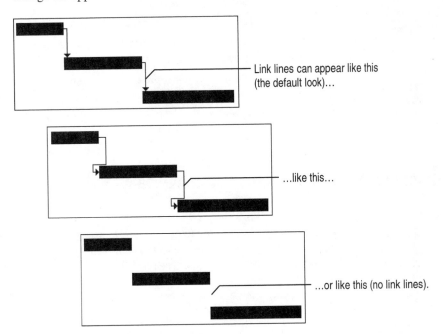

Link lines can appear like this (the default look)...

...like this...

...or like this (no link lines).

> **To change the appearance of link lines**

1   On the **View Bar**, click **Gantt Chart**.

2   On the **Format** menu, click **Layout**.

3   Under **Links**, click the link line style you want.

Change the Appearance of Nonworking Time

On the Gantt Chart view, nonworking time appears as a lightly shaded vertical bar in the timescale portion of the view. The shading tells you on which days of the week your resources don't work. If you want nonworking time to stand out more, or if you want its appearance to conform with your organization's standards, you can change the appearance of nonworking time.

➢ **To change the appearance of nonworking time**

1 On the **View Bar**, click **Gantt Chart**.

2 On the **Format** menu, click **Timescale**, and then click the **Nonworking Time** tab.

3 Under **Draw**, select whether you want the nonworking time bars to appear behind or in front of task bars or not at all.

4 In the **Calendar** box, select the base or resource calendar to which you want to apply the nonworking time format.

5 In the **Color** box, select the color of the nonworking time. In the **Pattern** box, select the pattern of the nonworking time.

Formatting the Gantt Chart View Automatically

Because of all the many ways you can format the Gantt Chart view, keeping track of what you can do and how to do it can be a problem. To help you format the Gantt Chart view, Microsoft Project provides the GanttChartWizard. The GanttChartWizard is a series of interactive dialog boxes that present you with a number of options for formatting various aspects of the Gantt Chart view. When you finish selecting the options you want, the GanttChartWizard formats your Gantt Chart view for you.

The GanttChartWizard can't format every aspect of the Gantt Chart view that can be formatted, but it can help you to format:

- Noncritical tasks.
- Critical tasks.
- The appearance of information for a category of Gantt bars.
- The color, pattern, and end shapes of Gantt bars for various task categories.
- Link lines.

➢ **To format your Gantt Chart view automatically**

1 On the **View Bar**, click **Gantt Chart**.

2 Click **GanttChartWizard** .

3 Follow the GanttChartWizard instructions.

FORMATTING THE TASK USAGE AND THE RESOURCE USAGE VIEWS

In Microsoft Project 98, the Task Usage view is entirely new and the Resource Usage view has been improved. Both views consist of a table, such as in a sheet view, and a timescale on which you can see work, cost, and other details broken down by day, week, month, or some other time period that you specify.

This section includes a procedure for changing the appearance of details. To format other parts of the Task Usage view or the Resource Usage view, such as text, the timescale, or gridlines, see the procedures in the "Formatting Items Common to Many Views" and "Formatting Items Common to Sheet Views" sections.

Change the Appearance of Details

To make important information stand out, you can change the appearance of the details in the timescale portion of the Resource Usage and Task Usage views.

The table portion of the Task Usage view. — The divider bar. — The details portion of the Task Usage view.

Task Name	Work	Duration	Details	T	W
⊟ Compact the soil	32 hrs	2 days	Work	16h	16h
			Cost	**$320.00**	**$320.00**
Selena	*16 hrs*		*Work*	*8h*	*8h*
			Cost	*$160.00*	*$160.00*
Tom	*16 hrs*		*Work*	*8h*	*8h*
			Cost	*$160.00*	*$160.00*

The task Work field is formatted as regular text.

The task Cost field is formatted as bold text.

All assignment fields are formatted as italic text.

➢ To change the appearance of details

1   On the **View Bar**, click **Task Usage** or **Resource Usage**.

2   On the **Format** menu, click **Detail Styles**, and then click the **Usage Details** tab.

3   In the **Show these fields** list, click the field you want to change.

   If the field you want does not appear in the **Show these fields** list, click the field in the **Available fields** list, and then click **Show**.

4   Under **Field settings for Work**, select a font (click **Change Font**), cell background, and pattern for the field.

5   To hide the details header column, click the **Usage Properties** tab, and then click **No** in the **Display details header column** box.

6   If you don't want to repeat the detail headers on all assignment rows, clear the **Repeat details header on all assignment rows** check box.

7   To display short detail header names, select the **Display short detail header names** check box.

FORMATTING THE PERT CHART

This section provides procedures on how to format the PERT Chart, including how to:

- Change the border style and other elements of PERT boxes.
- Display more or less detail.
- Change the appearance of link lines.
- Move multiple PERT boxes at once.
- Adjust for page breaks.

Change the Appearance of PERT Boxes

By default, PERT boxes are displayed with a clear and simple format: The upper half of each box contains a task name. The lower half of each box is divided into four fields, each of which contains a piece of task information. If this format doesn't meet your needs, you can change the appearance of PERT boxes. You can change the appearance of all PERT boxes or a category of PERT boxes; you can't change the appearance of one box only.

For instance, each category of task appears with a unique PERT box border. A thin black line encloses each noncritical task, a thick red line encloses each critical task, and a shadowed box encloses each summary task. If the default border for a particular category of task doesn't suit your needs, you can change the appearance of that border.

You can make PERT boxes the following sizes:

Some of the ways you can format PERT boxes:

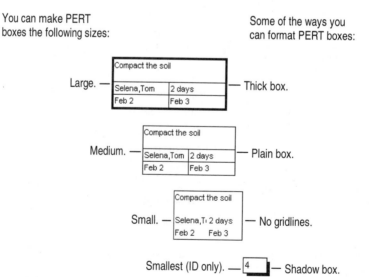

➤ To change the appearance of PERT boxes

1   On the **View Bar**, click **PERT Chart**.

2   On the **Format** menu, click **Box Styles**, and then click the **Borders** tab.

3   In the **Item to change** list, click the task category for which you want to change the border.

4   In the **Style** box, click a border style.

5   In the **Color** box, click a border color.

6   Click the **Boxes** tab.

7   In the **Size** box, click a size for the **PERT** box.

8   To remove the lines between the field information, clear the **Gridlines between fields** check box.

9   If you don't want to indicate tasks that are in progress or completed, clear the **Progress marks** check box.

Display More or Less Detail

The amount of your project you want to see will vary. To see a project overview, you'll want to view as many PERT boxes as possible at one time. To focus on details, you'll want to view a few tasks at a time. You can display as much or as little of your project at one time by zooming in and out.

➤ To display more or less detail

1   On the **View Bar**, click **PERT Chart**.

2   To see more detail (and fewer PERT boxes at a time), click . To see less detail (and more PERT boxes at a time), click .

Change the Appearance of Link Lines

After you link tasks, Microsoft Project displays link lines between the PERT boxes. By default, an arrow points toward the successor task. If the default look doesn't suit you, you can change the appearance of link lines. You can even hide link lines completely.

➤ To change the appearance of link lines

1   On the **View Bar**, click **PERT Chart**.

2   On the **Format** menu, choose **Layout**.

3   Under **Links**, select the type of link lines you want: straight lines or lines bent at right angles.

4   To remove arrows from the link lines, clear the **Show arrows** check box.

Move Multiple PERT Boxes at Once

To reposition multiple PERT boxes quickly, use one of the following methods:

- To move PERT boxes that are next to one another, select them with the pointer by dragging a box around the PERT boxes, and then drag the border of one of the PERT boxes.

- To move a summary task and its subtasks or a task and its successors, hold down SHIFT as you drag the border of the summary task box or the predecessor task box.

- To move nonadjacent tasks, click the border of each task you want to move, and then drag the border of one of the PERT boxes.

Prevent PERT Boxes from Crossing Page Breaks

If your project has many tasks, there's a good chance that some PERT boxes will straddle page breaks. A printout of the PERT Chart will show half of these boxes at the end of one page and the other half at the beginning of the next page. To give your PERT Chart an orderly appearance, you can prevent PERT boxes from crossing page breaks.

➢ **To prevent PERT boxes from crossing page breaks**

1 On the **View Bar**, click **PERT Chart**.

2 On the **Format** menu, click **Layout**.

3 Select the **Adjust for page breaks** check box, and then click **Layout Now** on the **Format** menu.

To hide page breaks on your screen, click **Layout** on the **Format** menu, and then clear the **Show page breaks** check box.

FORMATTING THE CALENDAR VIEW

This section provides procedures on how to format the Calendar view, including how to:

- Arrange task bars.
- Hide a category of task bars.
- Hide specific task bars.
- Change the bar type, pattern, and color of all task bars.
- Change the appearance of the timescale.

Arrange Task Bars

The narrow space within each Calendar row challenges you to keep task bars in a neat arrangement. You could try to rearrange task bars by moving them one at a time. But that can be time-consuming, and you might not end up with the result you want. A better way is to let Microsoft Project rearrange all task bars all at once, according to a predefined set of guidelines. This will result in an orderly arrangement. Then, if you need to, you can refine the arrangement by moving just those task bars that still aren't positioned where you want them, one at a time.

➤ To arrange task bars

1 On the **View Bar**, click **Calendar**.

2 On the **Format** menu, click **Layout**.

3 To display as many tasks as possible in one row without overlapping task bars, click **Attempt to fit as many tasks as possible**.

4 To arrange tasks in the current sort order, click **Use current sort order**.

5 To show task split lines, select the **Show bar splits** check box.

6 To have Microsoft Project automatically arrange task bars when you add or delete tasks, select the **Automatic layout** check box, and then click **OK**.

If you don't select the Automatic layout check box, then you must click Layout Now on the Format menu to rearrange the task bars.

7 If some tasks are not precisely where you want them, drag them to the desired locations.

Hide a Category of Task Bars

When several tasks occur on the same date, Microsoft Project stacks their task bars like pancakes one above the other within a Calendar row. If the Calendar row isn't high enough to fit all the task bars, Microsoft Project displays only some of the task bars. You can make sure that you can see the task bars for the tasks you're interested in by restricting the types of tasks that are displayed on the Calendar.

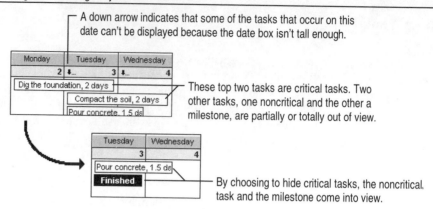

A down arrow indicates that some of the tasks that occur on this date can't be displayed because the date box isn't tall enough.

These top two tasks are critical tasks. Two other tasks, one noncritical and the other a milestone, are partially or totally out of view.

By choosing to hide critical tasks, the noncritical task and the milestone come into view.

> **To hide a category of task bars**

1 On the **View Bar**, click **Calendar**.

2 On the **Format** menu, click **Bar Styles**.

3 In the **Task type** list, click the task category you don't want to display

4 In the **Bar type** box, click **None**.

   Repeat steps 3 and 4 for each task category you don't want to display.

5 On the **Format** menu, click **Layout**, and then click **Attempt to fit as many tasks as possible**.

   The tasks in the remaining categories, including those that are out of view, will fill in the displayable area of the date boxes.

You can also use the following methods to display the task bars you want:

• On the **Project** menu, point to **Filtered for**, and then click a filter option.

• Display fewer, but larger, week rows by dragging the horizontal line between any two week rows up to increase the height of the week row. Or, adjust the height of the week rows to fit the greatest number of tasks scheduled on any date by double-clicking the horizontal line separating one week row from another.

Hide Specific Task Bars

When a Calendar row is too short to display the task bars for all of the tasks that occur on a given date, you can hide the specific task bars of those tasks you're not interested in at the moment. By hiding specific task bars, you may create enough room for the task bars you want to display. If hiding specific task bars doesn't create enough room, you may want to hide the task bars for a category of tasks.

> **To hide a specific task bar**

1 On the **View Bar**, click **Calendar**.

2 Select the task bar you want to hide.

3 Click **Task Information** , and then click the **General** tab.

4 Select the **Hide task bar** check box.

> **To display a hidden task bar**

1 Double-click the top row of a date on which the task will appear.

2 In the **Tasks occurring on** dialog box, double-click the task you want to display.

3 Click the **General** tab, and then clear the **Hide task bar** check box.

Change the Bar Type, Pattern, and Color of All Task Bars

To help you focus on a particular set of tasks, you can change the appearance of the task bars for all the tasks that belong to a predefined task category. For example, you can change the color, shape, or pattern of all critical task bars or all milestone task bars. You can also add information, such as the task start date, which appears within each task bar.

When you change the appearance of task bars for a category of tasks, you change the appearance of all the task bars for all the tasks in that category.

> **To change the bar type, pattern, and color of all task bars**

1 On the **View Bar**, click **Calendar**.

2 On the **Format** menu, click **Bar Styles**.

3 In the **Task type** list, click the task bar type for which you want to change the formatting.

4 Under **Bar shape**, click a bar type, pattern, color, and split pattern for the task type.

5 To add a shadow behind the bar, select the **Shadow** check box.

6 In the **Field(s)** box, click the information you want to appear within the bar.

   If you want more than one field to appear on the task bar, type a comma (**,**) after a field name, and then select another field name.

7 In the **Align** box, click the alignment you want to use to position the text within the task bars.

Change the Appearance of Headings, Date Boxes, and Rows

If the default appearance of the Calendar view doesn't meet your needs, you can change its overall look quickly. For example, you can change the monthly, weekly, and daily titles, such as changing February 1998 to Feb '98 or Monday to Mo or M.

You can also display 5-day or 7-day weeks, date boxes with different patterns, colors, and date formats, small representations of next and previous months, and more.

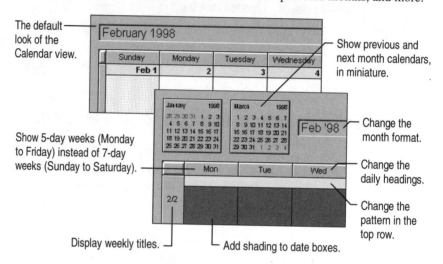

The default look of the Calendar view.

Show previous and next month calendars, in miniature.

Change the month format.

Show 5-day weeks (Monday to Friday) instead of 7-day weeks (Sunday to Saturday).

Change the daily headings.

Change the pattern in the top row.

Display weekly titles.

Add shading to date boxes.

> ## To change the appearance of headings, date boxes, and rows

1   On the **View Bar**, click **Calendar**.

2   On the **Format** menu, click **Timescale**, and then click the **Week Headings** tab.

3   In the **Monthly titles**, **Daily titles**, and **Weekly titles** boxes, click the title formats you want to use.

4   Under **Display**, click **7 days** to display a 7-day week or click **5 days** to display a 5-day week.

5   To add miniature calendars for the next and previous months, select the **Previous/Next month calendars** check box.

6   Click the **Date Boxes** tab.

7   Under **Top row** and **Bottom row**, select the information you want to display in the left and right portion of each row, and then select the pattern and color you want.

8   Click the **Date Shading** tab, and then click the name of the calendar you want to change in the **Show working time for** box.

9   In the **Exception type** list, click the type of date box you want to change, and then select a shade pattern and color.

You can change the column width by dragging any vertical line between two date boxes to the left to decrease column width or to the right to increase column width. To fit the displayed columns exactly to the width of the calendar area, double-click any vertical line between two date boxes.

FORMATTING THE RESOURCE GRAPH VIEW

This section contains only one procedure for formatting the Resource Graph view, a procedure on how to change the graph, pattern, and color on the view. You can also, however, change the appearance of text, gridlines, and the timescale. To find out how to format these aspects of the Resource Graph view, see the topics in the section "Formatting Items Common to Many Views."

Change the Graph, Pattern, and Color

The Resource Graph view is capable of displaying a graph of information for an individual resource and a graph of information for a group of selected resources at the same time. For instance, you can format each graph separately, to help you compare an individual resource's allocated work hours with the group's allocated work hours.

You can overlap bar graphs for individual and selected resources, use a different type of graph (such as a bar, area, or line graph), and change the graph color and pattern.

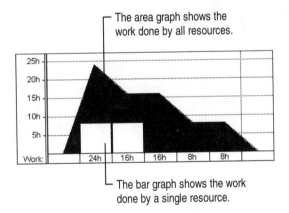

The area graph shows the work done by all resources.

The bar graph shows the work done by a single resource.

> ➤ **To change the graph, pattern, and color**

1 On the **View Bar**, click **Resource Graph**.

2 On the **Format** menu, click **Bar Styles**.

   The customizing options for the filtered (or selected) resource graph are on the left side of the Bar Styles dialog box. The customizing options for the individual resource graph are on the right side.

3 In the **Show as** boxes, click the styles you want to use to represent each graph.

   To remove a graph, click **Don't Show** in the **Show as** box.

4 In the **Color** boxes, click the colors you want to use for the graph.

5 In the **Pattern** boxes, click the patterns you want to use for the graph.

6 If you've chosen to show two bar graphs and you want the bars to overlap, type the overlap percentage in the **Bar overlap** box.

SORT A VIEW

By default, Microsoft Project lists tasks and resources in ascending order by ID number. But you may want to see tasks or resources in a different order. If, for example, you want to decrease the project length, you may want to list tasks from the longest duration to the shortest, to focus on reducing the longest durations first.

The sorting criteria you can choose are the Microsoft Project task and resource fields that are available. For instance, if you want to sort tasks by duration, you specify that the Duration field control the sort order.

The sorting you apply to a view is saved with that view. You can't sort in the PERT Chart view.

➢ **To sort a view**

1   On the **Project** menu, point to **Sort**, and then click the sorting option you want.

   To select a sorting option that doesn't appear on the Sort submenu, point to **Sort**, and then click **Sort by.**

2   In the **Sort by** box, click a field by which to sort your data, and then click **Ascending** or **Descending** to specify the sort order.

3   To sort by an additional field, click the fields in the first **Then by** box, and then click **Ascending** or **Descending** to specify the sort order.

4   To sort tasks within their outline structure so that subtasks remain with their summary tasks, select the **Keep outline structure** check box.

5   To permanently renumber your tasks based on the new sort order, select the **Permanently renumber tasks** check box.

   You can renumber your tasks only if you select **Keep outline structure** first.

6   To return your tasks to their original sequence, click **Reset**.

   If you've permanently renumbered your tasks, you can't return your tasks to their original sequence by clicking **Reset**.

13

Printing and Reporting

Most likely, you can share project information electronically in one or more of the following ways: by routing a project file across an e-mail system, by exchanging project information with a web site, by importing or exporting project information, or by linking project information between a project file and another kind of file (such as a spreadsheet file).

If a client, manager, or team member worked in a different site, town, or country, you might have no choice but to exchange project information electronically. But if you meet with project participants frequently, you might find it more convenient—even necessary—to print project information for them.

Among the reasons for printing project information are:

- Each Microsoft Project view and report presents a set of organized, related project information in an effective format. To review or distribute the information you want, you only need to select and print the right view or report.

- A printout can show more project information than can be displayed on a computer screen at one time.

- You can print everything from project overviews to very specific information. You can quickly specify exactly the information you want to share.

- A printout of project information fastened to a wall, bulletin board, or side of a computer monitor can serve as a helpful reminder. For example, a resource can use a printout of the tasks assigned to him or her as a checklist.

- Your organization may require you to distribute printouts and reports of some project information.

- Many people prefer to read information, especially lengthy or complex information, on paper.

- You may not be able to share project information electronically with some project participants.

Printing a completed project schedule and distributing it for review before the project begins is one of the main reasons for printing project information. But there are a number of reasons for printing project information at any time during a project. For example, you can periodically print status information for your managers, clients, and team members. If you want, you can include status information in status reports created in other programs, such as Microsoft Word. (See Chapter 15, "Sharing Project Information with Other Programs and Projects.")

If the schedule changes significantly, you may want to distribute a printout of the revised schedule to team members. You can also print project overviews for managers, task lists for individual team members, project costs to date, resource usage information, information about in-progress tasks and slipping tasks, and many other kinds of project information.

Using Microsoft Project views and reports, you can print exactly the project information required by a particular project participant. Views are discussed in Chapter 11, "Viewing the Information You Want: Using Views, Tables, Filters, and Details." A *report* is a predefined set of project information in a format that's ready for printing. Microsoft Project reports are made to be printed. Information you're likely to want to print is probably in one of the predefined reports. In many cases, all you need do is select the report that has the information you want and then print it. There are 25 predefined reports.

Whether you print a view or a report, you can specify exactly the information that appears by using tables and filters. You can also change the appearance of views and reports by making text bold, italic, and so on, adding headers and footers, adjusting margins, changing the page orientation, adding borders, specifying how large or how small information should appear on a printed page, and much more.

You might change the appearance of a view either to display it in a more effective way or to print it in a suitable format. Thus, information about changing the appearance of views resides in a "neutral" chapter, Chapter 12, "Making Your Project Look the Way You Want." Because there's only one reason for changing the appearance of a report, and that is to print the report with a certain look, you'll find information about changing a report's appearance in this chapter. For information about exchanging project information electronically—by using an e–mail system, an intranet, or the World Wide Web—see Chapter 10, "Updating Task Information by Using E-Mail and the Web."

PRINTING BASICS FOR VIEWS AND REPORTS

Printing a view or report can be as easy as clicking a Print button. The information in the view or report may be the information you want, and you may be happy with the default appearance. In that case, there are only a few things you should know before you print your project information.

This section covers the basics of printing views and reports, such as the differences between views and reports, the kinds of information you can print in views and reports, and the procedures for printing views and reports.

Comparing Views and Reports

One of the main differences between views and reports is that you can enter and edit information in a view. You can't enter or edit specific information in a report. You can however, apply different tables and filters to a report, similar to the way you apply tables and filters to views.

There are five types of views: sheet, graph, chart, calendar, and form views. There's at least one predefined Microsoft Project view of each type. When you create a new view, you base it on one of the predefined views.

There are four types of reports: task, resource, crosstab, and monthly calendar reports. (Like the Task Usage and Resource Usage views, a *crosstab* report shows information about tasks or resources broken down by time period.) There's at least one predefined Microsoft Project report of each type except the monthly calendar type. There are no predefined monthly calendar reports. When you create a new report, you base it on one of the four report types. You can create a monthly calendar report because Microsoft Project supplies the basic model on which to base your own monthly calendar reports.

You have many ways to change the appearance of most views. You have fewer ways to change the appearance of reports. For example, you can format a category of text but not an individual piece of text. And no matter what you do to a report, it will still look like, well, a report. Reports are made to look like reports, complete with report titles. That's their job.

When you print a view, you decide if you want to check the pages in the preview window first, to see how they'll look when printed. Microsoft Project automatically displays a preview of a report when you select the report (just before you print it).

One small difference is that you can print a view from the project window or the preview window. You can print a report from the preview window or the Custom Reports dialog box.

Print a View

The information you see on your screen is contained in a view. If you want to print the information you see on your screen, then print the view. You can print any view except form views and the Task PERT view.

➤ **To print a view**

To print a view quickly, click Print 🖨.

1   On the **View Bar**, click the view you want.

   To select a view that doesn't appear on the **View Bar**, click **More Views**, click the view you want in the **Views** list, and then click **Apply**.

2   On the **File** menu, click **Print**.

3   Select the printing options you want.

   You can cancel printing at any time by pressing ESC.

➤ **To preview a view before printing**

To preview a view quickly, click Print Preview 🔍.

1   On the **View Bar**, click the view you want.

   To select a view that doesn't appear on the **View Bar**, click **More Views**, click the view you want in the **Views** list, and then click **Apply**.

2   On the **File** menu, click **Print Preview**.

Print a Report

A report often contains a set of information that doesn't appear in any single view, or it might take time for you to specify the same set of information in a view that already exists in a report. In these and other situations, your best choice may be to print a report.

➤ **To print a report**

1   On the **View** menu, click **Reports**.

2   Click the report type you want, and then click **Select**.

   If you chose **Custom** as the report type, the Custom Reports dialog box appears. Click a report in the **Reports** list, and then go to step 5.

3   Click the report you want to print, and then click **Select**.

4   If a dialog box appears and asks you for specific values, enter the values, and then click **OK**.

   The report is displayed in the preview window.

5   Click **Print**.

Select a report category in the Reports dialog box...

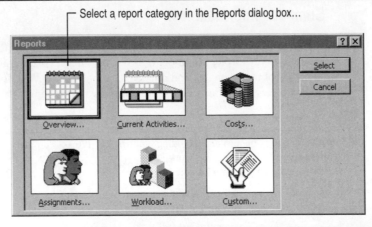

...and then select a specific report.

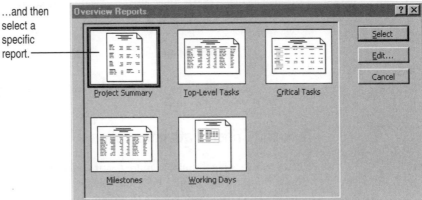

Examples of Project Information You Can Print

After you've created your project plan, you can print project information that's tailored to each recipient. For example, you can create summary level reports for management, projected cost reports for the accounting department, and individual task-level reports for each supervisor. Since all reports are based on the same core set of information, it's easy to print exactly the information that's needed.

Each of the following tables shows you which views and reports you can use when you want to print a particular kind of information. The views and reports listed in each table are only a sampling of the possible views and reports you can print in each information category.

Summary Information

Views and reports with summary information can show everything from a statistical summary of the project (number of tasks, resources, cost, duration, and so on) to a summary of major phases and milestones in the project. The following table lists several views and reports that show summary information.

To print	Use
A summary of the project, including number of tasks and resources, cost, work, duration, start and finish dates, and project notes	Project Summary report (in Overview reports)
A summary of major phases, with bar chart showing the start and finish dates	Gantt Chart view, with the outline collapsed
A summary of major phases, showing duration, start and finish dates, cost, and percent complete	Top-Level Tasks report (in Overview reports)
Milestones in the project and top-level summary tasks	Milestones report (in Overview reports)
Working and nonworking time	Working Days report (in Overview reports)

Task and Critical Path Information

When you want to get down to more detail about the tasks in the project, you can print information showing details about individual tasks instead of a project overview. The following table lists several ways to report on tasks in your project.

To print	Use
A list of tasks and durations, plus a bar chart of tasks and critical path	Gantt Chart view, with pattern changed for critical task bars
A list of critical tasks and their successors	Critical Tasks report (in Overview reports)
A flow chart that shows all tasks and the dependencies between them	PERT Chart view
Tasks and notes about the tasks	Task report (in Custom reports)
A list of tasks showing assigned resources grouped under each task, a table of task information, and a set of details about tasks and their assigned resources	Task Usage view or Task Usage report (in Workload reports)

To print	Use
A list of tasks and their work and costs	Task Sheet view, with Summary table applied
A list of tasks scheduled during a particular time period	Task report (in Custom reports) or Tasks Starting Soon report (in Current Activities reports)
A schedule of tasks printed on a calendar	Calendar view

Resource Usage Information

Views and reports that include resource usage information provide information such as the tasks each resource is assigned to, the amount of work allocated to resources, resource costs, and pay rates. The following table lists some of the views and reports you can print with resource usage information.

To print	Use
List of all resources assigned to work on the project	Resource Sheet view
A list of resources showing assigned tasks grouped under each resource, a table of resource information, and a set of details about resources and their assigned tasks	Resource Usage view or Resource Usage report (in Workload reports)
Resource work and cost	Resource Sheet view, with Summary table attached, or Resource Usage view showing work and cost
List of resources and the tasks to which each is assigned	Who Does What report (in Assignment reports), Resource Usage view, or Resource Usage report (in Workload reports)
List of resources, the tasks to which each is assigned, and the hours worked on each task during each week	Who Does What When report (in Assignment reports) or Resource Usage view
List of overallocated resources and task assignments	Overallocated Resources report (in Assignments reports)
A graph showing resource allocations, costs, and work over time for an individual resource, a group of resources, or both	Resource Graph view
A list of tasks an individual resource is assigned to work on	To-do List report (in Assignment reports)
A list of resources scheduled to work on tasks during a specified time period	Resource Usage report (in Workload reports)

Cost Information

Microsoft Project provides several ways to print cost information. You can print resource costs, task costs, cumulative costs, or a table showing the cash flow over time. Print cost information for team members who need to approve or keep track of project costs, such as your manager or members of the accounting department.

To print	Use
Task costs and totals	Budget report (in Cost reports)
A list of resources whose costs will exceed baseline cost	Overbudget Resources report (in Cost reports)
A list of tasks whose costs will exceed baseline cost	Overbudget Tasks report (in Cost reports)
Expected task costs	Budget report (in Cost reports)
A list of cumulative cost per task	Task Usage view, with Cumulative Cost details displayed in the timescale
A forecast of task costs, such as how much money will be spent on tasks and when	Cash Flow report (in Cost reports)
A forecast of resource costs, such as how much money will be spent on tasks and when	Resource Usage view, with Cost details applied
A summary of resource costs	Resource Sheet view, with Cost table applied
A list of tasks showing whether you're ahead of or behind schedule as compared with the actual costs incurred	Earned Value report (in Cost reports)
Cumulative resource cost over the life of the project	Resource Graph view displaying cumulative cost for all resources

Progress Information

Keeping track of project progress increases your chances or completing your project on time and within budget. The following table lists views and reports that include progress information you'll want to share with managers, task supervisors, and clients.

To print	Use
A list of tasks currently in progress, which shows the months in which each task occurs	Tasks In Progress report (in Current Activities reports)
A list of tasks that are schedules to start within a time period you specify	Tasks Starting Soon report (in Current Activities reports)
A list of tasks that haven't started yet	Unstarted Tasks report (in Current Activity reports)
A list of tasks that should have started by the date you specify but haven't	Should Have Started Tasks report (in Current Activities reports)
A list of tasks showing actual start and finish dates, percentage of each task completed, and actual and remaining task durations	Gantt Chart view, with Tracking table
A list of tasks that have been rescheduled to occur after their baseline start dates	Slipping Tasks report (in Current Activities reports)
A list of tasks with scheduled start and finish dates, baseline start and finish dates, and the differences between scheduled and baseline dates	Gantt Chart view, with Variance table
A list of completed tasks	Task Sheet view, with Completed Tasks filter
A list of completed tasks showing the time period in which each task occurred	Completed Tasks report (in Current Activities reports)

Specify the Print Range and Number of Copies

Microsoft Project provides a number of printing options. For example, if you want to print only the pages within a certain range, say, pages 3 to 5, you can print just those pages. You can also specify the number of copies you'd like of the entire or partial view or report.

There are different procedures for specifying printing options for views and reports.

➢ **To specify the print range and number of copies for a view**

1 On the **View Bar**, click the view you want to print.

To select a view that doesn't appear on the **View Bar**, click **More Views**, click the view you want in the **Views** list, and then click **Apply**.

2 On the **File** menu, click **Print**.

3 In the **Print range** box:

To print all the pages in the view, click **All**.

To print a range of pages, click **Page(s)**, and then enter the number of the first page in the range in the **From** box and the number of last page in the range in the **To** box.

4 In the **Copies** box, type the number of copies you want to print in the **Number of copies** box.

➢ **To specify the print range and number of copies for a report**

1 On the **View** menu, click **Reports**.

2 Click the report type you want, and then click **Select**.

If you chose Custom as the report type, click a report in the **Reports** list, click **Print**, and then go to step 5.

3 Click the report you want to print, and then click **Select**.

4 Click **Print**.

5 In the **Print range** box:

To print all the pages in the view, click **All**.

To print a range of pages, click **Page(s)**, and then enter the number of the first page in the range in the **From** box and the number of last page in the range in the **To** box.

6 In the **Copies** box, type the number of copies you want to print in the **Number of copies** box.

Set Up a Printer or Plotter

This topic assumes that your computer is already connected to a printer or plotter. If it isn't, consult the printer or plotter reference guide to help you connect your computer to the printer or plotter.

After your computer is connected to a printer or plotter, and before you can print views and reports, you have to set up your printer or plotter. If you've already done so or someone has done it for you, you can skip this topic. You can print on any printer or plotter supported by your system software.

If you use Microsoft Windows 95 or Microsoft Windows NT, you set up your printer for use with all your programs; you don't need to set it up just for Microsoft Project. You can, however, switch to a different printer—if you're connected to more than one printer, such as on a network—or change printer settings as you work in Microsoft Project. If your computer is connected to a network that includes several printers, those printers might have different capabilities (speeds, resolutions, colors, and so on). Microsoft Project enables you to specify which of those printers you want to use.

➢ **To select a printer or plotter and change its settings in Microsoft Project**

1 On the **File** menu, click **Print**.

2 In the **Name** box, click a printer or plotter name, and then click **Properties**.

3 Select the options you want to use, and then click **OK**.

4 Click **Close**.

SPECIFYING PRINT OPTIONS FOR VIEWS

Microsoft Project print options enable you to fine-tune the information that appears in printed views. This is not the same as specifying the core information that's displayed in views. To specify the core information that appears in a view, you select views, tables, filters, and details. (See Chapter 11, "Viewing the Information You Want: Using Views, Tables, Filters, and Details.") With print options for views, however, you can:

- Print information only about those tasks, resources, and assignments that occur within a specified date range.
- Print specific columns in sheet views.
- Print notes.
- Prevent blank pages from printing.
- Specify the number of weeks or months printed in the Calendar view.
- Print miniature previous and next month calendars in the Calendar view.

Specify the Date Range for a View

A number of views have timescales, such as the Gantt Chart view, the Task Usage view, the Resource Usage view, the Resource Graph, and the Calendar view. Normally when you print a timescale view, you print all the information that's available in that view for the entire project duration, from the project start date to the project finish date. Sometimes, however, you may want to print only the information that falls within a time period that's less than the project duration. In that case, you can specify the date range within which you want printed information.

You can't specify a date range for printing the PERT Chart, PA_PERT Entry Sheet, Task PERT, Task Sheet, or Resource Sheet views. (You can't print form views at all.)

➢ **To specify the date range for a view**

1   On the **View Bar**, click the view you want to print.

   To select a view that doesn't appear on the **View Bar**, click **More Views**, click the view you want in the **Views** list, and then click **Apply**.

2   On the **File** menu, click **Print**.

3   Under **Timescale**, click **Dates**.

4   In the **From** box, click the first date you want included in your view.

   In the **To** box, click the last date you want included in your view.

   If you specify a "to" date that falls in the middle of a page, Microsoft Project fills in the entire page, including information that occurs after the "to" date.

Print All Columns or Repeat Columns in a Sheet View

A printed sheet view (which is a view that contains columns of information, such as the Gantt Chart view or Resource Usage view) includes all portions of the view except for those columns that aren't completely visible on your screen. For example, if the Entry table is applied to the Gantt Chart view and only the Indicator, Task Name, and Duration columns are completely showing, then only those columns will be printed, along with the bar chart portion of the view. By moving the divider bar to the right, you can show—and print—more columns, but you still might not be able to print all of them and you might not print the bar chart portion at all. Instead of moving the divider bar, you can select an option that enables you to print all columns that are part of the view, even those that you'd have to scroll to or move the divider bar to see.

If a printed sheet view is more than one-page long, each successive page begins where the previous page leaves off. For example, if a 9-column Gantt Chart is 3-pages long, the first page may contain the first 6 columns, the second page may contain the last 3 columns and the first part of the bar chart, and the third page may contain the remaining part of the bar chart. On the second and third pages, you won't see which task name goes with each Gantt bar, because the task names will appear only on the first page. To help you avoid this problem and similar ones, Microsoft Project enables you to print the first several columns on each page.

➤ **To print all columns and repeat certain columns in a sheet view**

1   On the **View Bar**, click a sheet view.

    To select a sheet view that doesn't appear on the **View Bar**, click **More Views**, click the sheet view you want in the **Views** list, and then click **Apply**.

2   On the **File** menu, click **Page Setup**, and then click the **View** tab.

3   To print all columns, including those that are hidden behind a timescale (such as may occur in the Gantt Chart view or the Resource Usage view), select the **Print all sheet columns** check box.

4   To repeat a certain number of columns on each printed page, select the **Print first** check box, and then enter the number of columns in the **columns on all pages** box.

5   Click **Print**.

Print Notes with a View

To each task, resource, and assignment, you can add notes. In task views, such as the Gantt Chart view and the Calendar view, you can add notes to individual tasks. In resource views, such as the Resource Sheet view and the Resource Graph view, you can add notes to resources. In the Task Usage view, you can add notes to tasks and assignments. In the Resource Usage view, you can add notes to resources and assignments.

If notes about tasks, resources, or assignments have been added to your project plan, you can print those notes with the appropriate views. Notes are printed on the last page of a view. If you print a task view, task notes are printed. If you print a resource view, resource notes are printed. If you print the Task Usage view, both task and assignment notes are printed. If you print the Resource Usage view, both resource and assignment notes are printed.

> ➤ **To print notes with a view**

 1 On the **View Bar**, click a view.

 To select a view that doesn't appear on the **View Bar**, click **More Views**, click the view you want in the **Views** list, and then click **Apply**.

 2 On the **File** menu, click **Page Setup**, and then click the **View** tab.

 3 Select the **Print notes** check box.

Prevent Blank Pages from Printing in a View

A blank page is a page with no task, resource, or assignment information. By default, the Gantt Chart, PERT Chart, Task Usage, and Resource Usage views can be printed with blank pages. To save time and paper, you can prevent blank pages from printing. When you prevent blank pages from printing, blank pages appear shaded in the Print Preview window.

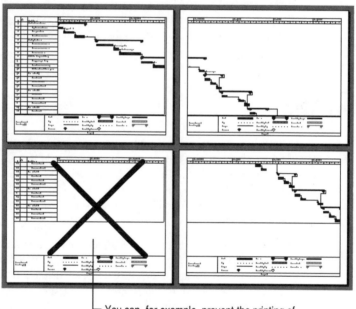

You can, for example, prevent the printing of Gantt Chart pages that have no Gantt bars.

➤ **To prevent blank pages from printing**

1   On the **View Bar**, click a view.

To select a view that doesn't appear on the **View Bar**, click **More Views**, click the view you want in the **Views** list, and then click **Apply**.

2   On the **File** menu, click **Page Setup**, and then click the **View** tab.

3   Clear the **Print blank pages** check box.

Specify the Number of Weeks or Months Printed in the Calendar View

The Calendar view displays the project schedule in a monthly calendar format, with rows of weeks. A printed Calendar view can be a useful way for task supervisors and resources to see which tasks need to be accomplished in a particular week or month. To make a printed Calendar even more useful, you can specify how many months or weeks you want to print on each page. You can print up to 2 months or up to 99 weeks on each page.

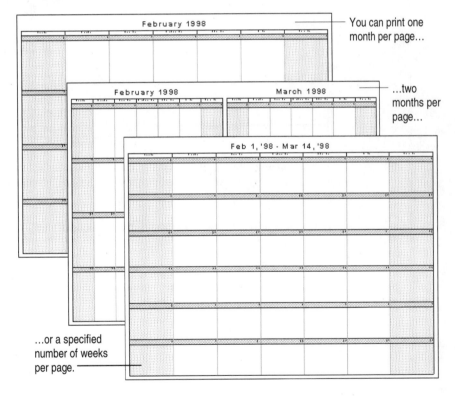

You can print one month per page...

...two months per page...

...or a specified number of weeks per page.

➢ **To specify the number of weeks or months printed in the Calendar view**

1 On the **View Bar**, click **Calendar**.

2 On the **File** menu, click **Page Setup**, and then click the **View** tab.

3 To specify months, click **Months per page**, and then click **1** or **2**.

 To specify weeks, click **Weeks per page**, and then enter the number of weeks you want to display.

Print the Previous and Next Month in a Calendar View

The calendars that you hang on your wall often show miniature versions of the previous and next month along with the current month. That way, you can quickly see a continuous connection between where you've been, where you are, and where you're going. The little next-month calendar is particularly helpful because it enables you to plan ahead.

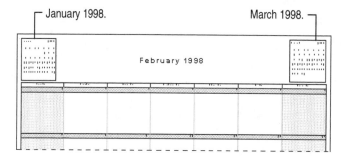

January 1998.
March 1998.

You can include this useful feature by choosing to print the previous and next month with the Calendar view. For example, if it's February, you can choose to also print miniature calendars of January and March.

➢ **To print the previous and next month in the Calendar view**

1 On the **View Bar**, click **Calendar**.

2 On the **File** menu, click **Page Setup**, and then click the **View** tab.

3 Select the **Print previous/next month calendars** check box.

SETTING UP PAGES FOR VIEWS

If you think of a printed view as being a framed picture, then print options affect the picture, and page setup features affect the frame. This section focuses on ways to affect the frame. It explains how to change page presentation by doing one or more of the following:

- Adjust the size of page margins.
- Add and remove page borders.
- Print pages in portrait orientation (vertically) or landscape orientation (horizontally).
- Add and remove headers, footers, and legends.
- Adjust page fit.
- Adjust the size of information that appears on a page (scaling).
- Insert and remove page breaks.

Adjust Page Margins in Views

Margins are the white space that surround the printed part of a page. There are four margins: top, bottom, left, and right. You can adjust each of these margins separately.

When you increase a margin, less information can be printed on a page, and a printed view may require more pages. When you decrease a margin, more information can be printed on a page.

➢ **To adjust page margins for a view**

1   On the **View Bar**, click a view.

    To select a view that doesn't appear on the **View Bar**, click **More Views**, click the view you want in the **Views** list, and then click **Apply**.

2   On the **File** menu, click **Page Setup**, and then click the **Margins** tab.

3   In the **Top**, **Bottom**, **Left**, and **Right** boxes, type the new margin settings.

Add and Remove Page Borders in Views

A page border is a rectangle drawn around all the information contained in a printed view. A border shows approximately where the margins begin; the larger the margins, the smaller the area encompassed by a border. You can choose to print a border around every page, print a border around outer pages (PERT Chart only), or print no border.

By default, Microsoft Project adds a border to each printed view. Only one border style is possible in Microsoft Project: a thin line.

➢ **To add page borders to a view**

1 On the **View Bar**, click a view.

   To select a view that doesn't appear on the **View Bar**, click **More Views**, click the view you want in the **Views** list, and then click **Apply**.

2 On the **File** menu, click **Page Setup**, and then click the **Margins** tab.

3 In the **Borders around** box, click **Every Page** or **Outer Pages** (for the PERT Chart only).

➢ **To remove page borders**

1 On the **View Bar**, click a view.

   To select a view that doesn't appear on the **View Bar**, click **More Views**, click the sheet view you want in the **Views** list, and then click **Apply**.

2 On the **File** menu, click **Page Setup**, and then click the **Margins** tab.

3 In the **Borders around** box, click **None**.

Print Pages Vertically or Horizontally in Views

Microsoft Project enables you to print pages vertically (portrait orientation) or horizontally (landscape orientation). For example, if all the columns of a sheet view won't fit on a vertically oriented page, you can try printing the view in landscape orientation.

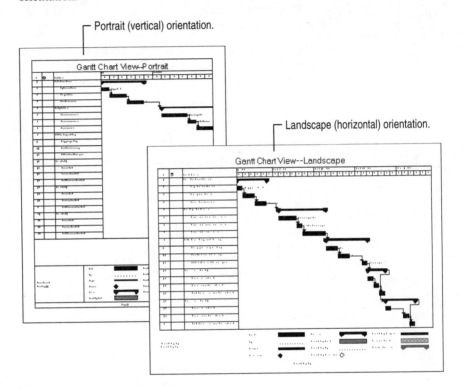

Portrait (vertical) orientation.

Landscape (horizontal) orientation.

> ## To change the page orientation
>
> 1 On the **View Bar**, click a view.
>
>   To select a view that doesn't appear on the **View Bar**, click **More Views**, click the view you want in the **Views** list, and then click **Apply**.
>
> 2 On the **File** menu, click **Page Setup**, and then click the **Page** tab.
>
> 3 Click **Portrait** (vertical) or **Landscape** (horizontal).

Add and Remove Headers, Footers, and Legends in Views

A *header* is text that gets printed at the top of every page. A *footer* is text that gets printed at the bottom of every page. Headers and footers make your printed views look more professional and often more useful. Examples of text that you can add to headers and footers are page numbers, the current date, the current time, the project file name, and your company name or company logo. You can also add a running page count (such as Page 1 of 3, Page 2 of 3, and Page 3 of 3).

A *legend* is an explanatory list that appears on every page of a printed view. Typically, a legend explains what each symbol in a view means. You can add legends only to the Gantt Chart, Calendar, and PERT Chart views.

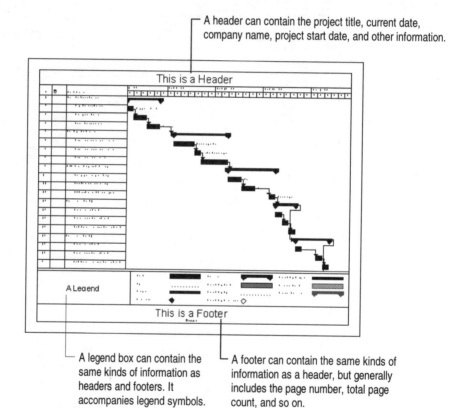

A header can contain the project title, current date, company name, project start date, and other information.

A legend box can contain the same kinds of information as headers and footers. It accompanies legend symbols.

A footer can contain the same kinds of information as a header, but generally includes the page number, total page count, and so on.

Add a Header, Footer, or Legend to a View

You can add text to a header, footer, or legend by typing it or pasting it. You can format the text before or after you add it. You can also insert graphic images. For information about inserting graphics into a header, footer, or legend, see Chapter 15, "Sharing Project Information with Other Programs and Projects."

You can add up to five lines of information to a header and up to three lines to a footer or legend. You can also adjust the width of the legend's text box from 0 to 5 inches.

> ## To add a header, footer, or legend to a view

1 On the **View Bar**, click the view you want.

   To select a view that doesn't appear on the **View Bar**, click **More Views**, click the view you want in the **Views** list, and then click **Apply**.

2 On the **File** menu, click **Page Setup**.

3 Click the **Header**, **Footer**, or **Legend** tab.

4 Under **Alignment**, click the **Left**, **Center**, or **Right** tab.

5 In the text box, type or paste text or insert or paste a graphic.

6 To add common information such as the page number, total page count, date, time, and file name, click the appropriate button below the text box.

   To add a running page count, type **of** between the Page Number symbol and the Total Number of Pages symbol:

   &[Page] **of** &[Pages]

   To see what kind of information you can add with a button, click the question mark in the upper-right-hand corner of the Page Setup dialog box, and then click the button.

7 To add information such as the project title, company name, project start date, and report name, select the information you want from the list below the text box, and then click **Add**.

8 To change the appearance of text, select the text you want to change in the text box, click $\boxed{\textbf{A}}$, choose the font options you want, and then click **OK**.

Remove a Header, Footer, or Legend from a View

A header, footer, or legend appears in a printed view only when you add information to the header, footer, or legend. To remove a header, footer, or legend, you only need to delete the text and/or graphical information that's in it.

When you delete the data in a legend's text box, only the legend's symbol box appears when you print the view. You can, however, prevent the entire legend from being printed by suppressing it when you print. When you suppress a legend, the information remains in the legend; the legend just doesn't get printed. You can also print a legend on a separate page after the view is printed.

➢ **To remove a header, footer, or legend from a view**

1   On the **View Bar**, click the view you want.

    To select a view that doesn't appear on the **View Bar**, click **More Views**, click the view you want in the **Views** list, and then click **Apply**.

2   On the **File** menu, click **Page Setup**.

3   Click the **Header**, **Footer**, or **Legend** tab.

4   Under **Alignment**, click the **Left**, **Center**, or **Right** tab.

5   Select the text or graphic, and then press DELETE.

➢ **To print a view without printing its legend**

1   On the **View Bar**, click the view you want to print.

    To select a view that doesn't appear on the **View Bar**, click **More Views**, click the view you want in the **Views** list, and then click **Apply**.

2   On the **File** menu, click **Page Setup**, and then click the **Legend** tab.

3   In the **Legend on** box, select **None**.

4   Click **Print**.

➢ **To print a legend on a separate page**

1   On the **View Bar**, click the view you want.

    To select a view that doesn't appear on the **View Bar**, click **More Views**, click the view you want in the **Views** list, and then click **Apply**.

2   On the **File** menu, click **Page Setup**, and then click the **Legend** tab.

3   In the **Legend on** box, select **Legend page**.

4   Click **Print**.

Adjust Page Fit in a View

When printed, the pages of some views fit together like pieces of a jigsaw puzzle: You have to place the pages correctly in a matrix of rows and columns to see the entire view. An example of a view that gets printed in jigsawlike pages is the Gantt Chart view (especially when it contains many tasks and linked Gantt bars).

A view that prints on several rows and columns of pages can be unwieldy. To make it easier to manage, you can reduce the size of the printed view by specifying how many pages tall and wide the printed view will be. If your printed view is, for example, three pages tall and two pages wide (for a total of 6 pages), you could reduce it by changing the setting to two pages tall. The view will fit on fewer pages, and the information on each page will decrease in size proportionately.

You can only reduce the number of pages tall and wide on which a view prints; you can't increase the number of pages. For example, you can't enlarge a three-page view to five pages. You can, however, enlarge a view by adjusting the size of information that appears on a printed page.

➢ **To adjust page fit in a view**

1   On the **View Bar**, click any view except the Calendar or Resource Graph.

    To select a view that doesn't appear on the **View Bar**, click **More Views**, click the view you want in the **Views** list, and then click **Apply**.

2   On the **File** menu, click **Page Setup**, and then click the **Page** tab.

3   Under **Scaling**, click **Fit to**.

4   In the **pages wide by** box, type the number of pages you want.

5   In the **tall** box, type the number of pages you want.

Adjust the Size of Information on a Printed Page in a View

For any number of reasons, you may want to change the size of the information that appears on each page of a view. If the information is difficult to read, you can increase its size. If the view prints on too many pages, you can decrease the size of the information and reduce the number of pages.

The default setting is 100 percent. If you decrease the setting to, say, 60 percent, you'll decrease the size of the information by 40 percent, print more information on each page, and perhaps print fewer pages. If you increase the setting to, say, 150 percent, you'll increase the size of the information by 50 percent, print less information on each page, and perhaps print more pages.

➢ **To adjust the size of information on a printed page**

1   On the **File** menu, click **Page Setup**, and then click the **Page** tab.

2   Under **Scaling**, click **Adjust to**.

3   In the **% normal size** box, type the percentage at which you want information to appear on your printed pages.

Insert a Page Break into a View

When a view prints on more than one page, information that should logically be together on the same page may appear on different pages. For example, a summary task might appear at the bottom of one page and its subtasks at the top of the next page. Microsoft Project automatically inserts page breaks after information on a page reaches the bottom margin.

To keep certain information together, you can insert page breaks exactly where you want them. That may mean that extra white space appears at the bottom of some pages—perhaps causing the view to print on more pages than it otherwise would have—but the convenience of seeing certain pieces of information together on one page may be worth the tradeoff.

You can insert manual page breaks into sheet views only. You can't insert manual page breaks into form views, the Resource Graph view, the Calendar view, the Task PERT view, and the PERT Chart view. You can, however, adjust page breaks in the PERT Chart view so that PERT boxes don't cross page breaks. (See Chapter 12, "Making Your Project Look the Way You Want.") By default, a page break that you insert appears as a dotted line that you can easily identify.

➢ **To insert a page break**

1   On the **View Bar**, click a sheet view.

To select a sheet view that doesn't appear on the **View Bar**, click **More Views**, and then click the sheet view you want.

2   In the **Task Name** or **Resource Name** field, select the task or resource that you want to appear at the top of a new page.

3   On the **Insert** menu, click **Page Break**.

Remove a Page Break from a View

If you inserted a manual page break in a view and then decided that you don't want it, or you want to break pages in a different place, you can remove the page break. You can remove manual page breaks individually or all at once. By default, manually inserted page breaks appear as dotted lines for easy identification.

You can also leave the manual page breaks in a view, but print the view without the page breaks by suppressing the page breaks when printing. For example, you might want to print a view on the fewest possible pages.

➤ **To remove an individual page break**

1   In the **Task Name** or **Resource Name** field, select the task or resource with which the page break is associated.

2   On the **Insert** menu, click **Remove Page Break**.

➤ **To remove all manual page breaks at the same time**

1   Select all the tasks in your view by clicking any column heading.

2   On the **Insert** menu, click **Remove All Page Breaks**.

➤ **To suppress page breaks when printing**

1   On the **File** menu, click **Print**.

2   Clear the **Manual Page Breaks** check box.

CHANGING THE CORE INFORMATION THAT APPEARS IN A VIEW

If none of the existing views contains the information you want to print or has a suitable appearance, you can edit an existing view, modify a copy of an existing view, or create a view from scratch (but based on an existing view). You also have many ways to change the appearance of a view.

For information about creating a view or modifying an existing view, see Chapter 11, "Viewing the Information You Want: Using Views, Tables, Filters, and Details." For information about changing the appearance of a view, see Chapter 12, "Making Your Project Look the Way You Want."

SPECIFYING PRINT OPTIONS FOR REPORTS

Microsoft Project print options enable you to fine-tune the information that appears in printed reports. This is not the same as specifying the core task, resource, or assignment information that appears in a report. To specify the core information that appears in a report, you select a report, table, and filter. With print options for reports, however, you can:

- Print notes, objects, work, and other additional information in task and resource reports.
- Group information by time interval in a task, resource, or crosstab report.
- Print column totals in a task or resource report.
- Print summary tasks in a task or crosstab report.
- Change the rows and columns in a crosstab report.
- Print the first column on every page of a crosstab report.
- Print column and row totals in a crosstab report.
- Specify the date range for a crosstab report.
- Print a monthly calendar for a specific resource.

Print Notes, Objects, Work, and Other Details in Task and Resource Reports

With most reports, you can print not only the core information in the report but additional information as well. The kind of additional information you can print depends on the kind of report.

With this kind of report	You can print this additional information
Task	notes, objects from other programs that are attached to tasks, predecessor tasks for each task, successor tasks for each task, assignment schedule fields, assignment cost fields, and assignment work fields
Resource	notes, objects from other programs that are attached to tasks, working and nonworking information from the base and resource calendars, cost rate information, assignment schedule fields, assignment cost fields, and assignment work fields

There are three resource reports in Microsoft Project: Overbudget Resources, Overallocated Resources, and Who Does What.

Some task and resource reports can include only some kinds of additional information. The Cash Flow, Project Summary, and Working Days reports can't include any additional information.

➢ **To print notes, objects, and so on in a task or resource report**

1 On the **View** menu, click **Reports**.

2 Click the report type you want, and then click **Select**.

If you chose Custom as the report type, click a report in the **Reports** list, click **Edit**, and then go to step 4.

3 Click the report you want, and then click **Edit**.

4 Click the **Details** tab.

5 If the report is a task report, then in the **Task** box, select the **Notes**, **Objects**, **Predecessors**, or **Successors** check box.

If the report is a resource report, then in the **Resource** box, select the **Notes**, **Objects**, **Calendar**, or **Cost Rates** check box.

6 In the **Assignment** box, select the **Notes**, **Schedule**, **Cost**, or **Work** check box.

Group Information by Time Interval in a Task, Resource, or Crosstab Report

In most reports, information is presented in a continuous list. You see unbroken information for the entire project. When the list is short, you can scan it and easily pick out relevant dates. When the list is long, however, scanning it and picking out important dates can be particularly difficult. To read information in a long report more easily and to focus on information in specific time periods, you can group the information by time periods you specify.

When you group information by time period, a date separates one group of information from another. For example, if you group information into one-week periods in the Unstarted Tasks report, the report will look something like this:

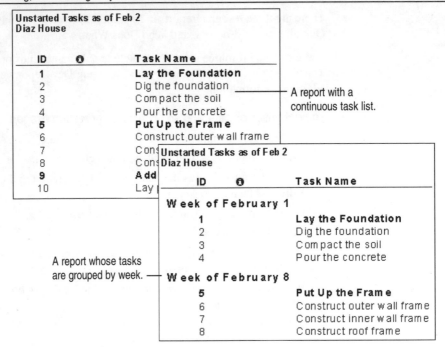

A report with a continuous task list.

A report whose tasks are grouped by week.

In addition to changing the basic time period unit, such as years, months, weeks, and days, you can also change the count of the time period. For example, in the Unstarted Tasks report, you can group information into one-week periods, two-week periods, three-week periods, and so on.

The default time period for most task and resource reports is the entire project. However, for the Tasks In Progress report and the Completed Tasks report, the default time period is months. Changing the time period may affect the number of pages on which a report is printed.

➤ **To change the time period for grouping information in a task or resource report**

1 On the **View** menu, click **Reports**.

2 Click the report type you want, and then click **Select**.

   If you chose Custom as the report type, click a report in the **Reports** list, click **Edit**, and then go to step 4.

3 Click the report you want, and then click **Edit**.

4 Click the **Definition** tab.

5 In the **Period** box, click the time period you want.

6 In the **Count** box, click the number of time periods you want reported as a single unit.

   The Count box is not active for the time period Entire Project.

When you change the time period in a crosstab report, each column represents the duration of the time period you specify. For example, if you select days as the time period and 3 as the number of time periods in each column, each column will represent 3 days.

You can change the time period in any of the Microsoft Project crosstab reports, which are the Cash Flow, Crosstab, Resource Usage, Task Usage, and Who Does What When reports. The default time period for the first four crosstab reports is weeks. However, for the Who Does What When report, the default time period is days.

➤ **To change the time period in a crosstab report**

1 On the **View** menu, click **Reports**.

2 Click **Custom**, and then click **Select**.

3 In the **Reports** list, click the name of a crosstab report, and then click **Edit**.

4 Click the **Definition** tab.

5 In the **Column** box, enter the number of time periods you want in each column.

6 In the box to the right of the **Column** box, click the time period you want.

Print Column Totals in a Task or Resource Report

By default, the total of the values in a column is not printed in a task or resource report. For example, if a resource report includes a Work column, that column will only show the number of hours worked by each resource; it will not show the total number of hours worked by all resources. You can, however, choose to print column totals. (You can only print column totals for those columns in which it makes sense to add the values in the column. For example, there's no total printed for a column that contains start dates.)

➤ **To print column totals in a task or resource report**

1 On the **View** menu, click **Reports**.

2 Click the report type you want, and then click **Select**.

   If you chose Custom as the report type, click a report in the **Reports** list, click **Edit**, and then go to step 4.

3 Click the report you want, and then click **Edit**.

4 Click the **Details** tab.

5 Select the **Show totals** check box.

Print Summary Tasks in a Task or Crosstab Report

A number of task and crosstab reports don't include summary tasks by default (some do). Including summary tasks is a good way to group tasks visually and to see which tasks belong to the same project phase. If you want, you can choose to print summary tasks in some task and crosstab reports. Each summary task is printed above the group of subtasks that belong to the summary task.

➢ **To print summary tasks in a task or crosstab report**

1 On the **View** menu, click **Reports**.

2 Click the report type you want, and then click **Select**.

If you chose Custom as the report type, click a report in the **Reports** list, click **Edit**, and then go to step 4.

3 Click the report you want, and then click **Edit**.

4 To print summary tasks in a task report, click the **Definition** tab.

To print summary tasks in a crosstab report, click the **Details** tab.

5 For a task report, select the **Show summary tasks** check box.

For a crosstab report, select the **Summary tasks** check box in the **Show** box.

Change the Rows and Columns in a Crosstab Report

A crosstab report consists of rows and columns of information. Each row contains information about a single item. Each column represents a period of time. The intersection of a row with a column shows you the total value of the item in the time period represented by the column.

For example, suppose a row contains the number of hours worked by a resource and each column represents a period of 1 day. Then the intersection of a row with a column shows you the number of hours of work the resource has on a specific day.

Each crosstab report comes with default rows and columns. For instance, by default the Resource Usage report shows resource work broken down by 1-week periods. To print different information in the rows and/or to break down the information by a different time period, you can change the rows and columns in a crosstab report.

The rows in a crosstab report can contain task information, resource information, or both. After you decide whether a report's rows will contain information about tasks or resources, you can choose the kind of task or resource information you want. For example, you can select Resources as the row, Work as the row information, and Days as the column to print a report showing the number of hours worked each day by each resource.

The Cash Flow, Crosstab, Resource Usage, Task Usage, and Who Does What When reports are the five crosstab reports available in Microsoft Project.

➤ **To change the row and column definitions in a crosstab report**

1   On the **View** menu, click **Reports**.

2   Click **Custom**, and then click **Select**.

3   In the **Reports** list, click the name of a crosstab report, and then click **Edit**.

4   Click the **Definition** tab.

5   In the **Column** boxes, enter the number of time units each column will represent, and then click the unit of time you want.

6   In the **Row** box, click **Tasks** or **Resources**.

7   In the box to the right of the **Row** box, click the information you want printed for the rows.

Print the First Column on Every Page of a Crosstab Report

If a crosstab report has more columns than can fit on one page, the spillover columns will be printed on other pages. On the second and third pages, you won't see which task or resource name goes with each row of information, because the task and resource names will appear only on the first page. To help you avoid this problem, Microsoft Project enables you to print the first column on each page of a crosstab report.

The Cash Flow, Crosstab, Resource Usage, Task Usage, and Who Does What When reports are the five crosstab reports available in Microsoft Project.

➤ **To print the first column on every page of a crosstab report**

1   On the **View** menu, click **Reports**.

2   Click **Custom**, and then click **Select**.

3   In the **Reports** list, click the name of a crosstab report, and then click **Edit**.

4   Click the **Details** tab.

5   Select the **Repeat first column on every page** check box.

This is the default option on most crosstab reports.

Print Column or Row Totals in a Crosstab Report

By default, the total of the values in a row or column is not printed in a crosstab report. The total for a column shows you the total value of a particular item for all tasks or resources in a particular time period. The total for a row shows you the total value of an item for a particular task or resource over the course of the entire project (or the date range you specify in the Print dialog box).

For example, if a crosstab report shows the number of hours worked by each resource each day, then a column total tells you how many hours all resources worked on a particular day, and a row total tells you how many hours a particular resource will work over the course of the entire project (or the date range you specify in the Print dialog box).

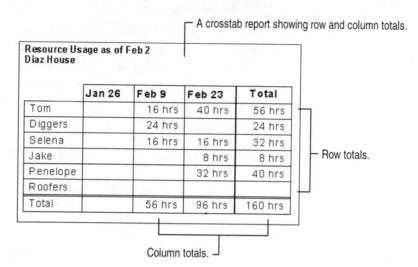

A crosstab report showing row and column totals.

Resource Usage as of Feb 2 Diaz House	Jan 26	Feb 9	Feb 23	Total
Tom		16 hrs	40 hrs	56 hrs
Diggers		24 hrs		24 hrs
Selena		16 hrs	16 hrs	32 hrs
Jake			8 hrs	8 hrs
Penelope			32 hrs	40 hrs
Roofers				
Total		56 hrs	96 hrs	160 hrs

Row totals.

Column totals.

The Cash Flow, Crosstab, Resource Usage, Task Usage, and Who Does What When reports are the five crosstab reports available in Microsoft Project.

> ### To print column or row totals in a crosstab report
> 1 On the **View** menu, click **Reports**.
> 2 Click **Custom**, and then click **Select**.
> 3 In the **Reports** list, click the name of a crosstab report, and then click **Edit**.
> 4 Click the **Details** tab.
> 5 Select the **Row totals** check box, the **Column totals** check box, or both.
>
>   In some crosstab reports, these boxes are selected by default.

Specify the Date Range for a Crosstab Report

The time-period columns of a crosstab report make up a kind of timescale, such as you find in the Gantt Chart view, the Resource Usage view, and other views. Normally when you print a crosstab report, you print all the information that's available in the report, from the project start date to the project finish date. Sometimes, however, you may want to print only the information that falls between a time period that's less than the project duration. In that case, you can specify the date range within which you want printed information.

The Cash Flow, Crosstab, Resource Usage, Task Usage, and Who Does What When reports are the five crosstab reports available in Microsoft Project.

➢ **To specify the date range in a crosstab report**

1   On the **View** menu, click **Reports**.

2   Click **Custom**, and then click **Select**.

3   In the **Reports** list, click the name of a crosstab report, and then click **Print**.

4   Under **Timescale**, click **Dates**.

5   In the **From** box, click the first date you want included in the report.

    In the **To** box, click the last date you want included in the report.

Print a Monthly Calendar for a Specific Resource

A monthly calendar shows the tasks that occur within a given month. A monthly calendar for a specific resource shows only those tasks assigned to the resource, which can help you and the resource keep track of the tasks that need to be accomplished each month. Although Microsoft Project doesn't include any predefined monthly calendar reports, you can create a monthly calendar report for a specific resource.

A monthly calendar report showing the tasks for one resource.

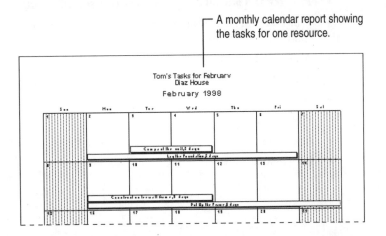

➢ **To print a monthly calendar for a specific resource**

1 On the **View** menu, click **Reports**.

2 Click **Custom**, and then click **Select**.

3 In the **Reports** list, click the name of the monthly calendar report you want to print, and then click **Edit**.

If you're creating a new monthly calendar report, click **New**, click **Monthly Calendar**, and then click **OK**.

4 If you're creating a new report, type a name for the report in the **Name** box.

5 In the **Filter** box, click **Using Resource**.

6 In the **Calendar** box, click the calendar you want to use for the resource.

You can use the Standard, 24 Hours, or Night Shift calendars or calendars you created yourself.

7 Click **OK**.

8 Click **Print**, and then click **OK**.

9 In the **Show tasks using** box, click the name of the resource for whom you want to print the monthly calendar.

SETTING UP PAGES FOR REPORTS

Reports are preformatted and ready to be printed. But you can fine-tune report-page appearance to suit your needs. This section focuses on ways to change the page presentation of reports. It explains how to:

- Adjust the size of page margins.
- Add and remove page borders.
- Print borders around details in a task or resource report.
- Print pages in portrait orientation (vertically) or landscape orientation (horizontally).
- Add and remove headers and footers.
- Adjust the size of information that appears on a page (scaling).
- Change the sort order.
- Print gridlines.
- Insert page breaks.
- Format report text.

Adjust Page Margins in a Report

Margins are the white space that surround the printed part of a page. There are four margins: top, bottom, left, and right. You can adjust each of these margins separately.

When you increase a margin, less information can be printed on a page, and a printed report may require more pages. When you decrease a margin, more information can be printed on a page.

➢ **To adjust page margins for a report**

1 On the **View** menu, click **Reports**.

2 Click the report type you want, and then click **Select**.

3 Click the report you want to print, and then click **Select**.

  If you chose Custom as the report type in step 2, click **Setup**, and then go to step 5.

4 Click **Page Setup**.

5 Click the **Margins** tab.

6 In the **Top**, **Bottom**, **Left**, and **Right** boxes, type the new margin settings.

Add or Remove Page Borders in a Report

A page border is a rectangle drawn around all the information contained in a report. A border shows approximately where the margins begin; the larger the margins, the smaller the area encompassed by a border. Only one border style is possible in Microsoft Project: a thin line. You can choose to print a border around every page or print no border.

➢ **To add or remove page borders in a report**

1 On the **View** menu, click **Reports**.

2 Click the report type you want, and then click **Select**.

3 Click the report you want, and then click **Select**.

  If you chose Custom as the report type in step 2, click **Setup**, and then go to step 5.

4 Click **Page Setup**.

5 Click the **Margins** tab.

6 In the **Borders around** box, click **Every Page** or **None**.

Print Borders Around Details in a Task or Resource Report

Details are notes, graphics objects imported from other programs, cost fields, work fields, successor tasks, predecessor tasks, and other pieces of information that aren't part of the core information that are normally included in a report. When you choose to include details in a report, you can print a border around them.

A task report showing borders drawn around details.

You can print borders around details in task and resource reports. You can't print borders around details in crosstab reports (the Cash Flow, Crosstab, Resource Usage, Task Usage, and Who Does When reports).

> **To print a border around details in a task or resource report**

1. On the **View** menu, click **Reports**.

2. Click the report type you want, and then click **Select**.

   If you chose Custom as the report type, click a report in the **Reports** list, click **Edit**, and then go to step 4.

3. Click the report you want, and then click **Edit**.

4. Click the **Details** tab.

5. Select the **Border around details** check box.

Print Pages Vertically or Horizontally in a Report

Microsoft Project enables you to print pages vertically (portrait orientation) or horizontally (landscape orientation). For example, if all the columns of a report won't fit on a vertically oriented page, you can try printing the report in landscape orientation.

➢ **To change the page orientation**

1 On the **View** menu, click **Reports**.

2 Click the report type you want, and then click **Select**.

3 Click the report you want, and then click **Select**.

   If you chose Custom as the report type in step 2, click **Setup**, and then go to step 5.

4 Click **Page Setup**.

5 Click the **Page** tab.

6 Click **Portrait** (vertical) or **Landscape** (horizontal).

Add and Remove Headers and Footers in a Report

A *header* is text that gets printed at the top of every page. A *footer* is text that gets printed at the bottom of every page. Headers and footers make your printed reports look more professional and often more useful. Examples of text that you can add to headers and footers are page numbers, the current date, the current time, the project file name, and your company name or company logo. You can also add a running page count (such as Page 1 of 3, Page 2 of 3, and Page 3 of 3).

Add a Header or Footer to a Report

You can add text to a header or footer by typing it or pasting it. You can format text before or after you add it. You can also insert graphic images. For information about inserting graphics into a header or footer, see Chapter 15, "Sharing Project Information with Other Programs and Projects."

You can add up to five lines of information to a header and up to three lines to a footer.

➤ **To add a header or footer to a report**

1   On the **View** menu, click **Reports**.

2   Click the report type you want, and then click **Select**.

3   Click the report you want, and then click **Select**.

   If you chose Custom as the report type in step 2, click **Setup**, and then go to step 5.

4   Click **Page Setup**.

5   Click the **Header** or **Footer** tab.

6   Under **Alignment**, click the **Left**, **Center**, or **Right** tab.

7   In the text box, type or paste text, add document or project information, or insert or paste a graphic.

8   To change the appearance of text, select the text you want to change in the text box, click $\boxed{\textbf{A}}$, choose the font options you want, and then click **OK**.

9   To add common information such as the page number, total page count, date, time, and file name, click the appropriate button below the text box.

   To add a running page count, type **of** between the Page Number symbol and the Total Number of Pages symbol:

   &[Page] **of** &[Pages]

   To see what kind of information you can add with a button, click the question mark in the upper-right-hand corner of the Page Setup dialog box, and then click the button.

10 To add information such as the project title, company name, project start date, and report name, select the information you want from the list below the text box, and then click **Add**.

Remove a Header or Footer from a Report

A header or footer appears in a report only when you add information to the header or footer. To remove a header or footer, you only need to delete the text and/or graphical information that's in it.

➢ **To remove a header or footer from a report**

1   On the **View** menu, click **Reports**.

2   Click the report type you want, and then click **Select**.

3   Click the report information you want, and then click **Select**.

If you chose Custom as the report type in step 2, click **Setup**, and then go to step 5.

4   Click **Page Setup**.

5   Click the **Header** or **Footer** tab.

6   Under **Alignment**, click the **Left**, **Center**, or **Right** tab.

7   Select the text or graphic, and then press DELETE.

Adjust the Size of Information on a Printed Page in a Report

You may want to change the size of the information that appears on each page of a report. If the information is difficult to read, you can increase its size. If the report prints on too many pages, you can decrease the size of the information and reduce the number of pages.

The default setting is 100 percent. If you decrease the setting to, say, 60 percent, you'll decrease the size of the information by 40 percent, print more information on each page, and perhaps print fewer pages. If you increase the setting to, say, 150 percent, you'll increase the size of the information by 50 percent, print less information on each page, and perhaps print more pages.

➢ **To adjust the size of information on a printed page**

1   On the **View** menu, click **Reports**.

2   Click the report type you want, and then click **Select**.

3   Click the report you want, and then click **Select**.

If you chose Custom as the report type in step 2, click **Setup**, and then go to step 5.

4   Click **Page Setup**

5   Click the **Page** tab.

6   Click **Adjust to**.

7   In the **% normal size** box, type the percentage at which you want information to appear on your printed pages.

Change the Sort Order in a Task, Resource, or Crosstab Report

By default, Microsoft Project lists tasks and resources in ascending order by ID number. But you may want to see tasks or resources in a different order. If, for example, you want to decrease the project length, you may want to list tasks from the longest duration to the shortest, to focus on reducing the longest durations first. Or, you may want to sort resources by how much they're overallocated.

The sorting criteria you can choose are the Microsoft Project task and resource fields that are available. For instance, if you want to sort tasks by duration, you specify that the Duration field control the sort order.

➤ **To change the sort order in a task, resource, or crosstab report**

1   On the **View** menu, click **Reports**.

2   Click the report type you want, and then click **Select**.

 If you chose Custom as the report type, click a report in the **Reports** list, click **Edit**, and then go to step 4.

3   Click the report you want, and then click **Edit**.

4   Click the **Sort** tab.

5   In the **Sort by** box, click the field you want to use as your primary sort criterion.

6   Click **Ascending** or **Descending**.

7   If you want to sort by a second and third sort criterion, click the field you want in the appropriate **Then by** box, and then click **Ascending** or **Descending**.

Print Gridlines Between Details in a Report

Having rows of information without horizontal lines separating one row of details from another can make it difficult to read the information in a report. A simple way to make it easier to read a report is to insert horizontal gridlines between details. You can print gridlines between any details in a task, resource, or crosstab report. In a task or resource report, gridlines separate task, resource, and assignment details, such as notes, objects, cost fields, work fields, and successor and predecessor tasks. In a crosstab report, gridlines separate resource details, task details, or both.

➢ **To print gridlines between details in a task or resource report**

1   On the **View** menu, click **Reports**.

2   Click the report type you want, and then click **Select**.

   If you chose Custom as the report type, click a report in the **Reports** list, click **Edit**, and then go to step 4.

3   Click the report you want, and then click **Edit**.

4   Click the **Details** tab.

5   Select the **Gridlines between details** check box.

The Cash Flow, Crosstab, Resource Usage, Task Usage, and Who Does What When reports are the five crosstab reports available in Microsoft Project.

➢ **To print gridlines in a crosstab report**

1   On the **View** menu, click **Reports**.

2   Click **Custom**, and then click **Select**.

3   In the **Reports** list, click the name of a crosstab report, and then click **Edit**.

4   Click the **Details** tab.

5   In the **Gridlines** box, select the **Between tasks** check box, the **Between resources** check box, or both.

Insert a Page Break in a Report

You can't insert a page break directly into a report. However, page breaks inserted in a view appear in reports that contain the same kind of information as that view. For example, if you select a task and then insert a page break in the Task Sheet view, the page break will occur before that task in the Task Report.

When you filter or sort information in a view or report, each page break remains with the task or resource selected when you inserted the page break. For example, if a task is not displayed when you apply a filter, the page break associated with that task does not appear in the view or report.

Format Report Text

On one day you may need to focus on critical tasks. On another day, you may want to point out overallocated resources to your supervisor. To visually distinguish a class of tasks or resources—or simply to change its appearance to suit your needs—you can change the appearance of tasks and resources in predefined categories.

When you change the appearance of a category of tasks or resources, you change the appearance of all the information for each task or resource in that category, all at once. For example, if you make a category of tasks on the Unstarted Tasks report bold, the entire row of text for each task in the category appears bold. The formatting you apply to text in one report does not transfer to another report.

You change the appearance of task and resource information by changing the font, font style, font size, and color. For information about fonts, font styles, and font sizes, see Chapter 12, "Making Your Project Look the Way You Want."

➢ **To format report text**

1 On the **View** menu, click **Reports**.

2 Click the report type you want, and then click **Select**.

   If you chose Custom as the report type, click a report in the **Reports** list, click **Edit**, and then go to step 4.

3 Click the report you want to format, and then click **Edit**.

   If you clicked Project Summary or Working Days, go to step 5.

4 Click **Text**.

5 In the **Item to Change** box, click the task or resource category whose text you want to format.

6 Select the font, font style, size, and color you want.

7 To underline the item, select the **Underline** check box.

8 To shade the item, select the **Shade** check box.

CHANGING THE CORE INFORMATION THAT APPEARS IN A REPORT

Each report shows a default set of information in its rows and columns. But sometimes you may want to print a report with a different set of information. Microsoft Project provides you with several ways to include exactly the information you want in each report. For instance, you can:

- Change the report name to one that's more suitable to the kind of information that's contained in the report.
- Change the table in a task or resource report.
- Change the filter in a report
- Modify a copy of a report.
- Create a report.
- Delete a report.

You can only change the appearance of text in the Base Calendar and Project Summary reports. You can't change the information they contain.

Change the Report Name

Some predefined report names may not tell you clearly what kind of information is contained in the report. Or, if you modified a report, you may want to give it a name that reflects the new information that it contains. In these situations and others, you can change the report name.

When you change a report name, you give the name to a copy of the original report. The copy, with the name you've given it, is added to the list of custom reports (in the Custom Reports dialog box). You do not delete the original report.

You can't change the names of the Project Summary, Working Days, or Base Calendar reports.

➤ **To change the report name**

1   On the **View** menu, click **Reports**.

2   Click the report type you want, and then click **Select**.

     If you chose Custom as the report type, click a report in the **Reports** list, click **Edit**, and then go to step 4.

3   Click the report you want to rename, and then click **Edit**.

4   Click the **Definition** tab.

5   In the **Name** box, type the new report name.

Change the Table in a Task or Resource Report

A *table* consists of a set of columns of related information. Each column displays a particular kind of information. A default table is attached to each task and resource report. For example, the Summary table is attached to the Completed Tasks report. To see other columns of information, you can apply a different table to the report. When you apply a different table to a report, the new table replaces the old table.

When you replace one table with another, you do not add information to or remove information from your project. You only change the project information displayed at the moment. Also, the list of tasks or resources on the report remains the same. Only the other columns of information change.

You can't apply tables to crosstab reports or to the Project Summary, Working Days, and Base Calendar reports.

➢ **To change the table in a task or resource report**

1   On the **View** menu, click **Reports**.

2   Click the report type you want, and then click **Select**.

    If you chose Custom as the report type, click a report in the **Reports** list, click **Edit**, and then go to step 4.

3   Click the report you want, and then click **Edit**.

4   Click the **Definition** tab.

5   In the **Table** box, click the table you want to apply.

Change the Filter in a Report

A *filter* is a set of criteria for displaying a specific group of related tasks, resources, or assignments. There's a default filter attached to each report. For example, the default filter for the Unstarted Tasks report is the Unstarted Tasks filter. If you want to show tasks or resources that meet a different set of criteria, you need to apply a different filter.

You can apply the filter that displays only those tasks or resources that share certain characteristics. For each filter, you can specify whether the filter displays only those tasks or resources that meet the filter criteria (and hides the tasks or resources that don't) or highlights the tasks or resources of interest in gray bands (while still displaying the other tasks or resources).

You can apply filters to task, resource, crosstab, and monthly calendar reports. The crosstab reports are the Cash Flow, Crosstab, Resource Usage, Task Usage, and Who Does What When reports. Specific reports you can't apply filters to are the Project Summary, Working Days, and Base Calendar reports.

> **To change the filter in a task or resource report**

1 On the **View** menu, click **Reports**.

2 Click the report type you want, and then click **Select**.

If you chose Custom as the report type, click a report in the **Reports** list, click **Edit**, and then go to step 4.

3 Click the report you want, and then click **Edit**.

4 Click the **Definition** tab.

5 In the **Filter** box, click the filter you want to apply.

6 To highlight filtered information, select the **Highlight** check box on the **Definition** tab.

Because Microsoft Project doesn't include any predefined monthly calendar reports, you must first create a monthly calendar report before you can apply a filter to it. When you create a monthly calendar report, you specify its default filter. Afterward, you can change its filter when you want to show a different set of tasks or resources.

> **To change the filter in a monthly calendar report**

1 On the **View** menu, click **Reports**.

2 Click **Custom**, and then click **Select**.

3 In the **Reports** list, click the name of a monthly calendar report, and then click **Edit**.

4 In the **Filter** box, click the filter you want to apply.

Modify a Copy of a Report

The predefined reports that come with Microsoft Project are designed to include the information you're most likely to want, in useful formats. However, if none of the predefined reports meet your information or formatting needs, but the report you want is similar to a predefined report, you can modify a copy of the existing report and save the modified version under a different name.

When you modify a copy of a report, the original, predefined report remains unchanged. You can create a copy of any predefined or custom report. The copy you create is displayed in the Reports list of the Custom Reports dialog box.

➢ **To copy a report**

1 On the **View** menu, click **Reports**.

2 Click **Custom**, and then click **Select**.

3 In the **Reports** list, click the report you want to copy.

4 Click **Copy**.

5 If you want to change the copied report's name, type a new name in the **Name** box.

6 If you're copying a task, resource, or crosstab report, specify the report content by entering the information you want in the appropriate boxes and selecting the options you want on the **Definition** and **Details** tabs.

   If you're copying a monthly calendar report, specify the report content by entering the information you want in the appropriate boxes and selecting the options you want on the **Monthly Calendar Report Definition** dialog box.

Create a Report

The predefined reports that come with Microsoft Project are designed to include the information you're most likely to want, in useful formats. However, if the report you want differs significantly from existing reports, you can create a new report. When you create a new report, though, you're constrained to basing the new report on one of the four basic report types: task, resource, crosstab, or monthly calendar. You can't make a new report look any way you want it to.

When you create a report, the new report is displayed in the Reports list of the Custom Reports dialog box.

➢ **To create a report**

1 On the **View** menu, click **Reports**.

2 Click **Custom**, and then click **Select**.

3 Click **New**.

4 Select a report type, and then click **OK**.

5 If you're creating a task, resource, or crosstab report, specify the report content by entering the information you want in the appropriate boxes and selecting the options you want on the **Definition** and **Details** tabs.

   If you're creating a monthly calendar report, specify the report content by entering the information you want in the appropriate boxes and selecting the options you want on the **Monthly Calendar Report Definition** dialog box.

Delete a Report

If you don't need a particular report, you can delete it. When you delete a report, you delete it from the project file only. A copy of it continues to be stored in the Microsoft Project global file, Global.mpt. Deleting a report does not delete information from your project file.

You can delete any predefined or custom report using the Organizer. Deleting a report in this way removes it from the project file, but not from the Global.mpt file.

➢ **To delete a report**

1   On the **View** menu, click **Reports**.

2   Click **Custom**, and then click **Select**.

3   Click **Organizer**.

4   On the right-hand side, in the list of reports available to the current project, click the report you want to delete.

The left-hand side of the Organizer lists reports that are available to all projects. Do not select a report from the GLOBAL.MPT list on the left unless you want to permanently delete it from Microsoft Project.

5   Click **Delete**.

6   Click **Yes** to confirm the deletion.

All predefined reports are listed in both the GLOBAL.MPT list and the project list. If you delete a predefined report, or any report, that's included in both files from the project file only, Microsoft Project will continue to display the report in the Reports list in the Custom Reports dialog box. Microsoft Project will remove a report from the Reports list only after it's deleted from both the GLOBAL.MPT list and the project list.

Part 5

Exchanging Information with Other Projects, Other Programs, and the World Wide Web

Sharing project information is necessary in every part of your job. At the beginning of a project, discussions with others help you to develop project goals and determine the tasks required to fulfill those goals. Later on, feedback enables you to track project progress. If you're managing several projects at the same time, you need to be able to collect and organize a great deal of project information to stay on top of each project. If project participants—supervisors, clients, or team member—require up-to-date project information, you need to be able to get them the information they need in a form they can use. A client might live on the other side of the country and not use the same software as you.

Part 5 is about sharing project information between projects and between the different kinds of programs people use during a project. It consists of two chapters.

Chapter 14, "Managing Several Projects at the Same Time," explains how Microsoft Project enables you to organize, work on, and share resource and task information between concurrent projects.

Chapter 15, "Sharing Project Information with Other Programs and Projects," explains how to exchange project information between different programs and other software tools. It discusses copying and pasting, OLE linking and embedding, importing and exporting, and creating links to information in other files or on the World Wide Web.

14

Managing Several Projects at the Same Time

If your situation is similar to that of many project managers, your biggest everyday challenge is juggling several projects at the same time. When your projects share resources, start and finish at different times, and confront budget constraints, chances are you'd rather make your first parachute jump than face the tangle of projects that awaits you at the office. But Microsoft Project can help you keep track of all your projects, put resources where they're needed most, and give you the best possible chance of completing all of your projects on time and within budget.

One way to manage several projects at the same time is to insert several project files into one *consolidated* project file. Each inserted project is represented as a single task. You can open each project to view and edit its tasks, resources, and assignments, the same way you can when a project resides in a separate file.

By using a consolidated project file, you can display all of your projects in the same window. In particular, you can quickly see which resources are working on which tasks and in which projects. Also, if a project is especially long and complex, you can create a separate project file for each major project phase and then combine them into a consolidated project. That way, you can focus on one phase at a time, while still seeing the big picture. In addition, if one phase or set of tasks occurs in many projects time and again, you can create a separate project file for it once and then plug it into any number of consolidated projects.

But consolidating projects is not the only help you get when you need to manage multiple projects. Microsoft Project also enables you to:

- Create a resource pool to make it easy to share resources among projects.
- Link tasks between projects, which is helpful when a task in one project is dependent on a task in another project.
- Open separate project files all at once, so that you can work with them at the same time without first inserting them into a consolidated project file.
- Create a project template, which contains the basic tasks that occur in many projects. Using the template, you can create projects quickly.

MANAGING SEVERAL PROJECTS IN ONE PROJECT FILE

Managing a number of projects at the same time requires you to keep track of each project's progress, resources, and costs. If each project is in a separate project file, you can focus on one project at a time, but you lose the big picture. Combine all those projects into one project, and you may end up with a huge file with hundreds of tasks, which can make it difficult to focus on one part at a time.

A better way to manage several projects at once is to consolidate them into one project file. To create a consolidated project file, you insert individual projects into one project file. In the Gantt Chart view, each project is represented by a summary task that you can expand to show all the other tasks in the project. A consolidated project enables you to focus on one project at a time and see an overview of all of your projects (all the ones you inserted, that is). By default, each inserted project retains its link to its source file. When you revise the source file, the inserted project is revised also.

You can insert all of the projects you're currently managing into one project file. Here, only the summary project titles of three inserted projects are showing.

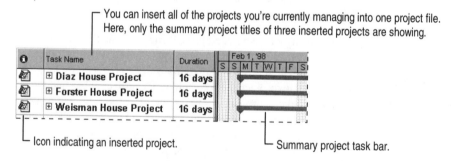

Icon indicating an inserted project.

Summary project task bar.

Consider consolidating projects when:

- You break a large, complex project into smaller project phases, with each phase residing in a separate project file. That way, the manager of each phase can focus on his or her tasks and update those tasks as necessary. The manager of the whole project sees the phases as summary tasks in the consolidated project file.

- You want updates in related, component projects of a larger project to be automatically reflected in the larger project.

- You're managing several projects that share the same resources and you want to check resource usage.

- You're managing a number of separate projects and want to see an overview of those projects.

- You want to create reports that include information from several projects.

- You have similar sets of tasks that occur in many projects. Rather than entering the tasks each time they occur in a project, you can create a project for each set of tasks, and then insert that project into a consolidated project as needed.

After you insert a project into a consolidated file, any changes you make to the source file appear automatically in the corresponding inserted project of the consolidated file, and vice versa. Format changes, however, are not transmitted between source and consolidated project files.

There are two ways to consolidate projects. You can customize as you consolidate your projects, which means you can specify the order of the inserted projects within the consolidated project.

If the projects you want to consolidate are already open in separate windows, you can use a quick method for consolidating those projects. When you use the quick method, Microsoft Project determines the order in which the inserted projects appear in the consolidated project file.

You can insert up to 1,000 projects in a consolidated project file.

Consolidate Project Files at a Specific Outline Level and in a Specific Order

A consolidated project file contains projects that have been inserted into it. If the inserted projects are unrelated or only loosely related, their order in the consolidated project file might not matter to you. But, for example, if each inserted project represents a project phase, you probably want the inserted projects to appear at the correct outline level and in the correct order.

The simplest way to make sure that projects appear where you want them is to insert each project one at a time into a consolidated project. The reason: An inserted project inherits the outline level of the task or project beneath which it's inserted. (A project inserted beneath a summary task will be indented one outline level with respect to the summary task.) When you insert several projects at the same time, they'll appear at the same outline level and in the same location in the consolidated project. If that's what you want, fine. But though you can change their order after you've inserted the projects, you won't be able to indent or outdent the inserted tasks with respect to each other (only with respect to the task beneath which they've been inserted). To insert each project at a different outline level, you'll need to insert the projects one at a time.

You can insert a project into any location in an existing project. If you're creating a new consolidated project file—that is, inserting projects into an empty project file—you can insert the first project, expand it to show all of its tasks, and then insert the next project into the first project, at the outline level and in the location you want. If you insert several projects at the same time, they'll be inserted at the same outline level and in the same location (regardless of whether you insert them into an empty project file or an existing project).

➤ **To insert a project file in a specific location in a consolidated project**

1 On the **View Bar**, click **Gantt Chart**.

2 Open a new or existing project file.

3 In the **Task Name** field, select where you want to insert the project.

   The inserted project will acquire the outline level of the task above the selected Task Name field (unless the task above is a summary task).

4 On the **Insert** menu, click **Project**.

5 In the **Look in** box, click the drive, folder, or World Wide Web location that contains the project files you want to insert.

   To insert several projects at the same time, they must reside in the same folder. You can, however, insert projects from one folder and then insert projects from another folder.

6 Hold down CTRL, and then click each project file you want to insert.

7 Click **Insert**.

   The projects will be consolidated in the order they are listed.

8 Repeat steps 3 to 6 for each folder that contains project files you want to insert into the consolidated project.

Consolidate Several Open Project Files at the Same Time

Microsoft Project enables you to work with a number of open project files at the same time. If you're managing several projects concurrently and you frequently have their project files opened at the same time, you may find it more convenient to consolidate those files into one project file. Microsoft Project provides a way to consolidate open project files quickly, without you having to insert them one at a time.

When you consolidate open project files, you can't specify the order or the outline location of each inserted project into the consolidated project. The projects are inserted at the same outline level in a new project file. You can, however, specify which of the open projects you want to consolidate (you don't have to consolidate all of them).

➢ **To consolidate open project files**

1   Open all the project files you want to consolidate.

2   On the **Window** menu, click **New Window**.

3   In the **Projects** list, click the project files you want to consolidate.

Hold down CTRL, and then click each project file you want to insert.

4   To have the consolidated project appear in a view other than the one currently displayed, click a different view in the **View** box.

Microsoft Project consolidates the projects in the order that they're listed in the Projects list.

Because each project is inserted into a new project file at the same outline level, you won't be able to indent or outdent the inserted projects with respect to each other. You can, however, insert a task above the topmost inserted project, and then indent and outdent the inserted projects with respect to this task.

Delete the Link Between an Inserted Project and Its Source File

When you consolidate project files, the inserted files are linked to their source files by default. If you revise the source file, the change automatically appears in the corresponding inserted project. If you revise the inserted project, the change automatically appears in the corresponding source file. If you do not want a change in the source file to be reflected in the corresponding inserted project, or vice versa, you can break the link between them. The inserted project will become wholly part of the consolidated project file.

> ➤ **To delete the link between an inserted project and its source project file**

1 In the **Task Name** field, double-click the project summary task of the inserted project.

2 Click the **Advanced** tab.

3 Under **Source project**, clear the **Link to project** check box.

Organize the Inserted Projects in a Consolidated Project

After you insert a project into another project, you can indent, outdent, and move the inserted project. After you insert open projects into a new project file, you can change their order but you can't indent or outdent them. They are inserted at the same outline level. If you insert a task above the topmost inserted project, all of the inserted projects can be indented with respect to that task.

In a consolidated project, an inserted project can behave as a normal task. For example, you can change the order of inserted projects by moving the inserted projects to different locations. When you move an inserted project, all of its tasks move with it (the same as with any summary task).

If you were to insert three projects into a new (empty) project file to create a consolidated project from scratch, you wouldn't be able to indent or outdent the inserted projects with respect to each other.

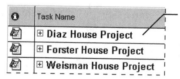

When you insert several projects at the same time into an empty project file (as you do when you consolidate open project files), you can change their order but you can't indent or outdent them.

If you insert a task above the inserted projects, then you can indent them with respect to this task.

	❶	Task Name
1		⊟ **My Projects**
2	📝	⊞ **Diaz House Project**
3	📝	⊞ **Forster House Project**
4	📝	⊞ **Weisman House Project**

As a workaround, instead of inserting projects into a completely empty file, you can insert one project at a time into an existing project, at the outline level and in the location you want.

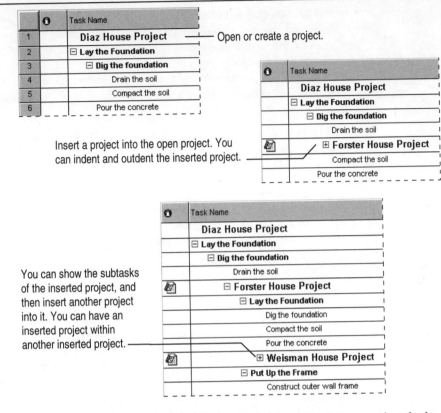

Open or create a project.

Insert a project into the open project. You can indent and outdent the inserted project.

You can show the subtasks of the inserted project, and then insert another project into it. You can have an inserted project within another inserted project.

In situations where you can indent and outdent inserted projects, a project that's outdented with respect to the project below it becomes a *summary project*. The projects below a summary project become the subprojects of the summary project. Each summary project displays cumulative information about the projects beneath it.

For information about how to move, indent, and outdent an inserted project or to show or hide the tasks of an inserted project, see Chapter 4, "Breaking Your Project into Phases, Tasks, and Milestones."

LINKING TASKS BETWEEN PROJECTS

Pretend you're managing a house construction project. As you develop the project plan, it's clear that the roof can't be put on until the frame's been built. There's a dependency between these two tasks. You might show that dependency by linking the tasks with a finish-to-start link.

But let's say that at the same time, you're also managing the construction of a second house, but you only have enough roofers to work on one house at a time. In that case, work on the second roof can't begin until work on the first roof has been completed. Two separate projects, but a task in the second project is dependent on a task in the first project. When you're managing several projects at the same time, especially if they're related, dependencies between tasks from different projects are common.

With Microsoft Project, you can link tasks between different projects. The tasks can be in completely separate projects or in projects that have been inserted into the same consolidated project file. The links between tasks in different projects work the same way as links do between tasks within the same project.

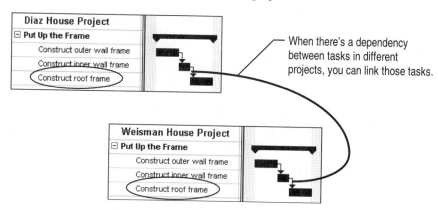

When there's a dependency between tasks in different projects, you can link those tasks.

When you link tasks by using the following procedure, a finish-to-start dependency is established by default. You can, however, change the link to a start-to-start, finish-to-finish, or start-to-finish link, and you can also specify lead and lag time.

➤ **To link tasks between projects**

1 Open both projects.

2 On the **Window** menu, click **New Window**.

3 Hold down CTRL, click the projects that contain the tasks you want to link, and then click **OK**.

4 On the **View Bar**, click **Gantt Chart**.

5 Position the pointer over the Gantt bar for the predecessor task and drag to the successor task in the other project.

   A finish-to-start task dependency is created. You can change this to a different type of task dependency.

6   Close the new window.

You don't need to save the project file that contains both projects. If you do save it, it will contain both projects and the link between them.

If the tasks you linked are not in a consolidated project, an external predecessor task is added to the project containing the successor task and an external successor task is added to the project containing the predecessor task.

SHARING RESOURCES AMONG PROJECTS

The several projects you're managing at the same time may use the same set of resources. You can add these resources to one project file at a time, but that's time-consuming. A faster way to share the same set of resources among different projects is to create a *resource pool*. A resource pool is a project file that usually contains resource information only, information about all the resources you want to share.

A resource pool enables you to:

- Quickly add resources to any project.
- Spend less time creating and updating resource lists. You create a resource pool once, and then share it with as many projects as you want. Also, by updating resource information in the resource pool, it gets updated in all the projects that share the pool.
- Share resources among many projects.
- Easily identify and resolve conflicts resulting from resources working on more than one project.
- Check resource usage and costs across all projects without opening each individual project file.
- Print reports about resource usage across projects.

You can share a resource pool among individual projects as well as among consolidated projects. You can also use a "real" project file, one that contains both tasks and resources, as your designated resource file.

A resource pool has a two-way link to the projects that share it. When you update information in the resource pool, you can update that information in all the linked projects. Likewise, if you update resource information in a project, you can update that information in the resource pool.

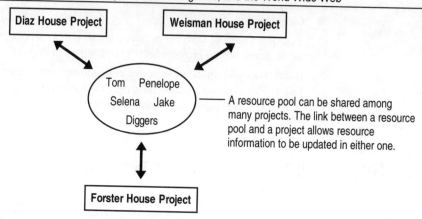

A resource pool can be shared among many projects. The link between a resource pool and a project allows resource information to be updated in either one.

When you add a new project to the group of projects that share a resource pool, that project may already contain resource information. In that case, the information in the resource pool takes precedence, by default. The resource pool information won't be overwritten by the resource information in the new project, unless you specify otherwise.

Create and Share a Resource Pool

When you know that several projects will use the same resources, you can save time by entering only task information in those projects and information about all the shared resources in a separate, resource-information-only project file. The project file that contains resource information only is the resource pool file. To share resources and resource information among several projects, you link the resource pool file to the project files.

If the resource pool file and a linked project file have resource information in common, the resource pool file takes precedence—its resource information won't be overwritten by the resource information in the project file, by default. You can, however, choose to have the project file take precedence.

➢ **To create and share a resource pool**

1   Open a new project file.

2   Enter information for each resource that is assigned to the projects that will share the resource pool.

3   Click **Save** .

4   In the **File name** box, type a name for the resource pool file.

5   Create the projects that will share the resource pool.

6   Open the projects that will share the resource pool.

7   Switch to one of the open project files.

8   On the **Tools** menu, point to **Resources**, and then click **Share Resources**.

9   Click **Use resources**, and then click the resource pool file in the **From** box.

10   To overwrite pool information with resource information from the selected project file (for resources that they have in common), click **Sharer takes precedence**.

11   Repeat steps 7 through 10 for each project that will share the resource pool.

Update Information in a Resource Pool

The link between a resource pool and a project file works both ways: When you update the resource pool, you can choose to have the updated information transmitted to the project file. When you update resource information in a project file, you can choose to update the resource pool. If you want the updated resource information from a project file to be included in all the projects that share a resource pool, you must update the pool.

➤   **To update information in a resource pool**

1   Open the project that shares the resource pool.

2   On the **Tools** menu, point to **Resources**, and then click **Update Resource Pool**.

OPEN SEVERAL PROJECT FILES AT ONCE: WORKSPACES

When you're managing several projects at the same time, you're probably working with their project files—the same project files—day after day. To work on those project files, you have to open them. If the projects are related, you could insert them into one consolidated project file. Then you'd just have to open one consolidated project file to work on all of your projects.

But if the projects aren't related, you might not want to insert them into a consolidated project file. Another way to save time opening project files that you frequently work on at the same time is to create a *workspace*. A workspace contains a list of project names that are linked to the project files you specify. You add the project files you want to the workspace. When you open a workspace, you open all the listed projects at the same time.

➤   **To create a workspace**

1   Open all the files you want to include in the workspace.

2   On the **File** menu, click **Save Workspace**.

3   In the **File name** box, type a name for the workspace file.

4   Click **Save**.

CREATING PROJECTS BY USING A PROJECT TEMPLATE

A project template is a good shortcut for quickly creating projects that have the same basic tasks. First, create the project template—it contains the basic tasks. Save the project as a template file. Then, each time you have a new project that's similar to the template you created, open the template file. When you save the template, you're automatically prompted for a new filename, so you don't have to worry about changing the template accidentally. Modify the copy of the template to match your current project needs.

Create a Project Template

You can make creating project plans nearly as easy as cookie-cutting by creating and using a project template. In a project template, you enter as much common task and resource information as possible, the kind of information that will likely be used in future projects. Then, when you need to create a project plan, you can do it faster by modifying a copy of the template, making only those changes that are specific to the new project.

➤ **To create a project template**

1 Create a project containing all the basic tasks.

2 Click 🖫.

3 In the **File name** box, type the template name.

4 In the **Save as type** box, click **Template**, and then click **Save**.

   If PlanningWizards are on, the Planning Wizard dialog box will appear.

5 Click **Save without a baseline**.

Create a Project Based on a Project Template

After you've created a project template file, you can use that template as the basis for your project plans. Each new project plan that's based on the template starts with the basic information you included in the template. For each project, you can revise, add to, or subtract from the basic information, according to the needs of the project.

➤ **To create a project based on a project template**

1 Click ⬚.

2 In the **Look in** box, select the folder that contains the template you want, click the template, and then click **Open**.

3 Change the details in the project.

4 Click ⬚.

5 In the **File name** box, type a name for the project file, and then click **Save**.

By default, the file is saved as a project file. ("Project" appears in the **Save as type** box.)

If PlanningWizards are on, the Planning Wizard dialog box will appear.

6 Click **Save without a baseline**.

15

Sharing Project Information with Other Programs and Projects

To manage some projects, the only software tools you'll need are Microsoft Project and the project file that contains your project plan. But when those tools aren't enough, Microsoft Project has the ability to "reach out" and work with a number of other software tools, such as other programs. Some of the reasons you may need to work with other software tools are:

- You want to use specialized programs to perform more calculations on project data than Microsoft Project can, and then include the results in your project plan. For example, a spreadsheet program may be able to perform more complex cost calculations than Microsoft Project.

- A client or someone you work with may not have Microsoft Project or another program that can open project files in a Microsoft Project file format. For example, a client who wants to see an electronic copy of your project plan may only have a database program.

- You want to include a portion of your project information in a file created in a program that doesn't support Microsoft Project file formats. For example, you may want to include task information in a status report created in a word-processing program.

- You want to access project information that resides in another source, such as a web site or another project file, from within your project plan.

- You want to archive, compare, or generate reports for several project files, which may best be accomplished in a database.

- You want to open a project file created with an older version of Microsoft Project.

You can accomplish all of these tasks and others by sharing project information. When you share project information, you either include information from your project plan in another software tool or include information from another software tool in your project plan. A software tool can be either another project file, a web site, or another program, such as a spreadsheet, word-processing, database, personal information management, or project management program.

To share project information with other software tools, you can:

- Copy and paste project information.
- Import or export project information.
- Create links to or embed project information.
- Create hyperlinks to project information.

This chapter focuses on sharing project information so that the information can be viewed, edited, calculated, and stored in a variety of programs and other software tools. Typically, the shared information consists of all or part of a project plan, though it can also be auxiliary information that augments a project plan, such as a project management document hyperlinked from a web site or a presentation linked from a presentation program.

This chapter does not discuss ways to exchange project information between people, such as across an e-mail system, an intranet, or the World Wide Web. For information about exchanging project information between people, see Chapter 10, "Updating Task Information by Using E-Mail and the Web."

How You Can Share Project Information

The sharing method you use depends on the amount, source, and format of the project information, as well as how you want to edit the information in the destination program, file, or web site. You can use the following methods to share project information.

To	Use
Copy small amounts of text or graphics information from one file and paste it into another file. You can edit the information in the destination file without changing the source file.	Copy and paste (which can be used between Windows programs only).
Quickly copy or move small amounts of information between two open files.	Drag-and-drop editing to drag selected information to another file (which can be used between Windows programs only).
Open all or part of a file created in another program in Microsoft Project.	Importing (use the **Open** command on the **File** menu).
Open all or part of a Microsoft Project file in another program.	Exporting (use the **Save As** command on the **File** menu).
Copy information from one file, paste it into another file, and update the copied information in the destination file automatically when you update the source file.	OLE linking (use the **Paste Link** option from the **Paste Special** command on the **Edit** menu to paste the information as a linked object). Can be used between OLE-supported programs only
Copy information from one file, paste it into another file, and edit the copied information in the destination file independently of the source file.	OLE embedding (use the **Paste** option from the **Paste Special** command on the **Edit** menu to paste the information as an embedded object). Can be used between OLE-supported programs only
Jump to information in another file, another part of the same file, or a web site.	Hyperlinks (use the **Paste as Hyperlink** command on the **Edit** menu or the **Hyperlink** command on the **Insert** menu or **Standard** toolbar to paste a hyperlink).

COPYING AND PASTING PROJECT INFORMATION

When you want to insert small amounts of text or graphical information from Microsoft Project into another Windows program or vice versa, you can copy and paste that information. For instance, you can copy and paste one or more cells, fields, or columns of information, as well as icons, logos, and other pictures. You can copy and paste between Microsoft Project files and sheet views, as well as between any two Windows programs. Typically, Windows programs can share copied information even if the destination program can't save files in the format of the source program.

Before you copy specific information, the file that contains that information must be displayed on your screen. The destination file can be opened before or after you copy the information. That is, you can copy the information in the source file, open the destination file or display the sheet view, and then paste the information. If you copy a second piece of information before pasting the first piece of information, the second piece of information will be pasted. Newly copied information replaces previously copied information.

It may be that you can copy and paste large amounts of information, such as many columns. But there's no accurate way to determine the amount of information that can be copied and pasted on an individual computer. As a rule of thumb, though, the more RAM memory your computer has, the more information you can copy and paste.

Copy Text from Another Program

If text information created in another Windows program can be used in your project plan, you can copy it from the source file and then paste it into a sheet view, such as the Gantt Chart view, the Resource Sheet view, or the Task Usage view. Text information can be either words or numbers and can consist of a single piece of calculated data, such as a cost calculated in Microsoft Excel, or it can consist of several cells, fields, or columns of information.

When you copy information from one cell or field to another, the destination field must be able to accept the type of information that's been copied. For example, if the copied information is numerical, the destination field must be capable of accepting numerical data.

➤ **To copy text from another program to a sheet view**

1 Open the source program and the source file.

2 Select the text, noting the size and type of the information.

3 Click **Copy**, or the program's equivalent command.

4 Open the Microsoft Project file into which you want to paste the text.

5 On the **View Bar**, click the sheet view into which you want to paste the text.

6 If necessary, apply a table with columns that match the order and type of the copied text.

7 If necessary, insert more rows to accommodate the entire text: Select the number of rows you're inserting, and then click **New Task** or **New Resource** on the **Insert** menu.

   Pasted rows replace existing rows. If you don't want to replace an existing row, be sure to paste copied information into a blank row.

8 To paste the text into new fields or rows, select the first field of the blank rows.

9 Click **Paste** .

Copy Graphics from Another Program

If graphical information created in another Windows program can be used in your project plan, you can copy it from the source file and then paste it into a Microsoft Project graphics area, such as the chart portion of the Gantt Chart view, a header, footer, or a legend, or a note. Examples of graphical information are company logos, pie charts, and graphs.

➢ **To copy graphics information from another program to a graphics area**

1   Open the source program and the source file.

2   Select the graphic.

3   Click **Copy**, or the program's equivalent command.

4   Open the Microsoft Project file into which you want to paste the graphic.

5   To paste the graphic into the **Gantt Chart** view, click **Gantt Chart** on the **View Bar**, and then click **Paste** 🖻.

6   To paste the graphic into a note, double-click a task, resource, or assignment in a sheet view, click the **Notes** tab, and then click **Insert Object** 🖼. Choose the options you want, and then click **OK**.

7   To paste the graphic into a header, footer, or legend, switch to a view that has a header, footer, or legend. On the **View** menu, click **Header and Footer**, and then click the **Header**, **Footer**, or **Legend** tab. Click the **Left**, **Center**, or **Right** tab, and then click **Insert Picture** 🖼. Select the graphic you want to insert, and then click **Insert**.

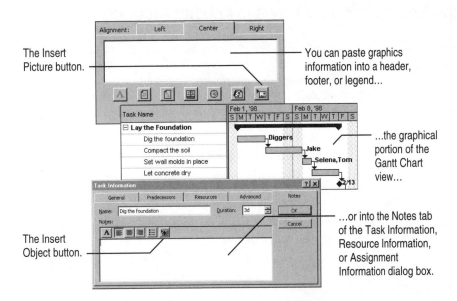

The Insert Picture button.

You can paste graphics information into a header, footer, or legend...

...the graphical portion of the Gantt Chart view...

The Insert Object button.

...or into the Notes tab of the Task Information, Resource Information, or Assignment Information dialog box.

Copy Microsoft Project Text to Another Program

When there are one or several fields or columns of information in your project plan that you want to include in the file of another program, you can copy and paste that information. Most often, you'll probably copy text from a sheet view, such as the Gantt Chart view, the Resource Sheet view, or the Task Usage view.

A field into which you paste text information may only accept information of a certain type. For example, some fields accept numerical information only; others, words only. When you copy several fields of information, those fields must match the order and type of the fields into which you're pasting the information. For example, if you copy information from Microsoft Project's Task Name, Duration, and Start fields, you must paste the information into fields that accept alphabetic characters, numbers, and dates, in that order.

➤ **To copy Microsoft Project text to another program**

1 In Microsoft Project, display the view and apply the table containing the text.

2 Select the text you want to copy.

3 Click **Copy** 🔲.

4 Open the destination program and the file into which the Microsoft Project text is to be pasted.

5 In the destination file, select the area where you want to insert the text.

6 Click **Paste**, or the program's equivalent command.

Copy Microsoft Project Views to Another Program

Your project reports and presentations can be made more useful as well as livelier by adding pictures of Microsoft Project views. You can add entire Microsoft Project views or selected view information as pictures into any program capable of displaying graphics information as images, such as word-processing, spreadsheet, and presentation programs. You can copy all views as pictures except for the Task PERT Chart and form views.

➤ **To copy a picture of a Microsoft Project view to another program**

1 In Microsoft Project, select the information.

2 Click **Copy Picture** 📷.

3 To copy the selected information as it would appear in print, click **For printer**, and then click **OK**.

Otherwise, the information is copied as it would appear on the screen.

4   Switch to the destination file into which you want to paste the information.

5   Click **Paste**, or the program's equivalent command.

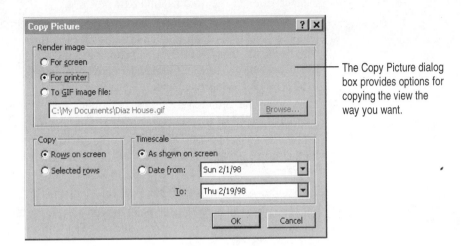

The Copy Picture dialog box provides options for copying the view the way you want.

IMPORTING AND EXPORTING PROJECT INFORMATION

When a file created in another program contains a significant portion of project information, you may want to open that file in Microsoft Project, where you can view, revise, or calculate project information by using Microsoft Project's particular features. You can open files created in a variety of other programs by *importing* those files.

When you or someone you work with wants to open a Microsoft Project file in another program, where the project information can be viewed, revised, or otherwise manipulated in ways that are particular to that program, you can *export* the file to the other program. You can export Microsoft Project files to a variety of programs.

Importing and exporting have certain benefits over other methods of sharing project information. For example, more programs support importing and exporting than object linking and embedding (OLE). Importing and exporting may be your only ways to share significant amounts of information with another program.

In addition, importing and exporting are often the best ways to share information with databases. For example, the only way to share project information with an SQL database (a database that uses the *structured query language*) is by importing or exporting the information. You can also store several projects together by exporting them to a single database. You can use the database to conduct cross-project analyses as well as to archive projects.

You follow the same basic process whether you import or export project information:

1   Identify information in one program, the source program, that you'd like to open in another program, the destination program.

Usually, the information is contained in a file that has a particular *file format*, which tells you what type of information is in the file. The file extension after the file name indicates the type of information that's in the file. For example, .MPP is the file extension for Microsoft Project files, .XLS is the extension for Microsoft Excel files, and .TXT is the extension for generic text files.

2   Identify the file format of the information in the source program.

Each program saves and stores files in a default file format. For example, the default file format for Microsoft Project files is .MPP. Often, the default file format for the source program is different than the default file format for the destination program.

3   Determine which file formats can be accepted by the destination program.

Each program can open only certain types of files. Although each program has a default file format, many programs, such as Microsoft Project, can accept and open files with other file formats.

4   Convert the information from the file format of the source program to a file format that's compatible with the destination program.

Programs do this part for you automatically, either when a file is opened in the importing program or saved by the exporting program. If the source program can't convert a file directly into the destination program's default file format, it may be able to convert the file into one of the other formats that the destination program recognizes. If so, the destination program can convert the intermediate file format into the default format.

When a file is converted from one format to another, the original file isn't changed. Rather, a copy of the original file is converted to the target format.

5   Open the file in the destination program.

Using Microsoft Project, you can import and export entire files or selected parts of files, depending on the type of program you're working with. For example, an entire project file can by exported to a database but not to a spreadsheet program. When you import or export selected information only, and not an entire project, you must use an *import/export map* to match a field of information in Microsoft Project to the corresponding field in the other program.

Most of the times that you import or export, you import or export a file. Even when you import or export selected parts of a file, the selected parts are usually "bundled" (automatically) into a file. In a few instances, however, the imported or exported information is not contained within a file; it remains "information" only. One of the most common examples of file-less importing or exporting is the exporting of information to an SQL database. (But there are file-based database programs, such as Microsoft Access, that do import and export files.) You can also append information to the end of an existing Microsoft Project file.

File Formats That Microsoft Project Can Import or Export

In addition to the default .MPP file format, Microsoft Project can open and save project files in a variety of other formats. For example, you can save information as a Microsoft Excel .XLS file that can be opened in Microsoft Excel. And you can open a Microsoft Access file that's in the .MDB format. You can even save project information in HTML (Hypertext Markup Language) format to display that information on a web site.

When you save project information in most formats other than Microsoft Project's "native" .MPP format, you can't save all of the information that's in a project file. For example, if you save project information as a Microsoft Excel .XLS file, the file can contain only information from Microsoft Project fields. An .XLS file can't, for instance, contain information that reconstructs Microsoft Project views and formatting.

You can, however, import or export entire projects, including view and formatting information, to databases. For example, you can export an entire project to Microsoft Access by saving a project file in the Microsoft Project database file format, .MPD, or in the Microsoft Access file format, .MDB.

In summary, you can import or export entire projects—all of the information that makes up a project, including view and formatting information—in the .MPP, .MPD, and .MDB file formats. When you import or export an entire project, you don't use an import/export map. If you use other file formats, such as .XLS, .TXT, and .HTM, you can import or export selected project information only. When you import or export selected project information, you must use an import/export map.

The following table summarizes the file formats you can use with Microsoft Project.

File format	Description
Microsoft Project file	The default file format for projects. Uses the .MPP extension.
Microsoft Project database	The file format for sharing project information with databases. Uses the .MPD extension.
Microsoft Project template file	The file format for projects that contain information you're likely to include in future projects. Uses the .MPT file format.
Microsoft Project Exchange	An ASCII format used with project management and other programs that support MPX. You can export field information only, but not an entire project. Some information specific to Microsoft Project 98 will not be saved. You can export only to the MPX 4.0 file format. You can import files that have the MPX 1.0, MPX 3.0, and MPX 4.0 file formats. Uses the .MPX extension.
Microsoft Access	The file format used by the Microsoft Access 8.0 database program. You can save an entire project or selected project information in this format. Uses the .MDB extension.
Microsoft Excel	The file format used by the Microsoft Excel spreadsheet program. You can export selected field information to this format, but not an entire project. Uses the .XLS extension.
Microsoft Excel Pivot Table	The file format used by the Microsoft Excel 5.0 and 7.0 spreadsheet programs for a Pivot Table. You can export field information to this format, but not an entire project. You can only export information from Microsoft Project to a Microsoft Excel Pivot Table; you can't import from it. Uses the .XLS extension.
HTML (Hypertext Markup Language)	The format used by browser programs on intranets and the World Wide Web. You can export field information to this format, but not an entire project. You can only export information from Microsoft Project to HTML format; you can't import from it. Uses the .HTM extension.
Text-only or ASCII	A generic file format used by word-processing and other programs. It is tab-delimited. You can export field information from a single Microsoft Project table to this format, but not an entire project. Uses the .TXT extension.
System list separator (CSV)	A generic text format used by word-processing and other programs, where information is separated by a system list separator. You can export field information from a single Microsoft Project table to this format, but not an entire project. Uses the .CSV extension.

About Import/Export Maps

Most often, the information you import or export is stored in fields. For example, in Microsoft Project, task names, durations, and start and finish dates are stored in fields. When you import or export selected project information, such as the information in the Task Name, Duration, Start, and Finish fields, you need to ensure that the data from a field in the source program gets inserted into the correct field in the destination program. You make sure that the fields from the two programs are correctly matched by using an *import/export map*.

An import/export map works like this: Suppose you want to export information from the Microsoft Project Duration field. In the destination program, the field that contains duration information is called Length. Using an import/export map, you specify that Duration's counterpart in the destination program is Length. That ensures that the information from Duration will be inserted into Length during export.

Microsoft Project comes with a number of predefined import/export maps that you can use in many common situations. You can also copy and modify a map or create a map from scratch. An import/export map can contain any combination of task, resource, and assignment information and can be filtered to allow only specific tasks, resources, or assignments in the exported file. You can use the same import/export map to import or export information, as well as use it for various kinds of programs.

Create an Import/Export Map

If none of the predefined or already created import/export maps matches the Microsoft Project fields you want to the fields in the other program, you can create your own import/export map.

Even though there are separate procedures for creating an import/export map for importing data and creating an import/export map for exporting data, after you create an import/export map, you can use it both for importing and exporting data.

➢ **To create a custom import/export map for importing data**

1   Click **Open** 📂.

2   In the **Look in** box, click the file you want to import.

3   Click **Open**, click **Selective data**, and then click **New Map**.

4   In the **Import/Export** map name box, enter the name you want.

5   Under **Data to import/export**, select the check boxes for the types of data you want to import.

6   In the options area, select any options you want (if options are available).

The title of the options area is different for each type of program you import from. For example, if you're importing data from Microsoft Excel, the options area is titled Microsoft Excel options.

7   Click the tab for the type of data you want to import.

For example, if you selected the **Tasks** check box, click the **Task Mapping** tab.

8   In the **Source worksheet/database table name** box, click the worksheet or table name from which you want to import.

If you select a table, Microsoft Project fills the From column with all the fields from the table. Any table field that matches a Microsoft Project field name will be automatically matched to the Microsoft Project field.

9   For any unmapped field in the To: Microsoft Project Field column, select or enter the Microsoft Project field that you want to map to the corresponding table field from the other program.

10 In the **Method for incorporating imported data** box, click an option.

11 To save the map, click **OK**.

> ### To create a custom import/export map for exporting data

1   On the **File** menu, click **Save As**.

2   In the **Save in** box, click the drive or folder in which you want to save the exported file.

3   In the **File name** box, enter the name for the file you want to create.

4   In the **Save as type** box, select the type of file (the file format) that you'd like the exported file to be.

5   Click **Save**, click **Selective data**, and then click **New Map**.

6   In the **Import/Export** map name box, enter the name you want.

7   Under **Data to import/export**, select the check boxes for the types of data you want to export.

8   In the options area, select any options you want (if options are available).

The title of the options area is different for each type of program you import from. For example, if you're importing data from Microsoft Excel, the options area is titled Microsoft Excel options.

9   Click the tab for the type of data you want to export.

For example, if you selected the **Task** check box, click the **Task Mapping** tab.

10 In the **From: Microsoft Project Field** column, select or enter the name of a Microsoft Project field.

Microsoft Project automatically fills in the corresponding fields in the **To** column with default names for those fields.

11 To change a default field name in the **To** column, type the name you want.

12 Repeat steps 10 and 11 for each field you want to export.

13 To export only certain tasks, click a filter in the **Export filter** box.

14 To save the map, click **OK**.

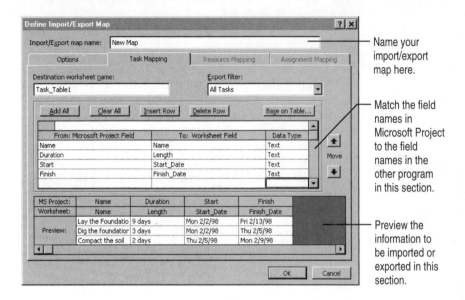

Name your import/export map here.

Match the field names in Microsoft Project to the field names in the other program in this section.

Preview the information to be imported or exported in this section.

Delete an Import/Export Map

If there's an import/export map you no longer need, you can delete it. Most import/export maps are stored in the global file (Global.mpt), but they can be moved to, and stored with, a project file. You can delete an import/export map from the global file and from a project file.

➢ **To delete an import/export map**

1 On the **Tools** menu, click **Organizer**.

2 Click the **Maps** tab.

3 To delete a map from the global file, click the map you want to delete in the **GLOBAL.MPT** list, and then click **Delete**.

   To delete a map from a project file, click the map you want to delete in the project file list (on the right), and then click **Delete**.

Import Project Information

Important project information may sometimes be created, calculated, or stored in programs other than Microsoft Project or in project plans created in previous versions of Microsoft Project. For example, you may store task and resource information in a database. Or, you may have created the project plan for a current project by using an earlier version of Microsoft Project. If you want to use information created in other programs or in earlier versions of Microsoft Project in the current version of Microsoft Project, you can import the information.

Typically, you import relatively large amounts of information that's in a file format that's not one of the "native" Microsoft Project file formats (which are .MPP, .MPX, and .MPT). Also, the information you import must reside in fields in the source program. You can import entire projects from databases and previous versions of Microsoft Project to create a new project plan. From all other kinds of programs, you can import only selected information (that is, information from fields you specify by using an import/export map). If you import selected information, you can create a new project file that contains the selected information or add it to the end of or merge it with the active project file.

To import project information from an ODBC database other than Microsoft Access, you must use a different procedure than the one described in this topic.

➢ **To import data**

1 Click **Open** 📂.

2 In the **Look in** box, click the folder that contains the file you want to import.

3 In the **Files of type** box, click the format of the file you want to import.

4 In the folder list, click the file you want to import, and then click **Open**.

   If you're importing an entire project in the .mpp, .mpx, or .mpt file format, Microsoft Project opens the file.

   If you're importing selected project information or an entire project in a file format other than the .mpp, .mpx, or .mpt, the **Import Format** dialog box appears.

5 To import selected project information, click **Selective data**, click an existing import/export map or create a new one, and then click **Open**.

   To import an entire project in a database that's in other than the .mpp, .mpx, or .mpt file format, click **Entire project**, and then select the project you want from the list.

If you open a project file created in Microsoft Project version 4.1 or 4.0, you may see differences in the calculated values of some fields.

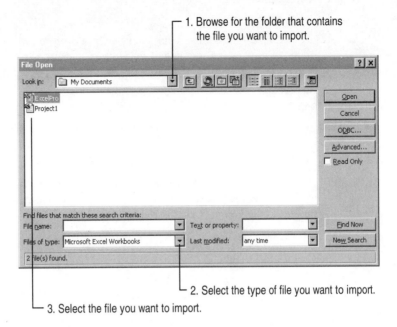

1. Browse for the folder that contains the file you want to import.

2. Select the type of file you want to import.

3. Select the file you want to import.

Import Project Information from an ODBC Database

Open Database Connectivity (ODBC) is an information-exchange standard for databases (and programs that incorporate databases in their innards, such as Microsoft Project). Databases programs that support ODBC can exchange information with one another.

Microsoft Access is a database program that supports ODBC, but Microsoft Project uses the same basic procedure for importing information from Microsoft Access that it uses for other kinds of programs. If you want to import information from any other ODBC database, you must use the procedure in this topic.

➢ **To import project information from an ODBC database**

1 Click Open 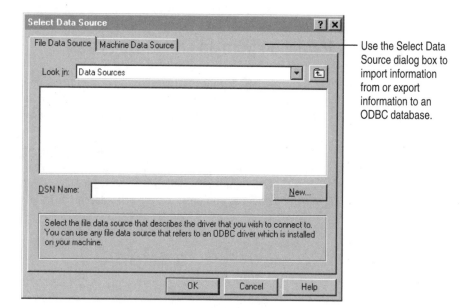.

2 Click **ODBC**.

3 To use a file data source, click the **File Data Source** tab, and then enter the file name or browse for one in the **Look in** box.

To define a new data source for any installed driver, click **New**, and then follow the instructions for defining a new data source.

4 Click the **Machine Data Source** tab, click the machine data source that contains the data you want to import, and then click **OK**.

5 If you need to log on to the ODBC data source that you selected, enter your logon ID, password, and any other information that may be required, and then click **OK**.

6 To import a complete project from the database, click **Entire project (includes all data, views, formatting, etc.)**, and then click the name of the project you want to import in the **Name of the project in the database** box.

To import only some of the data into your project, click **Selective data (allows you to import particular fields)**. In the **Import/export map to use for importing** list, click the name of the map you want to use for importing your data, or you can define a new map or edit an existing map.

7 Click **Open**.

Use the Select Data Source dialog box to import information from or export information to an ODBC database.

Export Project Information

Sometimes you may need to open part or all of your project plan in another program or even in a web site. For example, a client who wants to see your project plan may not have the current version of Microsoft Project. But perhaps the client has Microsoft Access or an earlier version of Microsoft Project. Or, maybe you want to use another program to store project files or calculate project data. In these situations and others, you can export project information from Microsoft Project.

Typically, you export relatively large amounts of information in a file format other than the Microsoft Project default file format, .MPP. You can export an entire project to a database or export only selected information (that is, information from fields you specify by using an import/export map) to spreadsheet, word processor, and project management programs, as well as to databases. You can also export project information to HTML documents on an intranet or the World Wide Web.

To export project information to an ODBC database other than Microsoft Access, you must use a different procedure than the one described in this topic.

➢ **To export project information**

1   On the **File** menu, click **Save As**.

2   In the **Save in** box, click the folder in which you want to save the exported file.

3   In the **File name** box, enter the name of the exported file.

4   In the **Save as type** box, click the format in which you want to export the file, and then click **Save**.

   If you're exporting an entire project in the .mpp, .mpx, or .mpt file format, Microsoft Project saves the file.

   If you're exporting selected project data or an entire project to a file format other than .mpp, .mpx, or .mpt, the **Export Format** dialog box appears.

5   To export an entire project (if you're exporting to a database, for example), click **Entire project (includes all data, views, formatting, etc.)** , and then enter the name of the project you want to export in the **Name to give the project in the database** box.

   To export selected project data, click **Selective data (allows you to export particular fields)**. In the **Import/export map to use for exporting** list, click the name of the map you want to use for exporting your data, or you can define a new map or edit an existing map.

6   Click **Save**.

1. Browse for the folder to which you want to export the file.

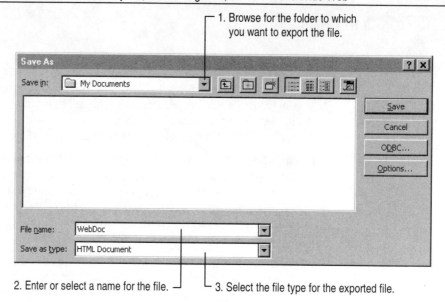

2. Enter or select a name for the file. ⌐ └ 3. Select the file type for the exported file.

Export Project Information to an ODBC Database

Open Database Connectivity (ODBC) is an information-exchange standard for databases (and programs that incorporate databases in their innards, such as Microsoft Project). Databases programs that support ODBC can exchange information with one another.

Microsoft Access is a database program that supports ODBC, but Microsoft Project uses the same basic procedure for exporting information to Microsoft Access that it uses for other kinds of programs. If you want to export information to any other ODBC database, you must use the procedure in this topic.

You can export project information to ODBC databases, such as Microsoft SQL Server and other programs that provide drivers with ODBC Level 1 to access their data files.

When you export to a database, Microsoft Project automatically makes the following changes to the names of Microsoft Project fields so that they are compatible with database field-naming conventions:

- Periods are deleted.
- Spaces are replaced with underscores.
- Forward slashes "/" are replaced with underscores.
- The percent sign "%" is replaced with the word "Percent".
- "Start" is changed to "Start_Date".
- "Finish" is changed to "Finish_Date".
- "Work" is changed to "Scheduled_Work".
- "Group" is changed to "Group_Name".

➢ **To export project information to an ODBC database**

1 On the **File** menu, click **Save As**.

2 Click **ODBC**.

3 To display the defined machine data sources for any ODBC drivers installed on your computer, click the **Machine Data Source** tab.

   To define a new data source for any installed ODBC driver, click **New**, and then follow the instructions for defining a new data source.

4 On the **Machine Data Source** tab, click the machine data source that contains the data you want to export, and then click **OK**.

   To use a file data source, click the **File Data Source** tab, and then enter or browse for a file name.

5 If you need to log on to the ODBC data source that you selected, enter your logon ID, password, and any other information that may be required, and then click **OK**.

6 To export an entire project, click **Entire project (includes all data, views, formatting, etc.)**, and then in the **Name to give the project in the database** box, enter a name for the project.

   To export only some of the data in your project, click **Selective data (allows you to export particular fields)**. In the **Import/export map to use for exporting** list, click the name of the map you want to use for exporting your data, or you can define a new map or edit an existing map.

7 Click **Save**.

If you want to perform cross-project analyses or simply want to archive your projects efficiently, you can store several projects in a single database.

➢ **To store several projects in a single database**

1 Open a Microsoft Project file that you want to store in a database.

2 On the **File** menu, click **Save As**.

3 In the **Save in** box, click the folder that contains the database in which you want to store the project file

4 In the folder list, click database name, and then click **Save**.

A dialog box appears, on which are described three options.

5 Click **Append**.

6 Click **Entire project (includes all data, views, formatting, etc.)** , and then enter the name of the project you want to export in the **Name to give the project in the database** box.

7 Click **Save**.

LINKING AND EMBEDDING PROJECT INFORMATION

Project information can consist of text and pictures created in Microsoft Project and in other programs. When you want to include project information in one program that's been created in another program while still maintaining the connection to the original, or source, program, you can *link* or *embed* the information. You can link and embed information (called an *object* when it's linked or embedded) between any two programs that support object linking and embedding (OLE) technology.

OLE technology lets you insert an object into your project plan and then either activate the source program (linking) or a special set of editing tools (embedding) from within the project plan to edit the inserted object. (Of course, you can also link or embed objects from Microsoft Project to other programs.) By linking or embedding, you get the combined power of the program that's providing the object and the project management features of Microsoft Project.

Link an object if you want the changes made to the object in the source program to be updated wherever the object exists. Create the object once. Link it to multiple places. Update it once, and (if you so choose) it's updated in each place to which you've linked it. When you link an object, the object is stored in the source file only, and your project plan (or destination file) contains only the name and "address," or path. Linking results in a smaller file than if you actually included the object in the project plan, such as by embedding it.

Embed an object if you want the changes you make to the object in the destination file to be independent of the changes you make to the original object in the source file. When you embed an object, updating the original object does not automatically update the embedded object; there's no link between the two. The object itself is included in the destination file. Embedding objects in a file can make that file large.

When you link or embed, objects can be placed in any graphics area, such as the chart portion of the Gantt Chart view; headers, footers, and legends of printed views and reports; and Note boxes. Text objects can be linked to sheet views.

Linking and Embedding Project Information from Other Programs

If there's information in another program that you want to include and update in one or more Microsoft Project files, you can link that information to as many project files as you want. When you link information, the information resides in the source file only. When you update the information in the source file, the information is updated in each project file to which it's linked. You can link both text and graphical information from a source program to a Microsoft Project file.

Link or Embed Text Information from Another Program to Microsoft Project

Other programs may contain text information you want to include in a project plan. Examples of text information are project costs and other values calculated in a spreadsheet program and task documentation stored in a word-processing program. If you update the information regularly and you want the updates to appear in each file that contains the information, you can link the text information as an object in the sheet view of one or more project plans. If you don't want updates in the source file to appear in the project files, you can embed the information.

The type of information that you link or embed within a sheet view must match the type of information already in the view that receives the text. For example, you can link numerical information to the Duration field, but not alphabetical information.

➤ **To link or embed text information from another program in a Microsoft Project sheet view**

1   Open the source program and the source file.

2   Select the object, noting the size, order, and type of the information.

3   Click **Copy**, or the source program's equivalent command.

4   Open the Microsoft Project file in which you want to create the link.

5   On the **View Bar**, click the sheet view in which you want to create the link.

6   If necessary, add columns or create a new table to make the view compatible with the order and type of information in the object.

7 If necessary, add more fields to the table to accommodate the entire object. (Select the number of rows you're inserting, and then click **New Task** or **New Resource** on the **Insert** menu.)

If there's not enough room in the sheet view, information already in the view may be replaced by the incoming object.

8 Select the field where the upper-left cell of the linked information should begin.

9 On the **Edit** menu, click **Paste Special**.

10 To create an embedded object, click **Paste**.

To create a linked object, click **Paste Link**.

11 In the **As** box, click a format.

For example, to paste the information as text, click **Text Data**.

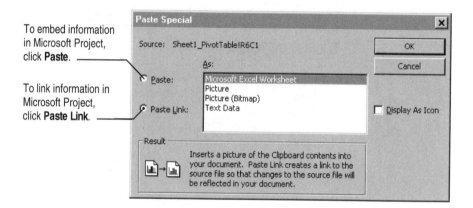

To embed information in Microsoft Project, click **Paste**.

To link information in Microsoft Project, click **Paste Link**.

Link or Embed Graphical Information from Another Program to Microsoft Project

Pictures can be worth a thousand words. For instance, a pie chart added to the Gantt Chart view might take the place of several paragraphs in a status report. At the very least, pictures can make printed views and reports more vivid and useful. When you want to include a picture from another program in one or more project files, you can link or embed the picture.

When you link a picture, the picture resides in the source program only. The Microsoft Project file to which it's linked contains only the path to the source file. By updating the picture in the source file, you update the picture everywhere it's linked. When you embed a picture, there's no link between the source file and the picture in the destination file. Updating the picture in the source file will not update the picture in the destination file. However, you can still edit the picture from within Microsoft Project.

You can link or embed a picture only to the Gantt Chart view or the Objects box. If you paste a picture into any other Microsoft Project graphics area, such as a note, header, footer, or legend, it will be pasted into your project file as a *static* (uneditable) picture.

➢ **To link or embed graphical information from another program in a Microsoft Project graphics area**

1 Open the source program and the source file.

2 Select the graphics object.

3 Click **Copy**, or the source program's equivalent command.

4 Open the Microsoft Project file in which you want to create the link.

5 Select the graphics area in which you want to create the link.

   To paste the object into the **Gantt Chart** view, click **Gantt Chart** on the **View Bar**.

   To paste the object into the **Objects** box, select the task or resource to which you want to attach the object. On the **View Bar**, click **More Views**. In the **Views** list, click **Task Form** or **Resource Form**, and then click **Apply**. On the **Format** menu, point to **Details**, and then click **Objects**.

6 On the **Edit** menu, click **Paste Special**.

7 To create an embedded object, click **Paste**.

   To create a linked object, click **Paste Link**.

8 In the **As** box, click a format.

9 To display the object as an icon representing the source program, select the **Display As Icon** check box.

Link or Embed an Entire File in Microsoft Project

Sometimes an entire file created in another program is important enough to include in a project plan. For example, you can include a presentation about your project right in the Gantt Chart view. Double-click the presentation object and, if it's linked to the source program, you can start the presentation. You can also link or embed entire spreadsheets, word-processing documents, and so on, to your project plan.

If you link the file, any changes to the source file appear in the inserted file. If you embed the file, changes to the source file do not appear in the inserted file.

Microsoft Project treats each inserted file as a graphics object. Therefore, you can link or embed entire files in Microsoft Project graphics areas only, such as the Gantt Chart view or a note. You can link or embed more than one file per selected task, resource, or assignment.

➤ **To link or embed an entire file in Microsoft Project**

1 Open a Microsoft Project file and select the graphics area into which you want to insert the file.

2 To insert the file in the **Gantt Chart** view, click **Object** on the **Insert** menu.

To insert the file in a task, resource, or assignment note, double-click a task, resource, or assignment on a sheet view. Click the **Notes** tab, and then click **Insert Object** 🖼️.

3 Click **Create from File**.

4 In the **File** box, enter the path and file name of the file you want to insert or click **Browse** to locate and select the file.

5 To embed the file, clear the **Link** check box.

To link the file, select the **Link** check box.

6 To display the file as an icon, select the **Display As Icon** check box.

If you do not select the Display As Icon check box, the entire contents of the file is displayed in the graphics area.

Linking and Embedding Project Information from Microsoft Project

As the main program you use to manage projects, Microsoft Project may be the source of information for other programs you use to control specific aspects of the project. For example, you may "feed" cost information from Microsoft Project to a spreadsheet file so that the spreadsheet program can perform complex cost calculations. You can also link or embed information from one Microsoft Project file to another Microsoft Project file.

If you want the information in other programs to be updated each time you update it in Microsoft Project, you can link the information. Linking is especially useful if you include the Microsoft Project information in several files. Then by updating the information once in Microsoft Project, you can update it in every file in which it's linked.

If you don't want the information in other programs to be updated, you can embed the information. When you embed information, you can edit it from within the program.

Link or Embed Microsoft Project Information in Another Program

When it's useful to include and edit Microsoft Project information in other programs, you can link or embed that information as an object. If you want the information to be updated in the destination program each time you update it in Microsoft Project, you can link the information. If you don't want the information to be updated in the destination program each time you update in Microsoft Project, you can embed the information.

You can link and embed entire views or selected information from views. But you can't link or embed graphical objects created in Microsoft Project into other programs.

For specific information about copying Microsoft Project objects into another program, see the documentation for that program.

➢ **To link or embed a Microsoft Project information in another program**

1   On the **View Bar**, click **More Views**.

2   In the **Views** list, click the view that contains the information you want to copy, and then click **Apply**.

3   Select the information you want to paste in the other program, and then click **Copy**.

To copy an entire sheet view, such as the Gantt Chart view, the Resource Sheet view, and the Task Usage view, click the blank button in the upper-left corner of the view, at the top of the **ID** field, and then click **Copy**.

To copy the PERT Chart view, the Resource Graph view, or the Calendar view, you don't need to select anything. Simply display the view, and then click **Copy**.

4   Open the program and file into which you want to paste the Microsoft Project information.

5   Select the location for the object.

6   Click the program's **Paste Special** command.

To embed the object, click the program's **Paste** option.

To link the object, click the program's **Paste Link** option, and then click the option to link the object as a Microsoft Project 8.0 object.

If you link or embed an entire Microsoft Project view into another program, the portion of the view that actually appears in the destination program depends on how that program scales or crops the view.

Link or Embed Project Information Between and Within Project Files

Different project plans that you create with Microsoft Project may have information in common. If you want to include information from one plan in one or more other plans, and you want to update or edit that information in the destination plans, you can link or embed the information.

You can create links to information between Microsoft Project files as well as to information from different areas within a single project file. You can also create multiple links to one object. You can create links to text only—between one sheet view and another—not to graphical objects.

➤ **To link or embed project information between or within project files**

1   Open the project file containing the text.

2   On the **View Bar**, click the sheet view that contains the text, and then select the text.

3   Click **Copy** 📑.

4   Open the project file in which you want to create the link.

5   On the **View Bar**, click the sheet view in which you want to create the link.

6   If necessary, add columns or create a new table to make the view compatible with the order and type of information in the object.

7   If necessary, add more fields to the table to accommodate the entire object.

    If there is not enough room, information already in the view may be replaced by the incoming object.

8   Select the field where the upper-left cell of the linked information should begin.

9   On the **Edit** menu, click **Paste Special**.

10 To create an embedded object, click **Paste**.

    To create a linked object, click **Paste Link**.

Drag Project Information from One Program or File to Another

You can copy information between Microsoft Project files or between a Microsoft Project file and a file in another program that supports object linking and embedding (OLE) by using drag-and-drop editing. This method will work only if the drag-and-drop editing option is turned on in both programs.

If you drag information into a field, the copied information must be the type of information that can be entered into the field. For example, you can drag a number into the Microsoft Project Duration field, but not a letter. Also, the copied information replaces the information in the field.

This topic on dragging project information between programs or files is included in the object linking and embedding section of the chapter because you can drag project information only between programs that support OLE. However, you can't link or embed information that you drag between Microsoft Project and another program.

➢ **To drag project information between programs or files**

1   Arrange the file windows so that both the source file and the destination file are open and visible.

   You must be able to see the information you want to drag as well as the location where you want to drop it.

2   Select the information, and then use the left mouse button to drag the information to the new location in the other file.

   To drag information from a Microsoft Project field, select the information, point to an edge of the field box (the cursor must be an arrow), and then use the left mouse button to drag the information to the new location.

If you have Windows 95 or Windows NT 4.x, you can drag the information to the destination program even if it isn't visible (though it must be open). After you select the information in the source program, hold down the left mouse button, and then drag the item to the destination program's button on the Windows Task Bar, which is usually located at the bottom of your screen. After a few seconds, the destination program will appear on your screen, and you can drag the information where you want.

Changing Linked and Embedded Objects

As your project progresses, you'll need to update the information you've entered in your project plan, such as task durations and start dates. You may also need to update any information you've linked to or embedded in your plan.

You can:

- Update linked information by updating the information in the source file.

  For information about how to update information in a source file, see the documentation that came with the source program.

- Edit embedded information (which is independent of the source program).

- Cancel the link to linked information.

Edit Information Embedded in a Microsoft Project File

Embedded information is information you inserted into a project file by choosing Paste Special from the Edit menu, and then choosing the Paste option. Embedded information is independent of the source file. You can change the source file without causing a change to the embedded information. You can, however, edit embedded information from within Microsoft Project by using the tools of the source program (or a similar set of special editing tools that appear when you double-click an embedded object).

➢ **To edit information embedded in a Microsoft Project file**

1 Open the Microsoft Project file that contains the embedded information you want to edit.

2 Double-click the object.

3 Edit the object using the source program commands.

4 On the **File** menu of the source program, click **Exit and Update** (or the program's equivalent command).

Cancel the Link to an Object in a Microsoft Project File

Information that you've linked to your project plan gets updated whenever the source file is updated. If you want linked information to be independent of the source file, you can cancel the link between the source file and the project file that contains the linked information. The information, however, remains in your project file.

After you cancel the link to text information you've inserted into a sheet view, you can edit that information the same way you edit information you've entered manually. But if you cancel the link to a graphics object in a graphics area, the object becomes a static picture; you can't edit it.

➢ **To cancel the link to an object**

1 Open the Microsoft Project file that contains the link you want to cancel.

2 On the **View Bar**, click **More Views**.

3 In the **Views** list, click the view that contains the link you want to cancel, and then click **Apply**.

4 Select the linked object.

5 On the **Edit** menu, click **Links**.

6 In the **Links** list, click the link.

7 Click **Break Link**.

Jumping to Project Information in Other Files and Web Sites: Hyperlinks

Other Microsoft Project files, files created in other programs, and web sites may contain "nice to know" information—information you'd like to access from your project plan but that doesn't need to appear in the plan. Examples of such information include project status reports, marketing documents, project management tips. You can access these kinds of information and many others by inserting *hyperlinks* in your project plan.

A hyperlink is text or an icon that you can click on to open another file or to jump to a web site. The destination can be almost any file, such as another Microsoft Project file, a word-processing document, a spreadsheet, or a database, or any web site on an intranet or the World Wide Web. You can even insert a hyperlink to your favorite stock market web site (if it's relevant to your work, of course).

Any number of project plans can have a hyperlink to the same file or web site. Updates to the destination file or web site show up immediately in each hyperlinked plan.

Insert a Hyperlink

When you want quick access to useful or long information that doesn't need to be incorporated into your project plan, you can insert a hyperlink to that information. You can insert a hyperlink to a web site on an intranet or the World Wide Web or to another file, including another project file. You insert a hyperlink with a particular task, resource, or assignment in a sheet view.

A hyperlink connects your project plan to a web site or file the way a phone number connects you to a particular person or organization. A phone number contains information that puts your call on the correct path to someone's telephone. Likewise, a hyperlink contains information that puts you on the correct path to a particular web site or file. The difference is that when you insert a hyperlink, you also specify the path.

To specify the path to a web site on an intranet or the World Wide Web, you use the following convention:

http://www.*<site name>*/*<file name>*

To specify the path to a file on your computer, you use the following convention:

<folder name>*<subfolder name>**<file name>*

To specify the path on a network server, you use the following convention:

*<server name>**<share name>**<folder name>**<subfolder name>**<file name>*

Be sure to include the full address of the destination file in your project file, and make sure there's a destination file located at the hyperlink address.

You can use the following procedure to insert the first hyperlink from a task, resource, or assignment. If you want to insert additional hyperlinks, see "Insert Additional Hyperlinks from a Task, Resource, or Assignment."

> ### To insert a hyperlink from a task, resource, or assignment in a sheet view

To view hyperlink addresses, display the Hyperlink table in a sheet view

1   Open the project file in which you want to create the hyperlink.

2   In a sheet view, select a task, resource, or assignment.

3   Click **Hyperlink** 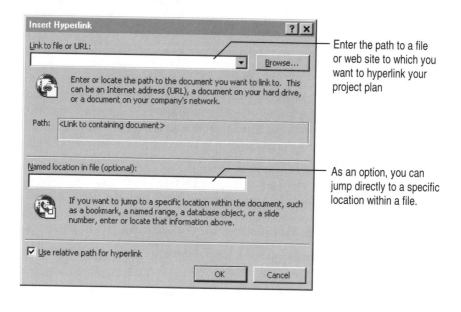.

4   In the **Link to file or URL** box, enter the address of the destination file.

If the destination file is located on your computer or on the network, click **Browse** to locate it.

If the destination file is located on a web site you've visited recently, click the path in the **Link to file or URL** box.

Enter the path to a file or web site to which you want to hyperlink your project plan

As an option, you can jump directly to a specific location within a file.

Insert Additional Hyperlinks from a Task, Resource, or Assignment

Perhaps it would be useful to access more than one document from a task, resource, or assignment in your project plan. For example, both a word-processing document and a web site may contain important information about a resource. If that's the case, then you can insert as many hyperlinks as there are files and web sites that you want to associate with the resource.

➤ **To insert more than one hyperlink for a task, resource, or assignment**

1 In a sheet view that contains the task, resource, or assignment, click the task, resource, or assignment.

2 Click **Task Notes**, **Resource Notes**, or **Assignment Notes** .

3 Click the **Notes** tab.

4 In the **Notes** box (under the row of 6 buttons), enter the addresses of the files to which you want to create hyperlinks. Add a space between each address, or enter each address on a separate line by pressing ENTER after you enter an address.

To enter the location of a file, such as on a computer or a network, type:

file:*<path><filename>*
For example, file:\\computername\folder\filename

To enter the location of a web site, type:

http:*<URL>*
For example, http://www.filename.com

When you insert a hyperlink in the **Notes** tab of the **Task Information**, the **Resource Information**, or the **Assignment Information** dialog box, a hyperlink icon appears in the **Indicators** field of the task or resource for which you inserted the hyperlink.

Go to a File or Web Site by Using a Hyperlink

When you want to display the file or web site associated with a task, resource, or assignment, you can go to, or *follow*, the appropriate hyperlink. The method you use for following a hyperlink depends on whether you inserted the hyperlink by using the Hyperlink command on the Insert menu or by using the Notes tab in the Task Information, Resource Information, or Assignment Information dialog box.

➤ **To follow a hyperlink you inserted by using the Hyperlink command**

1 Switch to a sheet view that contains the task, resource, or assignment to which you've added the hyperlink.

2 In the **Indicators** field, click .

To stop a hyperlink before it's followed, click **Stop Current Jump** on the **Web** toolbar.

➤ **To follow a hyperlink you inserted into the Notes tab**

1 Switch to the sheet view that contains the task or resource to which you've added the hyperlink.

2 In the **Indicators** field, double-click .

3 In the **Notes** box, click the hyperlink you want to follow.

Copy, Paste, or Move a Hyperlink

After you've hyperlinked a task, resource, or assignment to a file or web site, you may find it useful to hyperlink other tasks, resources, and assignments to the same file or web site. Instead of creating a new hyperlink for each additional task, resource, or assignment, you can copy, paste, or move the existing hyperlink.

➤ **To copy, paste, or move a hyperlink**

1 Switch to a sheet view.

2 On the **View** menu, point to **Table**, and then click **Hyperlink**.

3 In the **Hyperlink** field, select the task, resource, or assignment whose hyperlink you want to copy or move.

To select the field, click a field next to the hyperlink and then use the arrow keys to move into the Hyperlink field. If you click the hyperlink in the Hyperlink field, the file or web site to which the task, resource, or assignment is hyperlinked will be displayed.

4   If the hyperlink contains information in the **SubAddress** field, you need to also select the **Address** and **SubAddress** fields so that all three fields are selected.

To select multiple fields, click a field next to the **Hyperlink** field, hold down SHIFT, and then use the arrow keys to select all necessary fields.

5   To copy the hyperlink, click **Copy** .

To move the hyperlink, click **Cut** .

6   In the **Hyperlink** field, select the task, resource or assignment to which you want to add the hyperlink.

7   Click **Paste** .

Change the Destination of a Hyperlink

If the location of the file or web site to which you've hyperlinked a task, resource, or assignment changes, you can change the path within the hyperlink so that it connects the task, resource, or assignment to the new location of the file or web site.

➤   **To change the destination of a hyperlink**

1   In a sheet view, select the task, resource, or assignment that contains the hyperlink.

2   Click **Insert Hyperlink** .

3   In the **Link to file or URL** box, enter the new destination address.

4   If you want the hyperlink to jump to a specific location within the destination file, enter the location in the **Named location in file (optional)** box.

5   If you want a hyperlink to a directory to locate the linked file by using a path relative to the location where the project file that contains the hyperlink is saved, select the **Use relative path for hyperlink** check box.

If you want a hyperlink to a directory to use the same address regardless of where you save the project file that contains the hyperlink, clear the **Use relative path for hyperlink** check box.

Delete a Hyperlink

A hyperlink has outlasted its usefulness when it connects a task, resource, or assignment to outdated, insufficient, or irrelevant information. For these and similar reasons, you can delete the hyperlink.

The method you use for deleting a hyperlink depends on whether you inserted the hyperlink by using the Hyperlink command on the Insert menu or by using the Notes tab in the Task Information, Resource Information, or Assignment Information dialog box.

> **To delete a hyperlink you inserted by using the Hyperlink command**
> 1 Switch to a sheet view.
> 2 On the **View** menu, point to **Table**, and then click **Hyperlink**.
> 3 In the **Hyperlink** field, select the task, resource, or assignment that contains the hyperlink you want to delete.
>   To select the field, click a field next to the hyperlink, and then use the arrow keys to move into the field.
> 4 Press DELETE.

> **To delete a hyperlink you inserted in the Notes tab**
> 1 Switch to a sheet view, and then select the task, resource, or assignment containing the hyperlink.
> 2 Click **Task Notes**, **Resource Notes**, or **Assignment Notes** .
> 3 In the **Notes** box, select the entire text of the hyperlink.
> 4 Press DELETE.

Part 6

Customizing Microsoft Project Tools

Even if your desk is as messy as mine, your desktop is arranged to help you work efficiently. It may not have started out that way. Either your deliberate actions or "evolution" placed that smoky black pencil holder with its yellow, green, black, blue, and red pens and pencils within arm's reach, your computer in the middle of your desk, framed pictures of your loved ones just to the left of the computer or maybe at eye level on top of the monitor, and a carousel of paper clips, sticky notes, rubber bands, and scissors next to the tiered inbox and outbox trays, that bunk bed of lost causes.

Microsoft Project is like a desk filled with tools, tools that help you perform project management tasks. There are two kinds of tools that come with Microsoft Project. There are tools that enable you to enter, display, or print project information, such as views, reports, tables, and filters. And there are tools for performing the many detailed tasks required to manage projects and work with project files, such as menus and menu commands, toolbars and toolbar buttons, and forms and dialog boxes.

Part 6 describes how to customize the tools that enable you to perform the detailed tasks of project management—menus, toolbar buttons, forms, and so on—so that you can work with Microsoft Project as efficiently as possible. It also explains how you can automate repetitive tasks that you perform with Microsoft Project.

Part 6 consists of one chapter, Chapter 16, "Customizing Microsoft Project to Fit the Way You Work."

For information about how to customize views, reports, tables, and filters, see Part 4, "Viewing, Formatting, and Printing Project Information."

Part 6

Customizing Microsoft Project Tools

Customizing Microsoft Project to Fit the Way You Work

When you work with Microsoft Project, you use various sets of tools, including menus and menu commands, toolbars and toolbar buttons, and forms and dialog boxes in which you enter project information. Microsoft Project's many tools are designed and organized to fit the way the average user uses them.

But maybe you're not so average. Maybe it would be more convenient for you if the toolbar button that opens project files, , were on the right side of the toolbar instead of the left side, or if the Details command were on the View menu instead of the Format menu.

If some tools aren't organized in a way that enables you to work as efficiently as possible, you can reorganize them. But that's not all you can do. You can also:

- Show or hide the View Bar and toolbars.
- Add commands to menus.
- Create custom menus.
- Add a button to a toolbar.
- Change the image on a toolbar button.
- Move toolbars where you want them.
- Create custom forms for entering and editing project information.

In addition, if there are any series of actions that you perform frequently in Microsoft Project—such as clicking the Open toolbar button, selecting a certain file, and then clicking the Open button in the File Open dialog box—you can automate the series of actions by recording them in a macro. Macros can help you perform many complex tasks fast.

Whatever toolbars, toolbar buttons, menus, macros, and other tools you create in a project file, you can share with other project files by using the Microsoft Project Organizer. You also use the Organizer to delete and rename any tools you've made.

CREATING AND CUSTOMIZING MENUS AND MENU COMMANDS

A menu is a set of commands that often have related functionality. For example, the Edit menu consists of commands for editing task and resource information. Each command performs a specific action. On the Edit menu, the Copy Cell command copies a piece of information, the Paste command inserts copy or cut information into a cell, and so on.

The default menu structure might not suit you. For instance, you might want commands grouped differently or you might want to create a new menu. Microsoft Project enables you to customize menus and menu commands in a number of ways. For example, you can:

- Add a command to a menu.
- Delete a command from a menu.
- Create a command.
- Create a menu.
- Delete a menu.
- Reset a menu bar

The following illustration shows you some of the ways you can customize menus and menu commands.

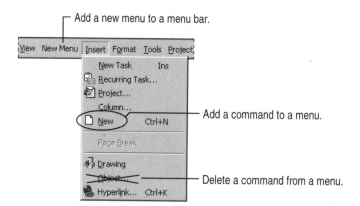

When you create or modify commands or menus, Microsoft Project saves them in your global file, Global.mpt. Any other project files you open on your computer using that global file will contain the new tools.

Add a Command to a Menu

A command performs a specific action, such as deleting a task, displaying a dialog box, or running a macro you've created. If a menu doesn't have a command you want, the command might be on another menu or it may be a custom command that hasn't yet been added to any menu. If the command exists, you can add it to any menu you want.

➤ **To add a command to a menu**

1   If the menu on which you want to add a command is not displayed, display the menu bar that contains the menu.

2   On the **Tools** menu, point to **Customize**, and then click **Toolbars**.

3   Click the **Commands** tab.

4   In the **Categories** list, click the name of the category containing the command you want to add.

   The commands in each category appear in the **Commands** list on the right side.

   If you're not sure which category a command is in, click **All Commands**.

5   In the **Commands** list, click the command you want to add to the menu, and then drag it to the name of the menu in which you want to place it.

   The menu will drop down, displaying its current commands.

6   Drag the new command to the location on the menu where you want it.

Delete a Command from a Menu

A menu may contain built-in or custom commands you don't use. To pare down a menu to those commands you do use, saving time selecting the commands you want, you can delete the unused commands from the menu. You can delete any command from any menu.

➤ **To delete a command from a menu**

1   If the menu bar from which you want to delete a command is not displayed, display the menu bar.

2   On the **Tools** menu, point to **Customize**, and then click **Toolbars**.

3   Click the **Commands** tab.

4   On the menu bar, click the menu command you want to delete, and then click **Modify Selection**.

5   Click **Delete**.

Create a Menu Command

Microsoft Project provides dozens of built-in menu commands to help you perform dozens of project management tasks. But if none of the existing commands has the functionality you want, you can create a command.

You can place a new command on any toolbar or menu, and then assign any Microsoft Project command, macro, or form to the command. Be aware that you should assign functionality to a new command before you edit its image (if you give it an image). Assigning functionality after you edit the image will remove any modifications you made to the image.

➢ **To create a menu command**

1   If the menu bar to which you want to add a new menu command is not displayed, display the menu bar.

2   On the **Tools** menu, point to **Customize**, and then click **Toolbars**.

3   Click the **Commands** tab.

4   In the **Categories** list, click **File**.

5   In the **Commands** list, click the command you want to add to the menu, and then drag it to the name of the menu in which you want to place it.

   (The command will probably have a default functionality associated with it, but you can change that functionality.)

   The menu will drop down, displaying its current commands.

6   Drag the new command to the location on the menu where you want it.

7   Click **Modify Selection**, and then click **Assign Macro**.

   In the Command box, you'll see the default functionality of the command

8   In the **Command** box, click a command, macro, or custom form, and then click **OK**.

   In the Command box, commands, macros, and custom forms are listed together in alphabetical order. Macros are preceded by "Macro" and custom forms are preceded by "Form."

   When you click a command, macro, or form, the new functionality replaces the old functionality.

9   Click **Modify Selection**, and then type the name of the new command in the **Name** box.

10 To change an existing image or create a new image, click **Edit Button Image**.

Create a Menu

Microsoft Project provides a number of standard menus, each one grouping a set of loosely related commands. But maybe you're tired of looking under each menu for those commands you use most frequently. To speed up your work, you can create a menu that has exactly the commands you want.

➢ **To create a menu**

1   If the menu bar to which you want to add a new menu is not displayed, display the menu bar.

2   On the **Tools** menu, point to **Customize**, and then click **Toolbars**.

3   Click the **Commands** tab.

4   In the **Categories** list, click **New Menu**.

5   In the **Commands** list, drag **New Menu** to the desired menu bar.

6   Click **Modify Selection**, and then type the name of the new menu in the **Name** box.

Delete a Menu

A menu bar may contain built-in or custom menus you don't use. To pare down a menu bar to those menus you do use, you can delete the unused menus from the menu bar. You can delete any menu from any built-in or custom menu bar.

➢ **To delete a menu**

1   If the menu bar that contains the menu you want to delete is not displayed, display the menu bar.

2   On the **Tools** menu, point to **Customize**, and then click **Toolbars**.

3   Click the **Commands** tab.

4   Click the menu you want to delete.

5   Click **Modify Selection**, and then click **Delete**.

Reset a Menu Bar

When you create, modify, or delete menus and menu commands, you're modifying the menu bar that contains those menus and menu commands. To restore a menu bar to its original configuration, you can reset it.

When you reset a menu bar, Microsoft Project deletes any custom menus and menu commands that you've added, adds menus and menu commands that you've removed, and restores all modified menus and menu commands to their original state. To save any custom or modified menus before you reset a menu bar, you can move the menus onto a built-in or custom toolbar. After you reset the menu bar, you can move them back.

➢ **To reset a menu bar**

1 On the **Tools** menu, point to **Customize**, and then click **Toolbars**.

2 Click the **Toolbars** tab.

3 In the **Toolbars** list, click the menu bar you want to reset.

4 Click **Reset**.

CREATING AND CUSTOMIZING TOOLBARS AND TOOLBAR BUTTONS

A toolbar is a set of toolbar buttons that either have related functionality or are frequently used together. Toolbar buttons are visual representations of commands. Whereas menu commands are hidden until you click a menu, toolbar buttons are always displayed (if you've chosen to show the toolbar they're on). A toolbar button is often, therefore, a shortcut to a command. You don't have to pull down a menu to get to it.

Microsoft Project provides you with twelve built-in toolbars, two of which, the Standard toolbar and the Formatting toolbar, are displayed by default. If the built-in toolbars or toolbar buttons don't meet your needs, you can customize them in a number of ways. For example, you can:

- Show or hide a toolbar.
- Move a toolbar.
- Add a button to a toolbar.
- Remove a button from a toolbar.
- Create a toolbar button.
- Create a toolbar.
- Change the image on a toolbar button.
- Reset a toolbar.

The following illustration shows you some of the ways you can customize toolbars and toolbar buttons.

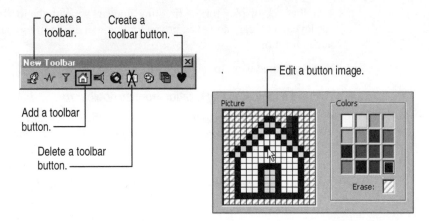

You can also show and hide the View Bar, which enables you to display some of the more commonly used views by choosing small representations of those views.

When you create or modify toolbars or toolbar buttons, Microsoft Project saves them in your global file. Any other project files you open on your computer that use that global file will contain the modified toolbars and toolbar buttons.

Show or Hide a Toolbar

By default, Microsoft Project displays the Standard toolbar (which has buttons such as Save, Open, Print, Copy, Paste, Link Tasks, and Assign Resources) and the Formatting toolbar (which has buttons and other tools such as Indent, Outdent, Font, Bold, and Filter). The buttons and other tools on these toolbars can help you perform many of the basic tasks you need to perform with Microsoft Project. Sometimes, however, you may need to use tools that are on other toolbars. Conversely, you may no longer need a toolbar that's displayed, so you can hide it to increase the work area. You can display any number of toolbars.

➢ **To show or hide a toolbar**

- On the **View** menu, point to **Toolbars**, and then click the toolbar you want to show or hide.

Move a Toolbar

A toolbar you display for the first time appears beneath the toolbars that are already displayed. You can, however, drag a toolbar to a different toolbar row or to any other screen location.

You have three ways to move a toolbar.

➢ **To move a toolbar to any location from the toolbar row**

- At the left side of a toolbar that's in a toolbar row near the top of the screen are two faint vertical lines. Position the pointer over these two lines, and then drag the left side of the toolbar to the location you want.

➢ **To move a toolbar from the toolbar row to the middle of the work area quickly**

- Double-click the two faint vertical lines at the left side of the toolbar.

➢ **To move a toolbar from the middle of the work area to the toolbar row quickly**

- Double-click the toolbar's title bar.

Show or Hide the View Bar

The View Bar, located on the left side of the screen, displays small images of the most commonly used views. To display any of these views quickly, you can click its image on the View Bar. The View Bar is displayed by default. You can hide it or display it.

➢ **To show or hide the View Bar**

- On the **View** menu, click **View Bar**.

Add a Button to a Toolbar

If a toolbar doesn't have a button (and accompanying function) that you want, the button might be on another toolbar or it may be a custom button that hasn't yet been added to any toolbar. If the button exists, you can add it to any built-in or custom toolbar you want.

➢ **To add a button to a toolbar**

1   If the toolbar to which you want to add a button is not displayed, display the toolbar.

2   On the **Tools** menu, point to **Customize**, and then click **Toolbars**.

3   Click the **Commands** tab.

4   In the **Categories** list, click the name of the category that contains the command (along with the button or other toolbar tool) you want to add to the toolbar.

If you're not sure which category the command is in, click **All Commands**.

5   In the **Commands** list, click the command you want, and then drag it to the toolbar on which you want the button displayed.

Remove a Button from a Toolbar

A toolbar may contain built-in or custom buttons you don't use. To pare down a toolbar to those buttons you do use, you can delete the unused buttons from the toolbar. You can delete any button from any toolbar.

➢ **To remove a button from a toolbar**

1   If the toolbar from which you want to delete a button is not displayed, display the toolbar.

2   On the **Tools** menu, point to **Customize**, and then click **Toolbars**.

3   Click the **Commands** tab.

4   On the toolbar, click the button (or other toolbar tool) you want to delete, and then click **Modify Selection**.

5   Click **Delete**.

Reset a Toolbar

When you create, modify, or remove toolbar buttons, you're modifying the toolbar that contains those buttons. To restore a toolbar to its original configuration, you can reset it.

When you reset a toolbar, Microsoft Project deletes any custom toolbar buttons that you've added, adds buttons that you've removed, and restores all modified buttons to their original state. To save any custom or modified buttons before you reset a toolbar, you can move the buttons onto a built-in or custom toolbar. After you reset the toolbar, you can move them back.

> ➤ **To reset a toolbar**

1   On the **Tools** menu, point to **Customize**, and then click **Toolbars**.

2   Click the **Toolbars** tab.

3   In the **Toolbars** list, click the name of the toolbar you want to reset, and then click **Reset**.

Change the Image on a Toolbar Button

Let's face it. It's a rare toolbar button image that clearly tells us what the button's function is. If you think a button should have a different image, one that's more meaningful to you, or you've changed the button's command and want to give it an image that matches its new function, you can change the button's image.

Microsoft Project provides more than 100 images you can choose from. You can apply an image as is. Or, if you want, you can modify its appearance by using the Microsoft Project Button Editor.

> ➤ **To change the image on a toolbar button**

1   If the toolbar that contains the button you want to modify is not displayed, display the toolbar.

2   On the **Tools** menu, point to **Customize**, and then click **Toolbars**.

3   Click the **Commands** tab.

4   On the toolbar, click the button you want to modify, and then click **Modify Selection**.

5   Point to **Change Button Image**, and then click the image you want.

Edit the Image on a Toolbar Button

If the image on a toolbar button is close to what you want, but not quite right, you can edit the image. When you edit the image on a toolbar button, you can change its colors one pixel at a time, and you can move the image to a different position on the button.

➢ **To edit a button image**

1   If the toolbar that contains the button you want to edit is not displayed, display the toolbar.

2   On the **Tools** menu, point to **Customize**, and then click **Toolbars**.

3   Click the **Commands** tab.

4   On the toolbar, click the button you want to modify, and then click **Modify Selection**.

5   Point to **Edit Button Image**.

6   Make the changes to the button image.

Reset a Toolbar Button

You can modify a toolbar button's appearance and functionality. If you've modified a toolbar button and want to restore it to its original appearance and functionality, you can reset it.

➢ **To reset a toolbar button**

1   If the toolbar that contains the button you want to reset is not displayed, display the toolbar.

2   On the **Tools** menu, point to **Customize**, and then click **Toolbars**.

3   Click the **Commands** tab.

4   On the toolbar, click the button you want to reset, and then click **Modify Selection**.

5   Click **Reset**.

Create a Toolbar Button

Microsoft Project provides dozens of built-in toolbar buttons to help you perform dozens of project management tasks quickly. But if none of the existing toolbar buttons has the functionality you want, you can create a toolbar button.

You can place a new toolbar button on any toolbar or menu, and then assign any Microsoft Project command, macro, or form to the button. Be aware that you should assign functionality to a new button before you edit its image. Assigning functionality after will remove any modifications you made to the button's image.

➢ **To create a toolbar button**

1 If the toolbar to which you want to add the button is not displayed, display the toolbar.

2 On the **Tools** menu, point to **Customize**, and then click **Toolbars**.

3 Click the **Commands** tab.

4 In the **Categories** list, click **File**.

5 In the **Commands** list, drag a button onto the toolbar.

6 Click **Modify Selection**, and then click **Assign Macro**.

The Command box displays the default command for the button you dragged onto the toolbar (and which should still be selected).

7 In the **Command** box, click a macro, command, or custom form, and then click **OK**.

In the Command box, commands, macros, and custom forms are listed together in alphabetical order. Macros are preceded by "Macro" and custom forms are preceded by "Form."

8 Click **Modify Selection**, and then type a button name in the **Name** box.

9 Press ENTER.

If you need to add an image to the button, see "Change the Image on a Toolbar Button."

Create a Toolbar

Microsoft Project provides you with a number of standard toolbars, each consisting of a set of toolbar buttons. But maybe you're tired of displaying each toolbar and searching along its length for those buttons and other tools you use most frequently. To speed up your work, you can create a toolbar that has exactly the buttons you want.

➢ **To create a toolbar**

1 On the **Tools** menu, point to **Customize**, and then click **Toolbars**.

2 Click the **Toolbars** tab.

3 Click **New**.

4 In the **Toolbar name** box, type a name for the new toolbar, and then click **OK**.

The new toolbar is displayed in the work area.

5 Add buttons to your custom toolbar.

You must add buttons starting from the left side a new toolbar. After you've added two or more buttons to a new toolbar, you can add buttons between buttons.

Delete a Toolbar

If you no longer need a toolbar, you can delete it. You can delete any built-in or custom toolbar from any project file. You can delete custom toolbars from the global file, but you can't delete built-in toolbars from the global file.

➤ **To delete a toolbar**

1   On the **Tools** menu, point to **Customize**, and then click **Toolbars**.

2   Click the **Toolbars** tab.

3   In the **Toolbars** list, click the name of the toolbar you want to delete, and then click **Delete**.

CREATING NEW FORMS FOR ENTERING AND VIEWING TASK INFORMATION

Forms are windows in which you enter information about selected tasks or resources. The Task Dependency dialog box is an example of a form.

You can create your own forms to enter the information that you're interested in. For example, if you're interested only in the percent work complete and task start dates, you can create a custom form containing the % Complete and Start fields. The information you enter in a custom form for tasks will be added to all the tasks that you selected before you displayed the form.

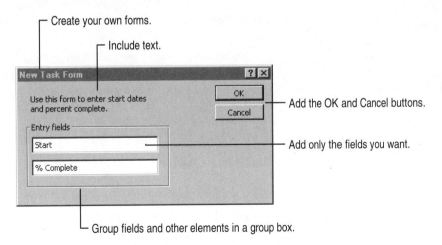

Microsoft Project enables you to work with custom forms in a number of ways. For example, you can create and display a custom form.

Create a Custom Form

Microsoft Project provides you with a number of forms for entering and editing project information. The Task Dependency dialog box is an example of a form. If you want a form in which you can enter or edit only the information you're interested in, you can create a custom form.

When you create a custom form, you can add:

- Text, as a title or to explain or describe something on the form.

- A group box, which can contain, or visually group, related text, buttons, and fields.

- Fields, meaning exactly those fields that appear in Microsoft Project views and dialog boxes, such as the % Complete field, the Resource Name field, and the Baseline Cost field.

- The OK and Cancel buttons, only if they don't already appear on the form.

Any custom forms you create are stored only in the active project file. You can, however, make them available to other project files by using the Organizer.

➢ **To create a custom form**

1   On the **Tools** menu, point to **Customize**, and then click **Forms**.

2   Click **Task** or **Resource**, and then click **New**.

3   In the **Name** box, type the name of the new custom form, and then click **OK**.

   To assign a shortcut key for displaying the form, enter the key in the **Key** box.

4   In the **Custom Form Editor**, click **Text**, **Group Box**, **Button**, or **Fields** on the **Item** menu.

   If you click **Button** on the **Item** menu, click **OK** or **Cancel**, and then click **OK**.

   If you click **Fields** on the **Item** menu, you must select a field in the **Field** box, specify its size (in the **Width** and **Height** boxes) and position on the form (in the **X** and **Y** boxes), and then click **OK**. (The "zero" of the x and y axes is the upper left-hand corner of the form.)

5   On the **File** menu, click **Save**.

6   On the **File** menu, click **Exit**.

To move a component in a form, drag it within the form.

To change the size of a component, drag the top, bottom, or side border. To change the size of a component so that it maintains its proportions, drag a border corner.

To edit a component, double-click the component to display the Item Information dialog box.

Display a Form You've Created

To use a form you've created, you need to display it.

➢ **To display a form you've created**

1   On the **Tools** menu, point to **Customize**, and then click **Forms**.

2   Click **Task** or **Resource**, click the form you want to display, and then click **Apply**.

AUTOMATING YOUR TASKS BY USING MACROS

Doing the same task over and over again in Microsoft Project can become tedious, especially if that task requires you to press a number of keys. You can replace most of those keystrokes by recording them in a macro. A *macro* is a small program that consists of a series of keystrokes or mouse clicks. When you record a macro, you determine which keystrokes it includes, and in what order, by performing those keystrokes one (hopefully last) time. The next time you want to perform the task that requires those keystrokes, you simply run the macro and let it do the work. Autopilot for project managers.

Microsoft Project provides you with a number of ways to work with macros. For example, you can:

- Record a macro.
- Run a macro.
- Interrupt a macro while it's running.

You can record a macro and perform other actions with macros without knowing any programming whatsoever. However, you can get the most out of macros if you know how to program with Visual Basic for Applications (VBA). The instructions for using VBA are beyond the scope of this book. If you'd like to know more about VBA, consult a VBA programmer or VBA reference guide.

Record a Macro

When performing a repetitive task in Microsoft Project requires a number of keystrokes, you can save time by letting Microsoft Project do the task for you. The way to do that is to record the keystrokes and mouse clicks in a macro. When you run the macro, Microsoft Project quickly performs the task for you, saving you time.

➢ **To record a macro**

1   On the **Tools** menu, point to **Macro**, and then click **Record New Macro**.

2   In the **Macro name** box, enter a name for the macro.

You must use a letter as the first character of the macro name. The other characters can be letters, numbers, or underscore characters. The macro name can't contain spaces or be a word that Microsoft Project reserves as a keyword.

3   If you want to run the macro by pressing a keyboard key, enter a letter in the **Shortcut key** box.

You can use any letter (but not number or special character) on the keyboard. You cannot use a key combination that's already used by Microsoft Project.

4   In the **Store macro in** box, click the location where you want to store the macro.

You can store the macro in the active project file only or in the Global file. If you want the macro to be available to the other projects that use the Global file, click **Global File**.

5   Type a description of the macro—its purpose or other information—in the **Description** box.

6   Click **OK**, and then perform the series of actions you want to record.

7   On the **Tools** menu, point to **Macro**, and then click **Stop Recorder**.

Run a Macro

To use a macro that you've created, you need to run it.

➢ **To run a macro**

1   Open the project that contains the macro.

2   On the **Tools** menu, point to **Macro**, and then click **Macros**.

3   Select the macro you want to run from the **Macro name** list.

4   Click **Run**.

Stop a Macro While It's Running

After you start a macro, you may realize that it's not doing what you want it to do, or you might want to examine its results after it's partly done. In either case, you can stop the macro part way through its run. After you stop a macro, you can continue it or end it.

➢ **To stop a macro before it finishes**

•   Press CTRL+BREAK.

SHARING AND DELETING CUSTOM TOOLS BY USING THE ORGANIZER

When you create a custom toolbar, menu, macro, form, or other tool that you find particularly useful, you might want to use it in other project files. The way to share custom tools is by using the Organizer.

The Organizer is a dialog box in which you can copy various Microsoft Project tools from one project file to another. You can also delete and rename those tools in the Organizer. In the Organizer, you can copy, delete, and rename forms, views, calendars, toolbars, tables, reports, menu bars, filters, and modules (such as macros).

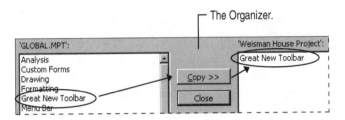

The Organizer.

When you modify or create menus, menu bars, menu commands, toolbars, toolbar buttons, and macros, the new or modified tools are saved in the global file, Global.mpt. These tools will be available in any project file that uses the Global.mpt file in which the tools are stored. Global.mpt is like a common reservoir of tools for the project files on one computer. That is, if you create a custom tool in one project file on your computer, it's likely that the tool will appear in all other project files on your computer.

However, a custom form is saved only with the project file in which you created it. To share a custom form with other project files, you can copy it to Global.mpt or to one project file at a time.

Copy a Custom Tool from One Project File to Another

If you create a custom tool that you find particularly useful, such as a custom toolbar or a custom menu, you can share it with other projects by using the Organizer to copy the tool from one project file to another. When you create custom tools other than custom forms, such as custom menus and toolbars, those tools are saved in a Global.mpt file and will appear in all project files that use that particular Global.mpt. However, if you want to share a custom tool with a project file that doesn't use the same Global.mpt as the project file in which you created the custom tool, you can copy the custom tool to the destination project file.

To copy a custom tool from one project file to another, both the project file where the tool resides and the project file to which you want to copy the tool must be open.

➤ **To copy a custom tool from one project file to another project file**

1   On the **Tools** menu, click **Organizer**.

2   Click the tab named with the category that contains the kind of tool you want to copy.

3   In the **GLOBAL.MPT** list on the left side, click the custom tool you want to share.

   If the custom tool only resides in the project file in which you created it, such as a custom form, click the project name in the **Available in** box.

4   In the **Available in** box on the right side, click the project into which you want to copy the custom tool, and then click **Copy**.

Delete or Rename a Custom Tool

To rename or delete a custom tool, you can access the tool in the Organizer. Before you can rename or delete a custom tool that resides in a specific project file, you need to open that file.

➤ **To delete or rename a custom tool**

1   On the **Tools** menu, click **Organizer**.

2   Click the tab named with the category that contains the kind of tool you want to delete or rename.

3   In an **Available in** box, display the file that contains the tool you want to rename or delete.

   That file might be the Global.mpt file or it might be a specific project file.

4   In the list that contains the tool, click the tool you want to rename or delete.

   To rename a project tool, click **Rename**, and then type a new name for the tool.

   To delete a project tool, click **Delete**.

Glossary

A

Accrual method   The method for determining when resource costs, the fixed costs for tasks, and actual costs are charged to a project. You can incur costs at the start or finish of a task or prorate them during the task.

Accrued cost   A cost that is charged all at once, either at the start or finish of a task, or gradually over the duration of a task. You select the accrual method.

Actual   Factual information about a project quantity as opposed to estimated information. For example, when you create a task, you enter its estimated duration. Later on, if you're tracking task progress, you can enter the task's actual duration.

Assignment   A task that's been assigned to a resource.

Assumption   An estimate or guess about what you expect will be true during a project. For example, you might assume that the cost of a particular material will stay the same during a project.

AutoFilter   In a sheet view, a filter that enables you to filter tasks or resources quickly based on a criterion in a specific column. Each column has an AutoFilter associated with it.

B

Base calendar   A calendar that shows the working days and hours for a group of resources (such as a department or a shift).

Baseline   A set of original, planned project information that you can save and compare with actual information as your project progresses. You can track project progress only if you set a baseline after you complete your project plan.

C

Calculated field   A field whose value is calculated and entered by Microsoft Project based on values in other fields. If you change a value in one of those other fields, Microsoft Project automatically recalculates the value in the calculated field.

Collapsing   The process of hiding the subtasks of summary tasks in a task outline, so that only the summary tasks are visible.

Combination view   A view that contains two views. The view in the lower pane displays detailed information about the tasks or resources selected in the upper pane.

Consolidated project file A project file into which other project files have been inserted. A consolidated file enables you to manage multiple projects from one project file.

Constraint A restriction you place on a task's start or finish date. For example, you can specify that a task must start on a certain date or start no earlier than a certain date.

Contour A specific distribution of work for an assignment over time. The default contour, "flat," distributes the same number of hours of work per day. You can apply different contours to different assignments.

Cost The total cost of a task, resource, assignment, or project.

Criteria Traits that distinguish one set of tasks or resources from all others. In a filter, criteria determine which tasks or resources are displayed or highlighted.

Critical path The sequence of tasks that has the latest finish date in a project. The critical path determines the project finish date. If any task in the critical path is delayed, the project finish date will also be delayed.

Critical task A task that, if delayed, delays the project finish date. All critical tasks are part of the critical path. By default, a critical task has zero slack time.

Current date line On the Gantt Chart view or the Resource Graph view, a vertical dotted line that indicates the current date.

D

Database The central storage area of all project information in Microsoft Project. When you display a view, you're looking at a portion of the information contained in the database.

Default value A typical value that Microsoft Project automatically inserts into a field. The default value may be one that the user is likely to enter into the field, thus saving the user time. Or, the default value might be entered because a value is required in the field so that Microsoft Project can use it to calculate values in other fields.

Delay time The amount of time inserted between overlapping tasks to resolve resource overallocations.

Dependency A condition that specifies the start or finish of one task relative to the start or finish of its predecessor task. For example, if two tasks are linked with a finish-to-start dependency, the condition is that one task can start only after its predecessor task is completed. Same as *link*.

Divider bar The vertical bar that separates the two portions of a view in the Gantt Chart, Resource Graph, Resource Usage, and Task Usage views.

Duration The length of time it takes to complete a task during normal working hours. To express a duration that stretches across nonworking time, use elapsed duration.

E

Earned value A method for determining whether tasks are on budget and on schedule based on actual costs incurred and actual progress to date. For example, if a task that's 50 percent complete has incurred 70 percent of its planned cost, the task would be said to be behind schedule.

Effort-driven scheduling This is the default scheduling method used by Microsoft Project to calculate duration, work, and resource units. With effort-driven scheduling on, you increase or decrease a duration by removing or adding resources.

Elapsed duration A task duration that includes nonworking time.

Embedding A method for copying information between two files, especially between files created in different programs. When you embed information, the information retains its "separateness" in the destination program. You can edit embedded information by using tools that are the same as or similar to the editing tools in the source program, even though the information does not retain a link to the source file.

Entered field A field in which you enter information, either by typing or selecting.

Expanding The process of showing the subtasks of summary tasks in a task outline.

Exporting Transferring information from Microsoft Project to another program, such as a database or spreadsheet program, and in a format compatible with the destination program, such as .MPD or .XLS.

F

Field A cell or box in a view that contains a particular kind of information about a task or a resource. In a sheet view, for instance, a field is the intersection of a row and a column.

File format The particular traits of a file that allow it to be opened in a particular program. Each program can open only files that are in certain formats. Each format is indicated by a specific file extension. For example, Microsoft Project can open files that are in the .MPP, .MPX, .MPT, .CSV, and several other file formats.

File name The name of a file, which usually consists of a given name and a file extension. For example, project.mpp could be the name of a file created in Microsoft Project. In Microsoft Project, a valid file name can have up to 255 characters, consist of any combination of letters or numbers, and can include the following characters: ! @ # $ % & ( ) - _ { } ' ~

Filter A tool that selects for display only those tasks or resources that match the filter's criteria. Tasks or resources that don't match the criteria are hidden. (Alternatively, a filter can be set to highlight the tasks or resources that match the criteria, while continuing to display the tasks or resources that don't.) See *AutoFilter, Criteria, Interactive filter,* and *Standard filter.*

Fixed cost A cost that doesn't change regardless of the task duration or how much work a task requires. The cost of a material required to do a task is an example of a fixed cost.

Fixed-duration scheduling A way to specify that the duration of a task remains the same regardless of how many resources are assigned to it.

Fixed-duration task A task whose duration is set to remain constant. Changes to the work or assigned resource units won't change the duration. See *Task type*.

Fixed-work task A task whose work is set to remain constant. Changes to the task's duration or assigned resource units don't change the amount of work required to complete the task. See *Task type*.

Fixed-units task The default setting for tasks. A task whose assigned resource units is held constant. Changes to the duration or amount of work don't affect the units. See *Task type*.

Flexible constraint A constraint that does not tie a task to a date, and allows Microsoft Project to move the task when the schedule changes. The flexible constraints are As Soon As Possible, As Late As Possible, Finish No Earlier Than (for projects scheduled from the start date), Finish No Later Than (for projects scheduled from the finish date), Start No Earlier Than (for projects scheduled from the start date), and Start No Later Than (for projects scheduled from the finish date).

Footer Text that appears at the bottom of every printed page. Examples of footer information are page numbers and current date.

Form A type of view that you use to enter, edit, or view detailed task or resource information. Examples of form views are the Task Form and the Resource Form.

Free slack The amount of time a task can slip without delaying another task.

G

Gantt bar A horizontal, rectangular bar on the bar chart portion of the Gantt Chart view. Each Gantt bar represents a task.

Gantt Chart A view that displays a table of task information in its left half and a bar chart showing a task schedule in its right half.

Global file The informal name for the Global.mpt file, which contains the tools used to perform tasks in Microsoft Project. It includes views, calendars, forms, reports, tables, filters, toolbars, menus, macros, and options settings. Typically, all the project files created on the same computer share the same Global.mpt file. For example, if you create a custom toolbar in one project file, it will appear in the other project files you create on your computer.

Goal One of the objectives you want to achieve in a project.

Graph A view that displays project information graphically. Examples of graph views are the Gantt Chart and the Resource Graph.

Graphic area Any area in Microsoft Project into which picture information from another program can be inserted. The graphic areas in Microsoft Project are the bar chart portion of the Gantt Chart view, notes, headers, footers, and legends, and the Objects box in form views.

Gridlines The horizontal and vertical lines that appear in most Microsoft Project views. By separating pieces of information or sections of a view, gridlines make it easier to read a view. Gridlines can be formatted, displayed, and hidden.

H

Header Text that appears at the top of every printed page. Examples of header information are project name, company logo, and the project start or finish date.

Hyperlink Text in one document (either a file or web site) that contains the address of another document. After you click a hyperlink, your computer displays the destination document. The address of the destination document is either a URL address or a UNC address. Hyperlink text is usually distinguished by a particular color.

I

Importing Transferring information from another program, such as a database or spreadsheet program, to Microsoft Project.

Import/export map A set of instructions for inserting information into the correct fields in a destination program. Essentially, an import/export map pairs a field in one program, which has a name, with the corresponding field in another program, which may have a different name.

Indenting In a task outline (such as on the Gantt Chart view), moving a task to a lower outline level by moving it to the right. Also known as demoting.

Indicators Icons in the Indicators column that serve as "flags" to important information about tasks or resources. By default, the Indicators column (for which no column title appears on screen) is located to the right of the ID column. When you point to an indicator, the task or resource information is displayed.

Inflexible constraint A constraint that ties a task to a date. If the schedule changes, the task's start and finish dates remain unaffected. The inflexible constraints are Finish No Earlier Than (for projects scheduled from the finish date), Finish No Later Than (for projects scheduled from the start date), Start No Earlier Than (for projects scheduled from the finish date), Start No Later Than (for projects scheduled from the start date). Must Start On, and Must Finish On.

Inserted project A project file that's inserted into another project file to create a consolidated project file.

Interactive filter A filter that displays a dialog box into which you must enter the filter criteria.

Interim plan A set of task start and finish dates that are saved with a project file. Saving interim plans periodically and comparing them with the baseline plan can help you track project progress. You can save up to 10 interim plans.

Internet A global computer network whose most visible component is the World Wide Web (WWW).

Intranet A computer network that resembles the Internet but exists only within an organization. An intranet may or may not be connected to the Internet.

L

Lag time The amount of time added between the completion of one task and the start of its successor task.

Lead time The amount of time that one task is being worked on before its predecessor task is completed. Work on the successor task overlaps work on the predecessor task. The amount of overlap is the lead time.

Legend An explanatory list that appears on every page of a printed view. Typically, a legend explains what each symbol in a view means.

Leveling Getting rid of resource overallocations by either delaying or splitting tasks that have overallocated resources assigned to them.

Link A dependency between tasks that specifies the start or finish conditions of a task relative to the start or finish of another task. For example, if two tasks are linked with a finish-to-start link, the condition is that one task can start only after its predecessor task is completed. Same as *dependency*.

Link line On the Gantt Chart and PERT Chart views, a line that links one task to another and shows the kind of dependency between the tasks.

Linking Can refer to one of two actions. When scheduling tasks, it refers to establishing a dependency between tasks. When including an object from one program in another program (object linking and embedding), it refers to establishing a connection between programs.

M

Macro In Visual Basic for Applications (VBA), an automated set of instructions you use to accomplish a specific task.

MAPI The acronym for Messaging Application Programming Interface. This is the standard programming interface proposed and supported by Microsoft for exchanging electronic messages.

Master project See *Consolidated project*.

Milestone A major event, such as the completion of a project phase, that indicates project progress. In Microsoft Project, a milestone is used as a marker and has a duration of zero.

N

Nonworking time Those periods of time when resources don't work. Examples of nonworking time are weekends, holidays, and vacations.

Note A usually brief explanation about a task, resource, or assignment that you can enter in the Notes tab of the Task Information dialog box, the Resource Information dialog box, or the Assignment Information dialog box.

O

Object In object linking and embedding (OLE), information from one document that's inserted into another document. The documents can be created by the same program or by different programs. A single object can be inserted into many documents. The object may or may not remain linked to its source program. If it's linked, then modifying the object in the source program modifies all inserted instances of the object also.

Object linking and embedding (OLE) The process of sharing information by linking or embedding it. When you link information, you insert the information into one or more destination documents, but the information remains linked to the source program. Updating the information in the source program updates it in the destination documents. When you embed information, you can also insert the information into one or more destination documents, but the information is not linked to the source program. You can, however, edit embedded information in a destination document by using editing tools associated with the source program.

Objects box An area of a form view into which you can link or embed objects, such as text or pictures from other programs.

Organizer A tabbed dialog box accessible via the Tools menu in which you can copy custom views, tables, filters, macros, toolbars, menus, and so on from one project file to another. You can also rename and delete custom tools.

Outdenting In a task outline (such as on the Gantt Chart view), moving a task to a higher outline level by moving it to the left. Also known as promoting.

Outline A list of tasks that shows some tasks subordinate to other tasks. The subordinate tasks, called *subtasks*, are indented with respect to the other tasks, called *summary tasks*.

Outline level The position a task occupies in the outline hierarchy. A task at outline level 1 occupies the highest outline level. All tasks below this task are subordinate to it. A task indented just once is at outline level 2, a task indented twice is at outline level 3, and so on.

Outline number A number used to indicate a task's level in the outline hierarchy. By default, outline numbers aren't displayed.

Overallocation The result of assigning more hours of work to a resource within a certain time period than the resource has available to work in that time period.

Overtime The number of hours of work performed by a resource beyond the resource's usual hours of availability.

P

Password A combination of characters that you can enter to display a project, the WebInbox, or a TeamInbox.

Per-use cost A cost that's incurred only at the particular times that a resource is used.

PERT analysis A process for determining a probable schedule from best-case, expected-case, and worst-case schedules.

Phase A group of tasks required to complete a major step in a project.

Plan A schedule of tasks and the task, resource, and cost information required to manage a project effectively.

Predecessor task A task on which another task depends. A predecessor task must start or finish before its successor task can start or finish.

Priority When you level overallocated resources, the place you give to a task in the leveling order. To level resources, you may prefer that low-priority tasks get delayed first. If delaying low-priority tasks doesn't resolve overallocations, Microsoft Project will delay the high-priority tasks.

Progress bar On the Gantt Chart view, a horizontal line drawn in the center of a Gantt bar to indicate the percent that a task is complete.

Progress line On the Gantt Chart view, a vertical, zig-zagging line that represents the degree to which tasks are ahead or behind schedule.

Project calendar A calendar of working and nonworking times used by the entire project. In actuality, it is the base calendar of base calendars. The default project calendar is the Standard calendar.

Prorated cost A cost that is incurred gradually over time as a task progresses.

R

Rate table A table that contains different pay rates for the same resource, such as increases or decreases in salary or different pay rates for different kinds of jobs.

Recurring task A task that occurs repeatedly and usually at regular intervals during the course of a project. An example of a recurring task is a weekly status meeting.

Report A detailed account of a particular aspect of a project that can include task, resource, calendar, or cost information, or some combination of these. Microsoft Project supplies 25 predefined and formatted reports (grouped into categories) that are made to be printed.

Resource allocation The assignment of resources to tasks in a project.

Resource calendar A calendar showing the working and nonworking times for an individual resource.

Resource group A set of resources that's usually grouped by job type and given a group name.

Resource list A list of the resources that are available to be assigned to tasks in a project. A resource list can include people, equipment, and supplies.

Resource pool A project file that usually contains resource information only. A resource pool is linked to the project files that share it.

Resource view A view that displays resource information. Examples of resource views are the Resource Sheet and the Resource Graph.

Resources The people, equipment, supplies, and services required to complete the tasks in a project.

Roll up On the bar chart of the Gantt Chart view, displaying subtask Gantt bars on summary task Gantt bars.

S

Scaling Increasing or decreasing the size of the printed image on a page.

Schedule A plan showing the sequence, start dates, finish dates, and durations of tasks in a project.

Scope The goals of a project, the tasks required to achieve those goals, and the amount of work required to perform those tasks.

Server A computer set up to be the central source of information or services for other computers.

Sheet view A view that includes a table of information. Examples of sheet views are the Resource Sheet view, the Gantt Chart view (which is also a graph view), and the Task Usage view.

Slack time (float time) The amount of time a task can slip before it delays another task (free slack) or the project (total slack).

Slippage The difference between a task's scheduled start or finish date and its baseline start or finish date, when the scheduled dates occur later than the baseline dates.

Sorting Putting tasks or resources in an order based on a particular criterion or set of criteria. For example, you can sort tasks by duration or by start date.

Split task A task on which work intermittently stops and then begins again. On the Gantt Chart view, the Gantt bar for a split task appears with gaps in it.

Status date A date that you set and use as a reference point from which to measure project progress.

Subproject See *Inserted project*.

Subtask A task that's indented under and is part of a summary task.

Successor task A task whose start or finish date depends on the start or finish date of another task. A successor task can't start or finish before its predecessor task has started or finished.

Summary task In a task outline (such as on the Gantt Chart view), a task that's at a higher outline level than the tasks beneath it. A summary task summarizes the information of its subtasks.

T

Table A group of columns of related information about tasks, resources, or assignments. Tables appear in sheet views.

Task One of the specific, concrete activities that needs to be completed to achieve project goals.

Task dependency See *Dependency*.

Task duration See *Duration*.

Task list A list of all the tasks required to achieve project goals.

Task type One of three types of tasks, in which either resource units, work, or duration is held fixed, and the other two quantities may vary. For example, in a fixed-units task, the number of resource units remains constant and work and duration may vary.

Task view A view that displays task information. Examples of task views are the Gantt Chart and the PERT Chart.

TeamInbox A web site either on an intranet or the World Wide Web where workgroup members can receive workgroup messages and manage their task lists.

Template A generic project that contains basic project information that's likely to be used in other projects. You can create projects faster by basing them on an existing template and then modifying the new project files.

Timescale An axis or line divided into evenly spaced time intervals. Timescales on the Gantt Chart, Resource Graph, Resource Usage, and Task Usage views enable you to see events over time or breakdowns of information per time period (for example, hours worked per day).

Total cost The total cost of a task, resource, or assignment over the life of a project.

Total slack The amount of time a task can slip without delaying the project end date.

U

UNC An acronym for Universal Naming Convention. UNC addresses are used to identify the locations of files that reside on network servers.

Underallocation The condition that exists when a resource is assigned to work fewer hours than that resource has available during a particular time period.

Units The percentage of a resource's available work hours that the resource is assigned to a task. For example, if a resource is available to do 8 hours of work per day and is assigned to work 4 hours on a task within one day, then the resource is said to be assigned at 50 percent units to that task.

URL An acronym for Uniform Resource Locator. A URL is the name or location of a site on the Internet. URLs are used in HTML documents to specify the destination of a hyperlink.

V

Variable cost A cost that changes, generally by increasing, over time. For example, the cost of a resource who gets paid an hourly rate is a variable cost.

Variance The difference between scheduled information and baseline information.

View A tool for displaying, entering, and editing project information. Views can display task or resource information and can be grouped into sheet, graph, chart, and calendar views.

W

Web browser A program that enables you to locate and display information on the World Wide Web.

Web server A computer that processes requests from other computers that want to display a web site. A web server can also contain web sites.

Web site Any location on the World Wide Web or an intranet that's formatted in HTML and is accessible from a web browser.

Work The amount of resource time required to complete a task. For example, if 2 resources each work 8 hours to complete a task, the task is said to have 16 hours of work.

Workgroup A set of resources and their manager who work on the same project and exchange task status information through the same electronic communications system.

Workgroup messages Special Microsoft Project messages that are used by workgroup members and the workgroup manager to exchange task status information.

Working time The time periods specified in a project, base, or resource calendar during which work can occur.

Working times calendar A generic name for project, base, and resource calendars. A working times calendar stores working and nonworking times.

Workspace A tool that enables you to open a number of separate project files at the same time. A workspace consists of a list of project names that are linked to the project files you specify. You add the project files you want to the workspace. When you open a workspace, you open all the listed projects at the same time.

World Wide Web The most visible component of the Internet, the World Wide Web consists of innumerable web sites.

Index